CW00822105

Guidelines for UK Government websites

Illustrated handbook for Web management teams

Cabinet Office
London

First published (online) 2002

The Office of the e-Envoy
Stockley House
130 Wilton Road
London SW1V 1LQ
guidelines@e-envoy.gsi.gov.uk

This document is available online via:
http://www.e-envoy.gov.uk/webguidelines.htm

Guidelines for the .gov.uk ***domain name registration*** are contained in section 1.9 via: *http://www.e-envoy.gov.uk/webguidelines.htm*

This document is also supported by a ***start-up kit***. This provides a small, self-contained, accessible and usable website template for training purposes and to assist in building an active website, available online via:
http://www.e-envoy.gov.uk/webguidelines.htm

The colour chart reproduced on the front cover represents Web safe colours described in paragraph 2.8.3

Foreword

by Andrew Pinder
e-Envoy

The Cabinet Office first published the Guidelines for UK Government Websites in December 1999. Releasing this updated version of the guidelines is acknowledgement of the fast-changing environment and the need for this to be a living document to provide effective best practice guidance to Government Web managers.

This updated version provides a detailed blueprint of best practice for building and maintaining well designed usable and accessible Government websites. They detail managerial, content and technical requirements, recommendations and suggestions for best practice. All of this is underlined by support of the recommendations from the World Wide Web Consortium.

Underpinning the importance of the need for conformance to best practice web design and management is that users expect content and services that are engaging, relevant to them and effective. The Internet has to be placed alongside other media as a means of providing information and services to the public and businesses.

Government websites need to be accessible and as easy to use as possible. They should be designed to load quickly, and take full account of the different levels of competence and equipment that the public may have when they go online.

These guidelines support these objectives and in particular efforts to improve the quality and inclusiveness of Government websites. The latest version of this document is available at:http://www.e-envoy.gov.uk/webguidelines.htm

April 2003

Executive summary

These revised guidelines grew out of the first edition, which was published in December 1999. This first version was commissioned by the Central IT Unit of the Cabinet Office and written by Cyberia, and underwent a lengthy consultation process. This second edition was commissioned by the Office of the e-Envoy as a result of advancements in technology and changes in government priorities. It builds on the previous version by updating, clarifying and extending the range of advice. This Executive summary is an extract from the Framework for senior managers published in 2001.

Achieving ambitions for current websites

The *Guidelines for UK government websites* support ambitions for current websites. We need to continue to progress from **informing** citizens to **interacting** with them and finally **transacting** with them. This framework document sets out key guidelines that should underpin all current government websites.

1. Government websites should be user focused. This means they are engaging; provide the information and services that users want; continually evolve to meet user demand; and achieve universal accessibility and usability.

2. Government websites must work together to join up the government and, in delivering this, adhere to the mandatory *e-Government Interoperability Framework* (e-GIF).

3. Government organisations must be working to provide their services online.

4. Users should be able to have reasonable expectations about the quality, accuracy and uniformity of government content using, for example, the UK online brand.

5. Government websites must raise citizen confidence by abiding by the law and explaining their terms and conditions to users. They should also be secure from intrusion and address the issues raised by the draft *Trust Charter for Electronic Service Delivery* (e-Trust Charter) guidelines, which clearly set out the rights of the citizen with respect to the information held by government.

6. Users expect communication on the Web to be two-way. Government websites should provide opportunities for users to contact officials, express their views or make enquiries.

7. Government websites should operate within a strategy that includes a full range of channels, such as Digital Interactive TV and mobile devices.

8. Government websites should have systems for evaluating their success and determining if they are meeting the needs of users, making alterations where appropriate.

9. Government websites must provide consistent metadata (data about data) about their documents, as outlined in the mandatory *e-Government Metadata Framework* (e-GMF). Managers should also promote the site and register it with search engines.

10. Government websites should be well managed with adequate resources; clear strategy, aims, and target audiences; publishing and business procedures in place; and a strategy for future development including moves to dynamic databases and other digital media.

The top 10 guidelines

This summary describes key guidelines that form the foundation of any government website. They are evolving and will continue to be updated over time.

1. Engaging, accessible, usable

1.1.   Government websites should be user focused. This means they:
- are engaging;
- provide the information and services that users want;
- continually evolve to meet user demand; and
- achieve universal accessibility and usability.
-

Why?

1.2.   Social exclusion policies: information have-nots should have access to services.

1.3.   Websites that do not identify and meet user needs cannot be effective.

1.4.   The Disability Discrimination Act means that you must take reasonable steps to change practices, policies and procedures that make it impossible or unreasonably difficult for people with disabilities to use your services. You must take reasonable steps to provide auxiliary aids or services, which would enable, or make it easier for people with disabilities to use your services. One aspect to note is the emphasis on usefulness. This may be taken to mean that services must not only be **accessible** but **usable** by people with special needs.

1.5. One of five key commitments of the *Modernising Government* white paper is responsive public services that meet the needs of all different groups in society.

1.6. Accessibility involves more than individuals with special needs. Some company firewalls strip out scripts, which is an issue for sites with a business audience.

1.7. New audiences will have different expectations for engaging and relevant content.

Issues

1.8. Accessibility means that a broad range of software and audiences, including business users and users with disabilities, can actually receive your online content and services.

1.9. The World Wide Web Consortium's (W3C) Web Accessibility Initiative (WAI) is an internationally agreed recommendation for website accessibility. Adopting their guidelines means that we do not have to invent a standard of our own. You are asked to comply with their Level A recommendation. This is defined in the *Web Content Accessibility Guidelines (WCAG)*. New sites or redesigned sites should comply. Each revision of the WCAG will be examined by the Office of the e-Envoy to confirm our continued support. See:
http://www.w3.org/WAI/Resources

1.10. WAI compliance alone will not give you a **usable** site. Usability means the site is easy to use by the intended audiences. For example the **structure of individual pages** may need to be made more understandable. It might mean that the **structure of the site** needs revision so that the site as a whole is more easily navigable.

Practical advice

1.11. Design should be professional, attractive and engaging depending on the needs of the different audiences.

1.12. Content aimed at the public must be written plainly and, where possible, be web-friendly: ie, at least 50 per cent shorter than printed text, broken up into lists and easily scanned.

1.13. Any formats or applications included in the e-GIF framework can be used. However hypertext mark up language (HTML) or other universally accessible alternatives must be provided to portable document formats (PDFs), JavaScript, Shockwave or other features that are less accessible. To be accessible, PDFs must be created as version 1.4 files using the latest Adobe Acrobat (currently version 5). PDF files created as earlier versions such as 1.3 will need to be amended or replaced. Even so, these files will be accessible only for users with Adobe Acrobat Version 5 readers. However, PDFs may be the best way to publish information in some minority languages that are not supported in HTML.

1.14.   All new or redesigned government websites should comply with the
        Web Accessibility Initiative's (WAI's) Level A recommendation for accessibility.
        This can be achieved by following the Priority 1 checkpoints of the Web Content
        Accessibility Guidelines. For example, alternatives should be provided to less
        accessible scripts or formats.

1.15.   The Disability Discrimination Act Code of Practice section 5 gives both
        explanations of what auxiliary services may be as well as some examples. Visit:
        http://www.disability.gov.uk/dda/finalcode.html

1.16.   A key aspect of this is providing alt tags to images that communicate important
        information. Images that are only decorative should be null tagged as "".

1.17.   Easyaccess pages found at the government portal www.ukonline.gov.uk are one
        model of how to write content and design a structure that is useful for some
        special audiences. See:*http://www.ukonline.gov.uk*

1.18.   Bespoke content that meets the needs and preferences of different target
        audiences will improve communications online.

1.19.   Accesskeys are keyboard shortcuts to particular kinds of information. For
        example hitting the 0 key could take the user direct to the menu of accesskeys.
        These shortcuts are helpful for people who have difficulty using a mouse. Some
        government websites are already implementing accesskeys. However, because
        there is no agreed standard, different accesskeys on different government sites
        lead to different options. The Guidelines recommend introducing a uniform menu
        of accesskeys for UK government websites. See Section 2.4 Building in
        universal accessibility.

1.20.   In the case of web-based kiosks and some other special circumstances, you
        may need further guidance on accessibility. In the first instance contact the
        Office of the e-Envoy at *webguidelines@e-envoy.gsi.gov.uk.*

---

*There are 2 million visually impaired people in the UK – can they access your site?
(RNIB 'Accessible Web Design')*

*"I would just like to see it look more interesting" – quote from an evaluation of a
government website.*

---

2. Working together

The guideline

2.1.   Government websites must work together to join up the government and, in
        delivering this, adhere to the mandatory *e-Government Interoperability
        Framework* (e-GIF).

Why?

2.2.   Users do not want to know which government body does what or what the
        approximately 1,000 separate government websites provide. They want simple

access to information and services organised around their needs not the needs of government organisations.

2.3.   Many transactions will be provided across departments. For this to happen, government needs to be able to share information and services. This requires a minimum set of technical policies and standards to achieve interoperability and seamless information flows. These policies and standards are set out in the e-GIF.

2.4.   Joined-up government in action is one of the keystones of the Modernising Government white paper, especially in the provision of electronic services.

Issues
2.5.   All important government documents should have a stable URL, so that portals and search engines can readily link to information.

2.6.   Departments must be considering how to work within the e-GIF framework and with the Government Gateway to provide online services.

Practical advice
2.6.   Departments should link to other relevant sites and deep link to relevant documents.

2.7.   Departments and their executive agencies should exchange links and clarify their

mutual roles.

2.9.   The UK online toolbar will link government home pages to a central site, and to important new announcements or documents on government websites

2.10.   All government sites should link to cross-government sites if appropriate. These include the Civil Service Recruitment Gateway site, the local government gateway info4local.gov, Inforoute and official legislation sites.

2.11.   Web managers are directed to the mandated e-Government Interoperability Framework.

3. Services for the citizen

The guideline
3.1.   Government organisations must be working to provide their services online.

Why?
3.2.   Government policy is to use IT to provide integrated, imaginative and convenient public services. For this reason the target is to make all government services available electronically by 2005.

3.3.   As commercial sites increasingly provide effective and easy-to-use online transactions, users will begin to expect the same from government.

Issues

3.4. Government bodies will need to identify the services most in demand by users and those which will bring the greatest cost-benefit to their organisations. The real aim is to provide services that people will want to use.

3.5. The provision of online services reaches deep into the business processes of the rest of the organisation. It is not only a content or IT issue.

Practical advice

3.6. Older PDF forms cannot be filled in electronically even when downloaded. Simple webforms are still the preferred alternative for forms.

3.7. Departments should now be looking at the business process and resource issues involved, and need to identify how they can best use the Government Gateway.

3.8. They must be working within the e-Government Interoperability Framework (e-GIF) to achieve this important target.

Twenty per cent of the UK electorate would vote online if they could. (Forrester Research)

"Overall I was quite impressed, but obviously you need more agencies to be able to accept electronic requests before this can be truly integrated (eg online birth registration)." ukonline.gov user comment.

4 Effective content

The guideline

4.1. Users should be able to have reasonable expectations about the quality, accuracy and uniformity of government content using, for example, the UK online brand.

Why?

4.2. Users should not have to learn an entirely new navigation system for each of the approximately 1,000 central government sites or to know which department does what.

4.3. Users have a right to expect that content will be up to date and current.

4.3. Users should be able to know that certain kinds of information such as contact addresses will be available from any government website.

4.5. Users expect to have news and new content highlighted.

4.6. We should be building relationships with citizens, trying to earn their trust so that we can meet their needs.

Issues

4.7. Government websites publish both high-level documents such as white papers and service-based information such as guidance. This means they are large and require updating and maintenance.

4.8. Many government documents are not aimed at the general public nor are they written to be read online. Web managers need to consider providing some content aimed at different audiences specifically written to be read online.

4.9. Information on government sites is subject to the conventions on government publicity, advertising and sponsorship.

Practical advice

4.10. Government websites should strive to be engaging to users and relevant to the different needs of different kinds of visitor to the site.

4.11. Government websites should provide the following minimum content:
- details of ministers and management boards;
- the organisation's aims and objectives;
- full contact information;
- complaints procedures;
- command papers;
- press notices;
- consultation papers;
- research reports;
- statistical information;
- published forms;
- recruitment policies;
- details of advisory groups.
- News and updated content should also be provided and, when updates occur, shown on documents.

4.12. Government information must not be polemical and must be procured in a proper way that achieves value for money. Guidance on government information is available from ***http://www.gics.gov.uk/handbook/index.htm***

4.13. The Easyaccess approach (as seen on the ukonline.gov portal) provides a structure and content that meets the needs of new or disorientated users as well as those with communication or visual difficulties. For example, often the elderly need an additional helping hand with complex sites when they are not familiar with the Web and may find learning everything at once difficult.

*A recent evaluation of a Devolved Administration site shows that users' top priorities were **speed of download** and **up-to-date, accurate information**.*

5 Building trust

The guideline
5.1.   Government websites must raise citizen confidence by abiding by the law and explaining their terms and conditions to users. They should also be secure from intrusion and address the issues raised by the draft *Trust Charter for Electronic Service Delivery* (e-Trust Charter) guidelines, which clearly set out the rights of the citizen with respect to the information held by government.

Why?
5.2.   This protects the government and helps build user trust.

5.3.   Some users are reluctant to give government information about themselves. This

reduces our ability to give them the information and services they individually need.

5.4.   Advertising and sponsorship partners must be selected so that trust in websites is not reduced.

5.5.   Security is an absolute necessity if users are to trust us with their details or make

online payments.

5.5.   Users' trust in the security of government websites will be reduced if these sites are hacked and defaced.

5.7.   Government websites should support efforts to build users' trust in the Web as a whole.

Issues
5.8.   Government webmasters must inform themselves about their legal obligations.

5.9.   Departments need to have a security policy and ensure that their web hosting service or in-house server is secure.

5.9.   Users must know what we are going to do with their data.

Practical advice
5.10.   Websites must have a policy on the following areas which is explained on the site: the Disability Discrimination Act, the Data Protection Act, copyright etc.

5.11   Goverrnment websites should address the issues raised by the draft *Trust Charter for Electronic Service Delivery* (e-Trust Charter) guidelines. Information about the e-Trust Charter can be found at:
http://www.e-envoy.gov.uk/publications/guidelines_index.htm_

5.12   All government websites should be securely hosted and regularly penetration-tested. Passing this test on a regular basis should be a condition of all hosting contracts.

5.13   Government websites should have a Platform for Internet Content (PICS) rating. This works rather like the ratings system for film, except that it allows users automatically to filter out sites with certain kinds of content. Web managers need to register the site with at least the Internet Content Rating Association (ICRA) PICS service. They will need to include the site's rating in metadata. For more information visit: ***http://www.w3.org/PICS/*** and ***http://www.icra.org***.

> *"(You'll) get yourself on some subversive anarchist list" female 50+ ABC1 user on why she distrusts giving government information about herself.*

6 Listening – two-way communication

The guideline
6.1.   Users expect communication on the Web to be two-way. Government websites should provide opportunities for users to contact officials, express their views or make enquiries.

Why?
6.2.   The Internet is two-way by its very nature. Websites that do not provide channels for electronic enquiries or comments will be regarded as trying to evade them.

6.3.   The Freedom of Information Act will require that enquirers be answered in their preferred format. This will include email.

Issues
6.3.   Departments need to decide how best to handle email enquiries and response to them.

6.5.   Web managers need to resolve the many issues of running discussion groups. Among these issues are resolving accessibility for people with disabilities to enable them to be included.

6.6.   The Freedom of Information Act will require that all enquiries be responded to within 20 days in the enquirer's preferred format.

Practical advice
6.7.   Full contact address information for the organisation should be provided.

6.8.   Full contact information including email addresses for enquiry points or individuals and maps showing 'how to find us' should be provided.

6.8.   Any discussion group should have a clear policy on what can and cannot be posted. Moderation is recommended.

"It's got to be seen as a two-way street – to me it's like they're going to do it anyway, but they'll throw the public a wee sweetie" – female 30-49, C1C2DE, Consensus Research for ukonline.gov.uk.

7 More than just the Web – multiple access channels

The guideline

7.1.   Government websites should operate within a strategy that includes a full range of technology channels, such as interactive digital television (DiTV) and mobile devices.

Why?

7.2.   The *Modernising Government* white paper commits government to keeping pace with technological change including the use of new channels.

7.3.   These new platforms will help us reach new audiences, sometimes audiences that we have difficulty reaching through PC-based digital media.

Issues

7.4.   It is possible to design websites that can also be viewed directly on DiTV . Some will need to be automatically transcoded. For others, transcoding may not be enough. Care should be taken to meet the different needs of television audiences.

7.5.   For many channels, such as wireless application protocol (WAP) or portable devices, bespoke information and services will be needed.

Practical advice

7.6.   Organisations have a responsibility to ensure that their information and services are available through digital media where appropriate, for example interactive television, kiosks and mobile devices.

Sixty to 75 per cent of UK households will take digital TV by 200t. By 2005 broadband Internet will be available to between 55 per cent and 75 per cent of households. (e-Government policy framework: interactive digital television, draft version, November 2001)

8. Is it working?

The guideline

8.1.   Government websites should have systems for evaluating their success and determining if they are meeting the needs of users, making alterations where appropriate.

Why?

8.2.   Public money is being spent – some means of verifying value for money and effectiveness is needed.

8.3.   Users' needs should drive the site.

8.3.   Uniform use of access statistics across government will allow a clearer picture of user needs across government to develop.

8.4.   The sale of advertising space or gaining of sponsorship when appropriate will be made easier if sites can prove they are attracting an audience.

Issues

8.5.   Different hosting services provide different access statistics. You need to be clear what access statistics you require when procuring hosting services or when setting up a server in-house.

8.7.   Raw data is not information. It must be converted to useful information about user behaviour or preference.

8.8.   Offline research will be necessary to find out the needs of the target audiences who do not visit your site or fill in feedback forms.

Practical advice

8.9.   Government websites should collect, as a minimum, the following statistics:

- number of users (visitors);

- number of visits (unique visits);

- number of page impressions.

- They should also collect these statistics:

- successful requests;

- unsuccessful requests;

- most frequently visited pages;

- least frequently visited pages;

- top entry pages; and

- top referring pages.

8.9.   Additional information on who is using the site, the level of data transferred and notice-of-error logs should be monitored. Other criteria for evaluating the site should be based on communication or service targets. Quarterly evaluations are recommended.

8.11.   It is acceptable to use cookies to identify or track users' use of the site. The site must contain a clear statement of policy on the use of cookies, and the site should still work when the cookies are turned off.

9. Can your site be found?

The guideline

9.1   Government websites must provide consistent metadata (data about data) on all new documents as outlined in the mandatory *e-Government Metadata*

Framework (e-GMF). Managers should also promote the site and register it with search engines.

Why?

9.2. Users may not be able to find your site unless you promote it and ensure search engines list it.

9.3. Search engines of many types use metadata to locate documents and pages within your site.

9.3. Metadata will improve the ease with which government information can be joined up.

9.5. Metadata will improve ease of archiving and retrieval.

Issues

9.6. There are millions of websites. You will need to promote your website as appropriate through online search engines and directories, and through such means as press releases, your stationery and brochures, and perhaps advertising.

9.7. Web managers are not subject specialists. The authors of documents should help provide metadata about the content of their documents.

Practical advice

9.8. Webmasters are directed to the published framework on government metadata: *http://www.govtalk.gov.uk/interoperability/metadata.asp*

9.9. Metadata should be added to hypertext mark up language (HTML) pages and documents in metatags.

9.10. Information should be based on the e-GMF framework.

9.11. The authors of the document rather than webmasters should increasingly provide Metadata. This includes classifying all pages and documents with terms from the *Government Category List*, due for publication in November 2001. This will work with your own organisation's thesaurus of keywords.

9.12. Don't abuse metadata. Adding subject terms describing every aspect of your organisation's work to every page may initially increase the number of visits but is frustrating for users. Metadata should be used to take users directly to the information they want, wherever on your site it may be.

9.13. Web managers should be familiar with how to register the site and additions to it with the major search engines/directories.

9.14. Is your URL memorable and easily understood? Is it within government guidelines? Advice on naming policy in the .gov.uk domain is available at: *http://www.ogc.gov.uk/naming/domains.html*

*Search engines are the leading way users in the United Kingdom locate websites.
Eightyone per cent said search engines helped them find sites. (Forrester Research)*

10. A well managed service

The guideline

10.1.   Government websites should be well managed, with:

- adequate resourcing;

- clear strategy, aims, and target audiences;

- publishing and business procedures in place;

- a strategy for future development including moves to dynamic databases and other digital media.

Why?

10.2.   Government websites typically publish more documents that are more detailed than commercial sites. Some sites now have roughly one 120,000 documents. Maintenance and updating alone is a logistical challenge.

10.3.   Government websites have different and more complex aims and requirements than commercial sites – only good management balances all these priorities.

10.3.   Good management may help retain skilled staff.

10.4.   Good management will ensure that sites plan for change, evolving to meet user needs and moving away from static hypertext mark up language (HTML) to more efficient, dynamic websites.

10.5.   Good management is the only way to build in and check for quality.

10.6.   Good management is not a technical web issue – it requires senior management involvement.

Issues

10.7.   Many government sites are not adequately resourced to carry out their publication tasks.

10.8.   A clear editorial policy needs to be supported by clear procedures.

10.9.   Legal obligations for Welsh language provision, archiving of public records and freedom of information may not be met if management is poor.

10.10. Requirements to provide online services, metadata on new documents, and Web Accessibility Initiative (WAI) Level accessibility may not be met, or maintained, if management is poor.

10.11. Some sites need to provide information in European Community languages. We also have a moral obligation to reach ethnic minority communities in the UK. To translate and update material in other languages requires clear procedures.

10.12. Specialist skills may be difficult to recruit and retain. Training your own staff is one option.

10.13. A full mix of skills is needed to set the goals for, brief designers of, and manage websites. These skills include communication strategy, content and publicity, marketing, IT, information science and business process.

Practical advice

10.14. Websites should:

- be developed in a coherent manner;

- be under the control of senior management with board members taking active responsibility;

- have active input and ownership from all units; and

- be supported by specialist expertise in technical, editorial, accessibility/usability and business process areas.

10.15. All staff should have ready access to the Internet and to their department's own websites. Training in preparation of documents for the Web should be available.

10.16. Set up sites to allow authors of information to input updates directly themselves.

10.17. Provision of minority languages in non-Roman alphabets will be difficult for a while. Web managers are advised to avoid graphic formats such as graphical interchange formats (GIFs) as some users turn these off. Portable document formats (PDFs) for non-Roman scripts are recommended. Anchor pages linking to all material in a particular language are recommended. This will make it easier to link all government information in these languages.

Conclusion

11.1. These guidelines have been adopted by the Office of the e-Envoy on behalf of 'government e-Champions, e-Communications Group. It is expected therefore that all departments and agencies developing government websites will make all reasonable efforts to comply with them. This pertains to all new sites and existing sites that are being revised.

11.2. The *Guidelines for UK government websites* includes *The Illustrated Handbook for Web management teams*. This handbook provides detailed advice and reminders for hands-on web managers with, for example, checklists, summaries, useful uniform resource locator (URL) links, example screenshots, sample coding and specimen terms and conditions and guidance on archiving websites.

11.3. A small, self-contained, accessible and usable website template supports the online version of this handbook. This is designed for training purposes and to assist in building an accessible website. The template is fully marked up in HTML4 with accompanying Cascading Style Sheets and sample Easyaccess pages. This is provided for re-use free of charge without restriction, provided the source is acknowledged.

Contents

4 HTML markup, other formats and scripting

5 Developments

6 Technical details and tutorials

Annexes

Specifying your website – checklist

Glossary

Index

Introduction

Digital media are becoming mass media. New audiences and new platforms are opening up new opportunities for government communications and services, allowing more personal and two-way communication than every before. More members of the general public are visiting government websites. In order to benefit from this, government needs to ensure that its own digital media offer a *best in class* experience to the user. For example, material aimed at professionals may not meet the needs of a general public audience. Users expect content and services that are engaging, relevant to them and effective.

In the future, owning a personal computer will no longer be the only way to interact electronically with the government. Users will the choice of interactive digital television, kiosks, game consoles and third generation wireless mobile devices. Access to government services may be available, for example, through public libraries, local UK online centres and post offices.

1 What is a UK Government website?

For the purposes of these Guidelines a UK Government website is one that is owned by and is managed by or for departments and agencies and other organisations detailed within the biannual Civil Service Yearbook.

2 How can these Guidelines help with website management

The *Framework for senior managers* outlines strategy and the top ten Guidelines. This handbook given detailed practical advice on how to achieve these and is intended for:

- hands-on web management teams,
- suppliers of design, development and Internet services, and
- staff requiring an introduction to the Web and how it works for government.

The Guidelines also cross-refers to other sources of policy and guidance, such as, e-government Interoperability Framework.

Electronic publishing via the Internet should be placed alongside other media as a means of providing information and services to the public, including citizens and businesses. This means that senior management should ensure that the necessary skills for professional electronic publishing are identified and the necessary resources provided and its use is integrated within the overall communication strategy.

There should be clear identification of responsibilities for ensuring the accuracy, legal compliance and currency of information on public sector sites. These principles underpin many of the sections of the guidelines.

The Guidelines draw attention to the recently revised Disability Discrimination Act's *Code of Practice on rights of access to goods, facilities, services and premises for*

disabled people and the requirement for information and services on the Internet to be as inclusive as possible. This Code of Practice is available from
http://www.drc.org.uk/drc/InformationAndLegislation/Page331a.asp

This means that our websites should be as convenient and easy to use as possible. That they should be designed in ways to minimise download times and should take full account of the different levels of competence and equipment which members of the public may have in their use of the Internet. This approach is not that of the lowest common denominator, but rather one that recommends to departments that they are continuously aware of how to provide options that offer an inclusive service. These Guidelines cover this in some details in section 2.4 and the technical guidance in Chapters 4 to 6 is written with these requirements in mind.

3 Compliance and implementation

These guidelines are intended to deliver Ministers' wishes that government websites should be of a high quality, easy to use and inclusive and that they should present a coherent impression of government activity. They acknowledge that content and presentational style may vary, but that basic technical features and good management practice should not. These Guidelines offer a range of good practice for the design of sites, which stresses the need for accessibility, usability, economy for the users and the minimum requirements for content including need to comply with some cross-government policies on information.

It is expected therefore that departments and agencies should make all reasonable effort to comply with these Guidelines. In the first instance, all new sites and the revision of existing sites should be compliant. The task of ensuring compliance of existing site will require an audit of the existing estate by web managers. This will enable departments to plan programmes for revising their sites. Web managers should also refer to the mandated e-government Interoperability Framework available at:
http://www.e-envoy.gov.uk/publications/frameworks_index.htm

In order to reduce duplication and help provide solutions, the Office of the e-Envoy is providing central infrastructure resources, such as, the Government Gateway and a secure hosting service. These resources with common design, applications and a hardware solution supported by implementation services should make it easier and more cost-effective for government organisations to purchase technical solutions. See section 1.1.2 **Planning your products and services**.

4 Authorship and maintenance

The maintenance of this document is the responsibility of the Digital Communications Team, e-Communications Group, Office of the e-Envoy. Enquires about any aspect of the document should be made to ***webguidelines@e-envoy.gsi.gov.uk***.

Whilst every effort has been made to ensure the information in these guidelines is accurate, we cannot accept responsibility for legal action taken based on this material. If you require a formal opinion on the law and its interpretation in any area and on electronic publishing and electronic services, please seek professional legal advice.

5 Acknowledgements and trademarks

This handbook was written by Neil Pawley from OGC (formerly the CCTA Internet Services) and Tom Adams and Geoff Ryman of the Office of the e-Envoy. They have been greatly assisted by colleagues from within specialist areas. The work has been validated by the UK office of the World Wide Web Consortium (W3C), Tim Levy an independent technical expert and Robin Brattel an independent web developer. Her Majesty's Stationery Office, The Information Commissioner, Treasury Solicitor's Department, COI Communications, Office of Government Commerce, Public Record Office, Welsh Language Board, the Royal National Institute for the Blind, Internet Content Rating Association and Nominet.UK have been consulted about the content.

The following is a lit of W3C terms claimed as trademark or a generic terms by MIT, INRIA, and/or Keio on behalf of the W3C, and a number of W3C icons are reproduced: W3C®, World Wide Consortium; CSS ™, Cascading Style Sheet specification; HTML (generic) HyperText Markup Language; Metadata (generic); WAI™, Web Accessibility Initiative; XHTML™, The Extensible HyperText Markup Language; XML (generic), Extensible Markup Language and PICSRules™. *http://www.w3.org*

The term Adobe is used to refer to Adobe software and products. Acrobat®, Acrobat® Reader™, are trademarks of Adobe Systems incorporated. *http://www.adobe.com*
IBM® is the registered trademark of IBM in the United States. *http://www.ibm.com*
Java and all Java-based trademarks are trademarks of Sun Microsystems, Inc in the United States, other countries, or both. *http://sun.com*
Microsoft®, Windows®, windows NT® and the Windows logo are trademarks of Microsoft Corporation in the United States, other countries or both. *http://www.microsoft.com*
Netscape and the Netscape N and Ship's wheel logos are registered trademarks of Netscape Communications Corporation in the US and other countries and are also trademarks of Netscape Communications Corporation and may also be registered outside the US. *http://home.netscape.com* .
The Watchfire Corporation owns Bobby™. *http://bobby.watchfire.com*
UNIX is the registered trademark of the Open Group in the United States and other countries.

6 Who should use this document

The Guidelines for UK Government websites – Illustrated handbook for web management teams focuses on improving our websites and is intended for:
- hands-on web management teams
- suppliers of design and development services
- staff requiring an introduction to the Web and how it works for the government.

Web managers working within Devolved Administrations or related bodies should review these Guidelines in the light of their own policies and legal and regulatory frameworks. This handbook is available online via -- *www.e-envoy.gov.uk/webguidelines.htm.*

1.1 Purpose of your website

The provision and ongoing delivery of a website, like all service delivery methods, is as dependent on the quality of its management infrastructure and controls as it is on the quality of information being provided. Additionally, the pace of technological development in the Internet arena demands that organisations move with the times and seek opportunities to take advantage of any new services on offer.

1.1.1 How should a website be considered by an organisation?

It is essential for the success of any website that it is recognised as an integral part of the organisation. It is a global, potentially low-cost communication and an (increasingly) transactional medium by which information and services can be made available at any time of day or night. As such, organisations need to consider how best the Internet can be used to provide access to information and to aid in the delivery of goods and services to customers.

A clear web management strategy is at the heart of developing this thinking. It must be an integral part of the organisation's Corporate Communications and e-Strategies.

There are three main categories of website:

- **Information orientated:** these cover departmental publications, publicity, recruitment, news, statutory information, promotional material, providing advice, requesting responses and feedback. They may, for example, provide an electronic catalogue to users. Queries and requests can be handled via email or forms. Orders, and necessary payment, can be fulfilled through the conventional procedures.

- **Operational:** these are transactional websites geared towards e-business and cover the whole online process, from service selection through ordering and confirmation to online payment. These may be integrated with departmental systems to enable electronic transactions with the public and other customers.

- **Campaign:** such websites will support a specific publicity campaign, working directly with press, TV and radio advertising. All the media reflect the same messages and images. They may also provide an electronic catalogue to users with requests being handled via email. Fulfilment can be handled through the conventional procedures.

Many websites may incorporate aspects of each of the above. In all three categories the principle of developing a relevant and effective management strategy applies. This section sets out the five key components of a web management strategy:

- **Purpose** – what is the website for?
- **Strategic and operational management** – who is the owner and who is responsible?
- **Information and other content management** – how will material and services be

provided and presented online?
- **Evaluation and ongoing development** – how should use and performance of the website be monitored and how should the results be used for future development?

1.1.2 What is the website for?

In establishing the aims of the website, each organisation must ensure that:

- users should be able to find your website;
- users are clear about who owns the website and what it is designed to achieve;
- navigation is clear and customer orientated, taking into account the needs of specific audiences;
- goods and services being offered by the organisation are effectively focused on the target audiences in terms of relevance and ease of accessibility
- visitors are able to access the information they seek as directly as is practicable;
- adequate security is in place when dealing with online transactions for the purchase of goods and services – and that neither the client nor the provider is compromised;
- contact points (whether email, forms-based or telephone) must be staffed and all enquiries answered within reasonable timescales;
  the information published is up to date, accurate and relevant to the website;
- content is clear, concise and appropriate;
- links are kept up to date that users can rely on the website being available and is fast enough.

The tasks to be addressed when setting the aims and objectives are:

- identification of your website's place in the organisation's overall communications strategy;
- identification of the audiences for your website, where possible on the basis of market research or dialogue with client groups;
- understanding and responding to users' satisfaction with the website;
- provision of resources, especially staff with the necessary skills, for the website team;
- integration of the website with business processes, which might include electronic dealings with the public, publication of information, recruitment and consultation;
- integration of the website into the department's strategy for electronic government and freedom of information;
- integration of web services with other systems where practicable;
- monitoring the development of the website and its success as a means of meeting departmental objectives.

To ensure that the aims and objectives of the website are achieved they must be applied to key roles in the organisation and placed under an appropriate management regime.

1.1.3 Benefits of publishing data on the Internet

Although publishing documentation on the Internet initially seems to be little different to publishing in any other medium, there are a number of special considerations that need to be borne in mind. There are almost as many permutations of monitor resolution, colour rendering, browser types, operating systems and user ability, as there are websites. Website Managers will have to consider many capabilities and standards to ensure that data is available to the widest audience.

There can be enormous benefits when documentation is published on the Internet, both for the publishing body and the general user.

1.1.3.1 Information access

A well designed website offers users a broader range of information than is available to them through conventional media, when they want it and in a form they can use.

To achieve this, the website should make use of the number of ways the web helps users find the documents they are looking for such as search engines, menus, navigational aids, indices and links between documents. Web navigation should also help users find the information they want within the document.

Some information such as menu pages and document summaries will have to be written specifically to be quickly scanned and understood.

It may be appropriate to make documentation available in a variety of differing formats. For example, some users may find it easier to download and print an entire document in Portable Document Format (PDF) and read it offline, whilst other may prefer to read it in online and on –screen in the form of a sequence of HTML pages.

1.1.3.2 Accurate and up-to-date

The web is easier to update or correct than print. Documents contained on the website can be a point of reference for both the public and your staff. Some departments provide a copy of their website on their intranet to facilitate this. A 'What's New' section should be included and constantly updated so that users have a constant and familiar route to new and updated information.

To achieve accuracy, the maintenance of documents after publication should be planned and resourced. Each document should adhere to the site template and all data should be formatted in a consistent way. Particular care should be paid to the Cascading Style Sheet, which may be used to control the formatting of the website.

1.1.3.3 Savings on print and distribution costs

Publishing data on the website should save on the printing, distribution and storing of printed documents and the wastage caused by overestimated print runs. Only the one copy needs to be maintained; as soon as a changed version is published it is available to everyone.

In order to achieve this publication in print and on the web should be part of one carefully planned publication process. This process should be audited regularly to ensure it is efficient.

1.1.3.4 Website maintenance and archiving

Web documents can also be a reliable source of older documents, developing into a useful archive.

This will be achieved if archived documents are given a stable URL and are clearly marked as being archived. It is important that electronic master copies of each document published on the website are kept. This not only makes the creation of new versions in other formats easy; it also maintains an archive version for historical purposes.

See **section 1.2.7** records management.
See **Annex L** Archiving websites.

1.1.3.5 Providing the call to action

A good publicity campaign issues a call for action – something the user is expected to do. A campaign website can give the user the chance to quickly and simply carry out that action, whether it is to set up an appointment, order more information, or enter the recruitment process for a public sector job.

1.1.3.6 Opening up consultation

Government makes policies and needs to collect informed views from organisations and individuals.   The web can provide this opportunity and provide another channel for the distribution of the background documents that people need in order to contribute to the debate.

1.1.3.7 Interactivity

The Web can speed up the process of individuals getting the answers they need. Websites could be used to direct enquiries to the right place in the organisation to get an answer. Email can speed up the process of responding to them.

1.1.3.8 Adapting to user needs quickly

Feedback and access statistics can tell web managers which pages are popular and which pages need further development. They can help identify gaps in information or services. A well-managed website will respond to user needs and use the flexibility of the web to revise the website.

1.1.3.9 Building individual relations with the citizen

Web technology provides a way for users to register interests and receive automatic updates of news and developments in the areas that interest them. Website content can be *personalised* to meet their interests and concerns, or provide local or national versions of information that are relevant to them.

1.1.3.10 Saving costs on services

Properly supported by business plans and backend systems, the web can be used to improve services and reduce the cost of providing them.

1.2 Management of your website

The key to effective website management is the development and implementation of a strategy designed to ensure that it remains focused on what the organisation is there to deliver as well as on what information and services the target audiences expect to be able to access.

1.2.1 Strategic and operational management

Effective website management can be defined under three categories:

- owning organisation – Web strategy and management team
- web service manager – Web Manager (aka Webmaster)
- information providers – content owners and the editorial team

1.2.1.1 The owning organisation

The owning organisation is responsible for establishing and maintaining the web management strategy and for ensuring that it integrates with wider strategic plans.

The equivalent of a senior editorial board is recommended. This will help ensure that key areas of the organisation bring a full range of necessary skills and awareness to the process of setting aims and objectives for the website. The owning organisation should also ensure that the resources are in place to achieve these aims. The following are examples of key areas of the organisation that should be represented.

- communications
- corporate services
- web service provision
- content provision
- resource provision
- technology provision.

1.2.1.2 Skill sets for setting web strategy

Communications: Executive Board
At this level the corporate communications policy is set. Therefore a clear framework covering how the organisation is to communicate information is required and is to be used to determine the subject matter to be covered by the website. This approach will clarify the areas of content control appropriate to both the Internet and Intranet.

This role does not require day-to-day involvement. It is more about clearly defining the parameters within which information is to be made available in the public domain and establishing appropriate control mechanisms for handling potentially sensitive information.

Corporate services: publicity and marketing
Publicity or marketing skills support the communication strategy, ensuring that audiences are identified and effective communication of messages and promotion of services takes place. Their understanding of the organisation's publicity and marketing strategy is integral to ensuring that the website communicates effectively and provides services users require.

Web service provision: Web management team
The web management team will know the opportunities and caveats of working with the web: what it does well and what can go wrong.

They can be a source of new ideas, and are likely to be able to keep an eye on the technological future.

As they represent the day-to-day management of the website they are also a source of practical advice on procedures, resourcing, scheduling, capacity, risks and benefits.

They are likely to be responsible for looking at access statistics and user feedback and are well placed to take an impartial view of customer needs versus organisational perceptions.

They are responsible for maintaining the structure of the website and understanding the limitations of staff time, Internet technology and the systems the organisation has in place.

It is likely that there will be one key manager responsible for content and another responsible for technical issues and developments. Both sides of the team should be represented on the editorial board.

Content owners
The people in the organisation who will want to publish to the web. What are their needs, issues, etc? What capacity do they have to amend and update content? It is important that a procedure is in place to control the correction and uploading of content, ie, who has final signoff before content goes live.

Resource provision
Because a website invariably impacts the whole organisation in terms of service delivery and business processes, it is essential that the resource implications are recognised and handled accordingly. Allied to this is the need to ensure that the technology aspects of the website are sufficiently and appropriately resourced and that future staff and equipment needs are planned in advance. This can be particularly difficult in an area notorious for its pace of change and evolution.

Material for the website (and other future communication technologies) has to be generated using specific software tools and languages. These create training and organisational requirements that need to be covered as part of the website management regime.

Finally, staff has to be recruited and trained and a purchasing budget will be necessary for software, equipment and consultants.

Technology provision:
All web services are dependent on technology solutions. Impartial technical advice and guidance is required to ensure that the most appropriate solution is used to meet customer service needs. It is essential that someone familiar with the technology should cover this area. However, given the diversity of IT solutions available in the marketplace, technological impartiality is essential and as such should be a key factor when selecting a suitable representative.

The establishment of a web strategy and management team comprising representatives that cover these roles will result in a more streamlined operational group. By operating in a more project-style management environment the team will be able to create and manage small teams geared towards delivering products on a customer-demand basis.

1.2.2 Web service management

A team of people will be responsible for ensuring that the website achieves its strategic aims. It does this through:

- measuring achievement against overall aims and objectives set by the organisation
- effective website operation
- effective content provision

This team should consist of people with a mix of publication, web and project management skills. A senior web manager is recommended to manage the team and ensure it carries out its tasks. A further division of labour between content and technical responsibilities is likely.

1.2.2.1 Meeting overall aims and objectives

Clear, formal and regular progress reports against the aims and objectives are recommended to ensure that:

- ongoing and proposed new developments for the website have been measured against the objectives, costed to ensure the best value and considered in relation to corporate developments;
- a business case has been prepared and approved to ensure sufficient resources (financial, time and people) have been allocated;
- projects for delivery are being managed within agreed tolerances (again tied to the business case).

Reports need not be onerous, with the emphasis being on reporting by exception. They will help inform the broader organisation of progress and give stakeholders the opportunity to raise concerns, issues and/or new developments.

The benefits of this process are:

- it provides a way to ensure continued adherence to delivery against set objectives;
- open and clear communication on developments throughout the organisation;
- accountability for development work against clearly defined resource limits;
- reduced risks on overlaps, duplication and failure to deliver against expectations.

1.2.2.2 Effective website operation

The website strategy should also determine the management, communications and security regimes that will drive the service. These objectives are also the criteria against which service level agreements (under formal contract where external commercial suppliers are party to service provision) are set.

The web management team should:

- manage the day-to-day operational interface with the Internet Service Provider (ISP)/hosting service in line with the agreed standards of service;
- ensure the security and reliability of the ISP/hosting service;
- determine the most appropriate technologies to be used for the production and availability of the information and/or goods and services;
- manage the procurement and subsequent contracts or Service Level Agreements with Internet Service Providers /hosting services;
- ensure that staffing levels are maintained for website content provision, in line with agreed standards of service;
- keep key stakeholders within the organisation informed of service performance against agreed targets and objectives.
- co-ordinate publishing of Internet information;
- set and maintain the organisation's design and editorial specifications for the Web (commonly called style guidelines);
- ensure that all information held on the website conforms to frameworks and standards set by the Cabinet Office, including the Government Web Guidelines and legislation, eg, copyright and data protection.
- ensure the website continues to work in a range of browsers and keep checking page links as they are easily broken;
- in partnership with the ISP, maintain the integrity of a website's structure, content and availability to agreed standards;
- monitor website activity including bandwidth usage, analyse usage statistics, review the regularity of updating information and report the findings to the relevant personnel.

The web management team can contribute towards effective transactions by ensuring that the website effectively exchanges data between the user and the organisation. They contribute to ensuring that transactions and authentication are secure. Effective transactions are likely to also require reform of other operational systems in order to accept electronic applications.

1.2.2.3 Effective content

The web management team is also the overall point of responsibility for ensuring that content:

- is line with the web management strategy
- takes its place in a clear and navigable website structure
- is consistent in style, intent and accuracy
- communicates effectively and meets users needs.

The relevant units can still carry out production of material across the organisation, but material can only be published once authorised by the appropriate posts in the web management team. The objectives for information providers must therefore be to ensure that:

- information is accurate, relevant and up-to-date;
- content held conforms to the style set down for the website;
- contact points (email, telephone or interactive form) are staffed, inputs received are actioned and responses given within agreed targets;
- metadata is provided for all new documents
- information is provided by the agreed deadline.

There should be sufficient controls in place to check that content:

- meets all editorial standards
- is in line with overall communication strategy
- is reviewed regularly by the information provider for currency and correctness
- is removed or archived when appropriate
- is easily accessible, navigable, with no broken links.

1.2.2.3 Effective service

All government websites must be working towards providing online information and services. The web management team's role here is to help ensure that data can be securely and effectively exchanged between the user and databases within the organisation and partner bodies. Effective service provision also involves reform of business systems in order to work with electronic data, security and authentication.

1.2.3 Conventions on government publicity

Websites maintained by UK Government departments and agencies, the Scottish Executive, the Northern Ireland Executive and the National Assembly for Wales are a form of publicity, and are subject to the conventions on government publicity and advertising.

These conventions are set out and explained at the following websites:

> **Guidance on the work of the Government Information Service**
> *http://www.cabinet-office.gov.uk/central/1999/workgis*
>
> **GICS handbook**
> *http://www.gics.gov.uk/handbook/index.htm*

In summary, they require that government publicity:

- should be relevant to government responsibilities;
- should be objective and explanatory, not tendentious or polemical;
- should not be party political, nor liable to misrepresentation as such;
- should be produced and distributed in an economical and relevant way, so that the costs can be justified as a proper expenditure of public funds.

These rules not only govern decisions on what should or should not be published on the Internet; they also apply to issues of content and style. For example, departments should take care when publishing ministerial speeches on the Internet to remove overtly party political content, such as direct attacks on policies and opinions of Opposition parties and groups.

See **section 1.3** Advertising and Sponsorship

1.2.4 Contingency planning

Whatever an organisation's line of business, there is always a requirement for contingency plans to cover a number of eventualities.

A government organisation can be thrust into the spotlight of the media at a moment's notice. You should ensure that your website has the capability to carry fast-developing stories and that its web hosting service would be able to deal with a sudden increase in the number of visitors.

A news development that requires immediate publishing on the web must not shortcut or bypass existing publishing standards. The contingency plan may suggest that it can be streamlined but the correct authorisation must be given before any information is published on the website.

Within this contingency plan there should a clear and easily accessible list of roles and responsibilities for each of the staff concerned in publishing emergency information. This list must be up-to-date and have contact numbers for each individual.

This same list of individuals to contact and a similar list of roles and responsibilities will be vital in any disaster recovery scheme. If the server is physically destroyed, severely hacked or ceases to function there should be plans already in place to restore service. If your organisation has an overall disaster recovery plan, then plans to restore website service should work within it.

Finally, you should ensure your contract with your server host writes preventative measures such as frequency of backup and the supplier's responsibilities in the event of a disaster.

See **section 1.12.3** Disaster recovery

> **IMPORTANT**
> The organisation's website may be the first port of call for many members of the public, and **incorrect data posted on the site in a hurry is worse than no data at all.**

1.2.5 Mirror (ghost)copy of website

The machine running the live website will usually reside at an Internet hosting datacentre. It is recommended that the web manager should keep one or more additional 'mirror' copies of the organisation's website on a local PC. This is in order to facilitate the development and testing of updates to the website's content and organisation prior to installing the changes on the live site.

One commonly adopted solution is for the web manager to establish a development environment and a second checking (or *staging*) environment in addition to the live website. It is possible to have the development and staging versions of the website on the same computer. However, it is important to keep the development and testing functions well separated regardless of whether the two mirror copies are on the same computer or separate ones.

Maintaining local copies of the website will also allow the complete and latest version of the site to be available at all times when only a dialled or slow speed connection to the Internet is available. It may also be desirable to automate the updating of the live website in order to minimise the time that it is unavailable while updates are being installed.

With a local development copy of the website, it is easy to see how any new documents will fit into the existing structure. Maintaining a staging copy of the website enables content and links to be checked and general usability to be tested prior to applying changes to the live website.

It is likely that a local PC's filesystem naming and organisation rules will be different from those used on the live server. In order for the development and test environments to be of value and easy to use, it is important they should replicate the directory and file organisation and naming used on the live website.   Often this can be achieved quite straightfordwardly by keeping all file and directory names and the references to them in hyperlinks within pages in lower case and always using relative URLs in internal hyperlinks (ie, reference all links from the root of the website). Refer to section **sections 1.9** and **3.2.3** for recommendations on directory and file naming schemes for websites. Following these recommendations will improve the chances that the live website directory structure and the files it contains can be copied to a PC where the site hyperlink navigation will work without having to make changes to all the files.

It is a role of the web manager to assess the technical requirements for the website development and testing environments in consultation with server managers. Typically the requirements will depend upon issues such as the size and complexity of the website and aspects of the regime under which it is managed, for example, whether it is being updated by more than one staff member or from multiple geographical locations.

1.2.6 Developing educational content

Where an organisation's website is developing online education content it is important that you refer to advice published by the National Grid for Learning.

- When planning web pages the content providers should be clear about whether they are likely to appear to a high proportion of children or young people.
- Consider carefully before linking from pages designed for children to pages where children are not the primary audience. Take special care when planning to link to external websites.
- Web managers should take steps to prevent any child from publishing their email address on your website or in a discussion group.

Web managers should also be aware of procedures that apply to the use of children's photographs on websites. You should be especially sensitive in the case of children or young people with special educational needs. If:

- You could readily identify an individual child by sight,
- or if the child is named.

Then you should:

- Have written consent to the publication of the photographs, signed by the parent of legal guardian.
- The consent should clearly include the Internet – it would not be sufficient to simply re-use consent that applied to a conventional publication.
- Retain the signed consent form.

When a website is directed at children or young people consider offering advice to them and their parents about safe surfing. See Home Office website at
http://www.wiseupthenet.co.uk/

The forthcoming Quality Framework document on 'What makes a good government website' explains what to do when children are involved in user research.

National Grid for Learning – Advice for Content Providers
http://www.ngfl.gov.uk/advice

NGfL Ground rules and Code of Practice
http://challenge.ngfl.gov.uk/

> **Keeping your child safe on the Internet (Home Office website)**
> *http://www.wiseuptothenet.co.uk/*

> **Jakob Nielsen's Alertbox – Kids' Corner: Website Usability for Children**
> *http://www.useit.com/alertbox/2002414.html*

1.2.7 Records management

Records Management is the systematic control and management of recorded information resources within an organisation to ensure that the business, legal, regulatory and other requirements for the retention of authentic, evidential records are met.

There are also useful management concepts familiar to records management professionals that are of use to managing large volume information resources. Examples include retention management (usually achieved using schedules), protective marking of sensitive material (eg on Intranets), corporate fileplans etc.

The underlying principle of records management is that records are kept for a period appropriate to their use. Specific procedures follow this principle to assist in its achievement in a systematic and structured way.

Records occurring on websites should be managed in the context of other information resources and records in government and not in isolation. Certain web content across government **will** have the status of records and should be identified and managed accordingly to manage business risk and comply with legal and regulatory obligations. Some will be required to be preserved for long periods for these reasons or to satisfy the archival preservation requirements of the Public Records Acts (see **section 1.10.5**).

Managing records in the electronic environment is demanding. Issues of retrieval, migration, authentication and preservation replace pressure on storage space in the traditional hard copy environment. Adding disk space may be a cheap option in the short term, but migrating the content to new platforms and ensuring media refreshment occurs at regular intervals are extremely costly.

This has a significant consequence on the management of web resources and the Public Record Office has published guidance on how these issues might be addressed: *Managing web resources: managing electronic records on websites and Intranets* available from: *http://www.pro.gov.uk/recordsmanagement/standards/default/htm*.

See **Annex L** Archiving websites.

1.2.8   Management documentation

Whether the organisation's website has been produced internally or by a design agency, it is important that each element of the construction is fully documented.

Personnel within the website management team will eventually move on and need to be replaced. Without adequate formal documentation a great deal of time will be lost in new staff determining, eg, what markup to use in order to maintain a consistent look and feel.

A number of standards should be developed for the life cycle of a website or document, covering many of the following:

- the management structure that a document must be passed through before it can be published;
- the production of HTML pages, whether they are manually constructed or dynamically generated from a database;
- the production of other document formats, such as PDF and RTF from the source document;
- the organisational publishing standards, eg housestyle covering colour usage, font specifications, logo placement, writing styles, etc;
- the lifespan control of on-line documents;
- the organisation's designated web authors and their roles and responsibilities;
- the management and storage of archived documents, both electronically and paper based (records management);
- the management of the web-hosting service-provision contract;
- the administration of the web server (if controlled internally);
- the information back-up routine that has been adopted;
- the management of existing third party contracts for publishing or design work;
- records of software and license agreements that are used by the website team,
- the administration and use of any escrow agent(s);
- the maintenance of an asset register of all domain names/sub-domains registered by/owned by the organisation, eg, date registered, when to be renewed, and corresponding IP numbers;
- record of permissions granted by third parties for you to link to their website(s);
- record of intellectual property rights permissions obtained, eg, for text, graphics, audio or video materials used;
- manage passwords keeping a record for emergency situations.

1.3 Sponsorship and advertising

Advertising on the web is envisaged as being a revenue stream for government websites. It can reduce the cost of providing government information and services, which saves the taxpayer money or results in better quality services and faster delivery of information and services on-line. It is a perfectly legitimate thing to do as long as the guidelines are adhered to.

Sponsors fund parts of a government publicity project, or support it by providing services or equipment. They do this in exchange for visible acknowledgement. This can be understood as implying a closer relationship than advertising. Therefore particular care is needed to make clear that both your Department and your website retain their independence in every way.

Over time, it is likely that advertising and sponsorship will become increasingly important as ways of funding the provision of information and services or developing websites. It is expected that guidance here will need to be regularly revisited, as markets develop.

1.3.1 Contract management

The management of advertising or sponsorship arrangements can be established using the following routes:

- in-house management of web space to be made available for advertising or other means of publicity agreed under a sponsorship agreement, or
- the use of a third party supplier to manage the advertising or sponsorship web space on your behalf.

The available costs, benefits and expertise are key factors when deciding which route will suit your organisation. All must be examined and included in the evaluation of the business case for making use of advertising or sponsorship to raise potential commercial revenues.

1.3.2 Advertising

Using the Internet for advertising falls into two distinct categories:

- *Selling* advertising or sponsorship space on your website, and
- *Buying* advertising space on other websites.

Advice on buying advertising is covered in **section 1.3.3**.

Selling advertising space on Government websites is not an easy task. This is a rapidly evolving and fiercely competitive area and a dedicated, trained resource is required to managed, sell and promote this service. You are advised to source help from specialist agencies, eg, COI Communications.

The full value should be obtained from the sale of advertising on government websites.

Departments and agencies need to judge carefully the balance between the effort required to achieve the maximum value and the income that is earned. Payment for web advertising may not be based on space alone, but on the number of page downloads or 'clicks on the ad'. Alternatively, an advertiser may wish to sell 'button space' on your website. These are fixed graphics with links to the advertised organisation's own website or campaign, paid for at a fixed rate for a fixed period of time, sometimes regardless of the number of page impressions or 'clicks through'.

Advertisers may expect there to be a link between known user interest and who sees the advert. You will probably need to be able to prove levels of access (refer to **section 1.4** Evaluation and **section 1.5** Focusing on user needs).

- in designing pages, you should ensure that advertisers' brands do not compete with or detract from the effectiveness, integrity and appearance of their own branding or that of the government as a whole.
- attention should be given to avoid any implication of endorsement of products or services or of contradiction between government messages and those of advertisers.
- Website users are often irritated by pop-up advertisements and related technologies (variously referred to as 'interstitials', 'superstitials') and particularly by those that draw animations within the main window overlaying the page content. It is therefore recommended that advertisements on government websites should be confined to the use of banners and buttons.
- where banner and button advertising space is included in Web pages, it is recommended the dimensions should conform to those of the industry-standard Interactive Marketing Units (IMU) defined by The Interactive Advertising Bureau (IAB) at ***http://www.iab.net/iab_banner_standards/bannersource.html*** Advertisers should be advised to bear in mind the range of connection speeds used by visitors to government websites and the implications for viable file sizes of advertisement content.
- with images and animations ensure use of the <alt> attribute to describe the function of each visual and ensure that the overall guidance in **section 2.4** and **section 2.9** is followed;
- if you are using information about user behaviour to sell advertising space, you must not breach your own website's published privacy statement (see **section 1.10**) and if in any doubt you must ask the advice of your Data Protection Officer.

1.3.3 The buying of advertising space on other websites

As the market place is in constant evolution and having a strategic approach to Internet advertising is required. Unlike traditional advertising space, the Internet does not benefit widely from independent audience audits. Traffic claims can be variable and you must ask for specific information – page impressions, from where specific information and pages are requested, etc – and make judgements on the effectiveness of an individual site against the site operator's claims.

In line with your overall media communications strategy specialist agencies are best placed to carry out the following tasks for you:

- planning an internet advertising campaign using various sites and methods of reaching your target audience;
- negotiating the approved plan to ensure maximum value for money;
- implementing the approved plan to ensure that the adverts appear on time and in the right place, and
- optimising campaigns through identification of the most appropriate web pages to be used for advertising, analysis of page impressions and 'click through' and the published performance of individual sites.

This is a specialist area and you are advised to refer to the *Guidance on the Work of the Government Information Service* ***http://www.gics.gov.uk/handbook/guidance/giswork/index.htm***. This gives detailed guidance on the propriety, value for money and procedural criteria that must be met by every paid publicity proposal, and includes web advertising. Value for money and procedural guidance is in paragraphs 25–32 of the guidance. Paragraph 28 stipulates that the principal source of advice in a department is the Head of Information, who should be given sufficient time to comment. Annex A ***http://www.gics.gov.uk/handbook/guidance/giswork/annexa.htm*** is the guidance on propriety in Government publicity and advertising. Annex C – ***http://www.gics.gov.uk/handbook/guidance/giswork/annexc.htm*** the guidance on the use of direct marketing would apply to any push techniques, including viral marketing.

The Head of the Government Information and Communication Service is the central contact on this guidance. He or she will advise if the matter needs further consideration by the Machinery of Government and Standards Group or the Head of the Home Civil Service.

1.3.4 Sponsorship

Sponsorship may be a useful means of saving public expenditure. Like all government publicity projects, websites should observe the guidance given in the Cabinet Office *Guidance for Departments on Sponsorship of Government Activities*. This document can be found online at ***http://www.gics.gov.uk/handbook/guidance/sponsorship.htm*** or published in the *Directory of Civil Service Guidance*. These guidelines should be consulted in full. Like all government guidelines they are subject to amendment and update.

In general, sponsorship:

- must avoid any suggestion that the sponsors will be sympathetically regarded for other purposes;
- must be seen to add significant benefit;
- should add to, not replace, core funding for the project
- cannot be given by firms which are involved in significant commercial negotiations with the department or are licensed/regulated by it;
- should be sought in an open and even handed manner between organisations in a particular field, using the appropriate public sector procurement methods to secure the contractual arrangements;
- must not be an endorsement by Government of the sponsor or its products or services;

- must not dilute the effectiveness of your website or the message that lies behind it. Sponsors cannot influence, the messages of Government communication in their business area;
- must not bring adverse publicity to the project;
- must be of websites and not of individual Ministers or civil servants;
- does not place a Minister or a Department under an obligation to a sponsor.

Sponsorship of individual amounts, including value-in-kind, of more than £5,000 must be disclosed in Departmental Annual Reports.

To measure the value of in-kind sponsorship, where the sponsor provides goods or services that benefit of the project, Departments should consider the opportunity cost, ie, how much it would have cost the department if it had paid for the support provided. Ongoing costs should also be taken into account for the lifetime of the sponsorship agreement.

Returns to the sponsor must be specified in writing as part of the sponsorship agreement. The agreement should cover, for example, the display of the name of the sponsor or whether there is to be a link to the sponsor's website.

Credit to a sponsor must never create confusion about branding or your website's identity.

Credit to a sponsor should only occur on those parts of your web space where the sponsor is directly contributing to its provision. This should be specified in the sponsorship agreement.

Acknowledgement should be concise. A company logo, if used, must not distract from clear branding of your website's own identity or any government branding. A sponsor's logo must comply with the universal accessibility and graphics requirements of these guidelines (refer to **section 2.4** and **section 2.9**). A company logo must be seen as appropriate and must not be of a size that is visually or perceived to be visually larger or more important than any official or campaign logo. A link to the sponsor's own web page is perfectly okay. To retain your audience, you may wish to have it open in a new browser window.

If these guidelines have been followed, then no specific disclaimer for this instance of sponsorship should be necessary. It should be evident that the source of sponsorship is appropriate. It is, however, your responsibility to ensure that this relationship cannot be misinterpreted.

In the case that a disclaimer is necessary to avoid the semblance of an inappropriate relationship with the company, then it should be placed next to the credit line in the same heading level and typeface and on the same page. This is because disclaimers that are a link away from a credit have not in practice proved to be effective at avoiding the appearance of a problem.

It would be useful if the government's policy on sponsorship is included were the disclaimer information just off the home page together with an assertion that all sponsorship of the site meets these criteria.

1.3.5 The commercial value of credits

The giving of credit to suppliers of web services that you employ directly within the functionality of your website can have commercial value. Significant reductions to the cost of features such as search engines can be negotiated especially if logos and links to suppliers' sites are granted.   The value will vary with the popularity of the specific web pages (as shown in page impressions), and the relevance of the service to your readership.

The giving of credit to suppliers of web services, for example, by name, by email address, particularly if within your metadata will also have commercial value. Reductions to costs should be negotiated.

Guidance for Departments on Sponsorship of Government Activities
http://www.gics.gov.uk/handbook/guidance/sponsorship.htm

A central Cabinet Office contact point for advice is:
020 7276 2472

COI Communications website
http://www.coi.gov.uk

1.4 Evaluation

The evaluation of your website must not be overlooked. You need to judge the effectiveness of the website's content, design, navigation and underlying technology. There are many ways to do this but for many web managers, the most important will be access statistics derived from the web server logs. These can help measure the size of the audience and the patterns of how they use the website. They can reveal if the website is reliably delivering pages. However, it is important to understand the limitations of these statistics.

1.4.1 Evaluation and website metrics

Is the web strategy working? Does the navigation get people to the information they need? Is the server reliable? Measuring audience satisfaction, looking at feedback, understanding access statistics without measures such as these you will not be able to demonstrate value for money, or that you are meeting the needs of users and the aims of management. Therefore, regular (quarterly will be sufficient), formal evaluation exercises of both the content and the technology are strongly recommended.

Evaluation of website design and content can be carried out by drawing on:

Website access statistics provided by the ISP/hosting service provider. (The ISP/hosing services provider may either supply the raw web server logs or the results of their having been processed by analysis software);

- Responses via feedback tools (forms, databases, email addresses) ;
- Feedback from contributors to the website;

- Conventional audiences research, for example, focus groups and professionally authored online questionnaires.

The effectiveness of the website can also be judged by measuring achievement in other ways. For example, one recruitment website was evaluated on:

- The number of recruits that applied via the website
- Their performance of web recruits measured against that of staff recruited by other means
- The cost per recruit measured against the cost per recruit of publicity in other media.

If the ISP/hosting service supplier provides the results of analysing the web server logs as opposed to providing the unprocessed raw logs, the minimum information that should be required from them is statistics on:

- number of unique users (visitors)
- number of visits ,and

- page impressions (page views).

Some examples of other relevant metrics that can be identified from web server logs are:

- error message counts (indicating that pages and other content were not served successfully); and
- traffic analysis focussing on peak times (to assess bandwidth requirements) and 'dead' times (should it be necessary to switch the site off while maintenance is carried out) see **section 1.4.8** for a graphical summary.

For definitions of these terms, see **section 1.4.7** Understanding the terminology.

Additional useful information can include:

- successful requests;
- unsuccessful requests;
- most frequently visited pages;
- least frequently visited pages;
- top entry pages;
- top referring websites.

This information can be used to do such things as:

- identify the most popular content,
- review the navigation system for example, identifying orphaned pages,
- identify referring websites (the sites from which users arrive at your website),
- audit the level of response to electronic forms,
- assess the effectiveness of marketing/PR campaigns in bringing traffic to the website,
- provide information on users' platforms and browsers
- identify users' DNS domains and thus visits from abroad or from within government

It is, in addition, recommended that web teams should:

- give more importance to visitors, unique visits and page impressions than to hits;
- take as much notice of error logs as of any other statistics;
- determine who is using the website the most;
- monitor current bandwidth use, and attempt to project future requirements;
- archive server logs to use for monitoring trends over time.

The web strategy and management team should ensure, at the procurement stage, that ISPs/hosting services are offering to provide a full range of server log information.

It is acceptable to use HTTP cookies or session identities to track visitors' paths through the website (and this will be essential in e-transactional sites). The website should contain a clear statement of policy on the use of cookies.

Good practice dictates that the need for attention to the accuracy and timeliness of information will increase as the level of activity of a site increases.

Web managers should, in the interests of open government, consider publishing a summary of usage statistics on their websites.

See **section 3.2** Legal issues
See **section 3.8** Understanding user statistics
See **section 3.11** Procurement

1.4.2 Understanding user statistics

Website usage statistics are generally obtained by analysing the server logs. A typical HTTP server log contains in a log entry for each HTTP request (or hit) on the server. This entry will contain information about the web resource requested and the browser to which it was served. Software can be used to analyse and process these log files and provide a picture of the traffic to the website. Typically, in addition to the information in **section 1.4.1**, this will include information such as:

- the number of visitors,
- visitor duration and traffic pattern,
- visitor origin including which country, when it can be identified,
- visitor IP address,
- visitors' technical preferences, such as browser type and version, platform.

This analysis will also indicate:

- traffic peaks and troughs against time of day and day of the week (see graphical summary in **section 1.4.8**),
- average daily user load,
- what obstacles may turn visitors away,
- which pages get high traffic,
- which directories are getting high traffic,
- which graphic files are acceptable in terms of size and download time,
- type of browsers (user agent) being used.

There is a wide range of software available for processing and analysing the potentially huge amount of raw data contained in web server logs. This ranges from the commercially available Webtrends product family through to 'shareware' packages such as Wusage and free software like Analog.

http://www.webtrends.com
http://www.boutell.com/wusage/
http://www.statslab.cam.ac.uk/~sret1/analog/

1.4.3 Using a server log file

A standard HTTP server log entry may look like this:

```
193.63.182.194 [03/March/2001:11:30:35]
'GET/webguidelines/index.htm HTTP/1.0' 200 35000
```

What this means:

- 193.63.182.194 is in principle the IP number of the client's (the visitor's) host name or computer making the request. In fact it may actually be the IP number of a 'proxy' device that made the HTTP request on behalf of the real user. Such devices include the web content caching appliances that ISPs are increasingly deploying ('perimeter caches') and the firewalls that are typically deployed between corporate networks and the Internet. See **section 1.4.5** Not the whole picture!
- 03/March/2001 indicates the date of the access.
- 11:30:35 indicates the time (hours:minutes:seconds) of the access.
- 'GET/webguidelines/index.htm HTTP/1.0' is the request that the browser sent to the server.
- 200 is the HTTP status code with which the request completed (code 200 means that the file was served successfully. See **annex I** Common HTTP server status codes.
- 35000 is the size in bytes of the file that was transferred to the client's browser.

Depending upon the logging capabilities of the web server software and how the web server logging has been configured, web server logs may contain a large amount of additional information such as:

- HTTP_REFERRER this records the URL of the web page that referred the visitor to the current page. This actually records how a user (client) makes their way through your website.
  For example, from ***http://www.e-envoy.gov.uk/webguidelines/whatsnew.htm***

- USER_AGENT this records the program name and version number of the browser that the user (client) employed. For example, Microsoft Internet Explorer/4.04 (Windows 95).

1.4.4 Advanced techniques

Log files can be further analysed through advanced techniques. For example:

- **Sessions** and **visits** – the identification of sequences of page requests from individual users.
- **Session** and **visit duration** the measurement of the length of time that individual users spend viewing a website
- **Categorisation** – a process whereby similar items, eg URLs, browsers, platforms, a specific directory, are grouped together for pattern matching.
- **Aggregation** – a process by which all combinations of entities and their resulting measurements are combined.

See **section 1.4.5** Not the full picture!

Other website server software may also keep logs that can provide useful insights to the way visitors use your website. For example, it may be possible to configure search facility software to record the search terms that visitors have used when they are attempting find information on your website. This information can be useful when considering whether there are areas of the site that are not easy to find and can help with organising navigation. It also may indicate what other information users are expecting to be on the website, which would be of use when considering whether additional content should be included on your website.

1.4.5 Not the full picture!

Your should be aware that there are limitations to the information that can be discovered from the analysis of Web server log files .The principal issues are:

- *Most ISPs use dynamic IP addressing*. This means they maintain a pool of IP addresses from which an IP number is 'loaned out' to each dial-up call for the duration of the call. A particular IP number will therefore be used by many different users and a particular user may appear at your website with many different IP numbers. The firewalls used at the interface between the Internet and corporate networks typically use a process named Network Address Translation (NAT) which has a similar effect. Firewalls also often use a process named Port Address Translation (PAT). With PAT, many users behind the firewall 'share' a single Internet IP number. The result of all this is that a specific IP number only rarely corresponds to a specific user and it is inappropriate to attempt to base estimates of the number of visitors to your website on a count of the different IP numbers found in server log files alone.
- *Caches* – almost all ISPs and many corporate users deploy 'perimeter caches' to conserve their Internet connection bandwidth and improve the speed with which web pages can be served to their users. These are often set up to work 'transparently' regardless of whether users have configured their browser's cache settings. . Perimeter caches work by storing a copy of pages fetched by the client systems on whose behalf they are deployed. Subsequent requests for pages from other users behind a cache will be served from the cache if it already has a copy of the page. This may be done without any further reference to the origin server. Therefore web pages may be served to users without the creation of any record being captured in the origin server's log file. (See **section 1.4.6** Downstream caching and pixel tagging).
- *Dynamic proxies* – dynamic IP addressing and perimeter cacheing make the identification of page requests from specific users uncertain. This uncertainty is further compounded by the fact that some organisations assign proxy devices such as perimeter caches dynamically during the course of a user's Internet session. The result is that a sequence of page requests that is in fact from a single user may appear to come from several users even during the course of a single visit or session. AOL is an example of an organisation that uses dynamic proxying.
- *Cookie manipulation* – users can delete, or otherwise manipulate cookies stored by their browsers. Browsers can convert persistent cookies to session cookies. Cookies cannot therefore be relied upon as the basis for accurately measuring the

number of users of a website or for identifying users that revisit a website ('repeat users').

- **Browsers** -- some browsers are known to incorrectly identify the referring URL by indicating the previous page that the client was viewing even if the user recalled a bookmarked URL or typed a URL in to their browser' as opposed to following a link on the displayed page.
- **Anonymisers** -- some clients use 'anonymisers' which deliberately send false browser and referrer data, see **section 1.4.5.1** User agent masquerading.

All of these issues mean that there have to be reservations concerning the reliability of estimates derived from standard web server logs of the number of users of a website or of their browsing behaviour when they visit a website. The Internet advertising industry develops and promotes standard website traffic metrics and methodologies for calculating them. It is recognised that the measurements are flawed for the reasons outlined above, however, it is believed that the metrics provide the basis for comparing one website's usage with another on the basis that these issues will affect all websites to broadly the same extent. There is, however, no sound basis for this belief.

The Joint Industry Committee for Web Standards in the UK and Ireland (JICWEBS) as the body created by the UK and Ireland media industry whose aim is to ensure independent development and ownership of standards for measuring use and effectiveness of advertising on electronic media
http://www.jicwebs.org

The International Federation of Audit Bureaux of Circulation's (IFABC) Web Standards Committee promotes similar aims on a worldwide basis.
http://www.ifabc.org

1.4.5.1 User agent masquerading

The term 'user agent masquerading' refers to browsers that transmit an incorrect browser identification string in the requests that they send to servers. Some browsers just do not properly identify themselves and are therefore not being identified in server log file records. Deliberate masquerading is also used for a number of reasons:

- Some websites alter the content they serve based on the browser identification string, so masquerading can be used to work-around this.
- Some websites reject requests from browsers that they are not intended to work with, so masquerading can be used to work-around this.
- Some users simply wish to remain as anonymous as possible.

1.4.6 Downstream caching and pixel tagging

Copies of Web pages served to browsers are often 'captured' by content caching systems. 'Downstream' caching systems are typically operated by third parties such as the ISPs and other organisations through whose networks the pages travel on their route to users' computers. These caching systems are able to serve pages of which they hold copies in response to subsequent requests for them without reference to the origin server.

From an Internet-wide perspective caching content downstream close to the browsers is a good thing: serving content to topologically nearby browsers is quicker and consumes less network resource than transmitting it from the origin servers. It also reduces the load on the origin servers.

In order to have a website inter-operate properly with downstream caches (for example, to avoid out-of-date pages being served to users), it is important that appropriate cache control directives are included in the HTTP headers of the content that it serves. Getting this right normally involves having your server administrator configure the web server software appropriately. Note that it is not appropriate to attempt to control downstream caches by using `<meta http-equiv ...>` HTML mark up elements because the special purpose appliances typically used for caching only act upon HTTP directives in the content headers.

There is an important consideration with regard to website traffic measurement arising from the increasing deployment of downstream caches on the Internet. Typically, there will be no record of pages served from downstream caches in your traffic log. As downstream caches are increasingly deployed on the Internet, standard origin web server logs tend to underestimate the number of your pages that have actually been viewed by users.

1.4.6.1 The pixel tag approach

One way of achieving a more accurate page view counts in origin web server logs is to ensure that every page contains a content element whose HTTP headers mark it as non-cacheable. This can be achieved by including a tiny transparent image referred to as a **pixel tag** in each HTML page. This pixel tag is typically served from a directory the contents of which the web server has been configured to serve out with HTTP headers marking the content as non-cacheable.

In a pixel-tagging regime, page impressions served (including those served from downstream caches) can be estimated by counting the number of pixel tags served. If more detailed information is required about which pages have been served, then all or a part of the page's own URL can be included as a query string on the end of the pixel tag.

1.4.6.2 Examples of pixel tagging

A basic pixel tag could be generated by including the following image element in HTML pages (conventionally just before the closing </body> tag):

```
<img src="/nocache/trans.gif" width="1" height="1">
```

In this example, the directory named 'nocache' resides at the root of the web server. The web server would be configured to include HTTP headers marking any files served out of the 'nocache' directory as non-cacheable. The file named 'trans.gif' would be a one pixel square transparent GIF image.

If it is required to track actual pages visited by users. In this case, the pixel tag for example, in the file at www.e-envoy.gov.uk/insideoee/index.shtml, would be:

```
<img src="/nocache/trans.gif?insideoee/index.shtml"
width="1" height="1">
```

1.4.7 Understanding the terminology

browser	is the web browser (also known as 'user agent') used by a visitor (client) to access your website
bytes transferred	the number of bytes transferred to the client's browser as a result of the request
entry resource	the first web page viewed as part of a visit to your website
exit resource	the last web page viewed as part of a visit to your website
hit (or request)	a browser request for any one web resource (page element), for example a web page or a graphic. A web page containing two graphics will take three hits to display that web page in a client's browser
hits per visit	the number of hits occurring in a given visit to your website
page impressions	a file or a combination of files sent to a user as a result of that user's request being received by the server. For example, one web page that contains three frames and 2 graphic files will generate one page view but 5 hits. Also known as 'page requests ', 'page views' or 'page accesses'. Where service providers, search engines or other organisation cache content, page impressions served from these caches may not be recorded on the originating website.
page view per visit	the number of page accesses occurring in a given visit to your website
platform	the operating system used by the visitor to your website, eg, Windows ME
session	*[industry-standard definition]* A series of page impressions served in an unbroken sequence from within the website to the same user. A session begins when a user connects to a website, continues while page impressions are served in a continuous sequence from within the website, and ends when the user leaves the website.
user	this is defined as the combination of an IP address and an 'heuristic'. The user agent string is usually employed as the 'heuristic'. Because of the use of dynamic IP number assignment, NAT, PAT, perimeter cacheing and dynamic

	proxying this definition may overstate or understate the real number of users visiting a website. Alternatively, websites may use cookies and/or registration Ids as the basis for identifying user numbers. Often also referred to as 'unique user'.
unique user duration	*[industry-standard definition]* The total time in seconds for all visits of two or more page impressions, divided by the number of unique users making such visits. In order to measure user duration, a first and last page impression record must exist for each visit. Therefore, users making visits of only one page are excluded, since no interval can be established. This metric is sometimes referred to as 'website stickiness'
user agent	the browser and platform used by a visitor when accessing your website
visit	*[industry-standard definition]* a series of one or more page impressions served to one user, which ends when there is a gap of 30 minutes or more between successive page impressions for that user.
visit duration	*[industry-standard definition]* the total time in seconds for all visits of two or more page impressions divided by the total number of visits of two or more page impressions.

See **Annex I** Common HTTP server status codes.

1.4.8 Graphical example of traffic analysis

The following bar graphs summarise the level of page requests over a seven-day period and separately the level of traffic represented hourly over the 24-hour period:

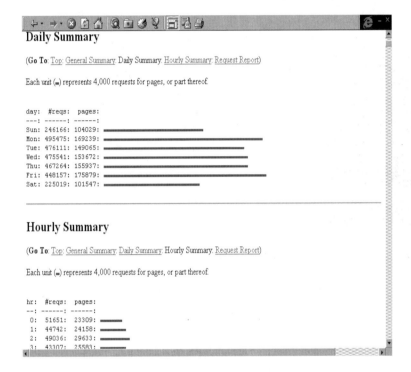

Checklist: Auditing and statistical analysis

The dynamic nature of the Internet environment makes it essential for the web team to carry out frequent monitoring of the performance and use of the website if high standards are to be maintained. It is also important that regular and authoritative reports on performance and usage are available to senior managers.

The Information Manager or editorial board should ensure that arrangements are in place for the following analysis and, where necessary, for maintenance of the appropriate standards of performance.

	Description
	Standards of performance over a modem connection 28.8 / 56.6 kbps over an open line and via a typical domestic ISP/hosting service. This is in order to replicate the access experience of a large number of users
	Checking using different browsers and screen resolutions, and with features such as scripts and images disabled
	Link checking. Broken links should be fixed within one working day
	Monitoring error messages: as much notice should be taken of error logs as of any other statistics
	Traffic analysis, focusing on peak times (to assess bandwidth requirements) and dead times (should essential maintenance require the website being down for a short time)
	Server log file analysis
	The minimum information which should be required from hosts are statistics on, eg: ▪ Number of users (visitors) ▪ Number of visits (unique visits or sessions) ▪ page impressions and also ▪ successful requests ▪ unsuccessful requests ▪ most frequently visited pages ▪ least frequently visited pages ▪ top entry pages ▪ top referring websites This information should be used to identify the most popular content, to review the navigation system (eg identifying orphaned pages), to review referring websites, to audit responses to web-inspired email and electronic forms and to assess the effectiveness of marketing/PR campaigns. The information is also likely to be useful as a source of information on website performance, the quantity of documents requested, visitors' electronic distribution, the number of visitors and the platforms that visitors use, including browsers and screen resolution
	Web teams should give more importance to unique visitors and page impressions than to hits
	Determine who is using the website the most

	Collect information from usage statistics on the types of browser being used to access the website
	Archive logs for as long as possible
	Ensure at the procurement stage that ISPs/hosting services are offering to provide a full range of server log information
	It is acceptable to use cookies to track visitors' paths through the website (and this will be essential in e-commerce websites). The website should contain a clear statement of policy on the use of cookies
	Consider publishing usage statistics on your website

1.5 Focusing on user needs

When initiating a website project there are some basic questions that need to be addressed, all of which will affect its usability. Technology that would be seen as suitable for one sector of the marketplace will not be ideal for another.

The language used within the document, the format of the document itself and the style of presentation will all have a direct effect on the users of your website.

1.5.1 Marketplace

It is vital to know who your target audiences are and how they will access your information. This information will determine how you design and prepare the electronic publication.

However, targeting information on a website is very different from the targeting of conventional publicity and information.

Conventional marketing is effective at getting the information to the intended audiences. Leaflets are sent only to mailing lists of the target audience, or displayed in places they are likely to visit. Advertising is placed in magazines or in TV programs that appeal to the target audience.

This leaves design and text in conventional publicity free to concentrate on the task of communication with particular kinds of people.

Anyone with access to the Web can show up at your website, whether your information is for them or not. Websites have to do their own targeting by directing users to the information or services that are for them.

Some industry experts suggest that the different levels of a website should have different aims.

Information on the **upper levels** of a website will be targeted at a very broad general audience. The aim is to help users swiftly find what is relevant to them… or move on. Design should aim to be professional and sufficiently engaging for a broad audience. In this context Government sites should aim to:

- Make immediately plain that this is a government site
- Make clear what the owning organisation does
- Make clear the kind of content and services on the site
- Build trust in the authority, accuracy and currency of the information
- Build trust in the security and effectiveness of the transactions on offer
- Direct regular users to content that is new on that particular site
- Offer access to the rest of government sites
- Send different kinds of interested users to content that is aimed at them.

Middle layers of the site can be for people with some interest in content or services. This level of the site should aim to:

- summarise information or available transactions
- provide enough details or facts to satisfy mild interest
- provide enough details for people with strong interest to select the detailed information that is for them or who wish to apply for the service.

Middle levels of the site can also be a good place for key messages aimed at the general public. Writing and design can in this case be more clearly targeted at the target audience.

Lower levels of the site will tend to provide the detailed information that government sites so often make available. Here the aim is to:

- secure the interested user's agreement to read the information
- and offer users the choice of reading onscreen or different file formats to download.

An exception to this approach is likely to be a website that works as part of a publicity campaign. As advertising is likely to be driving an interested audience to the site, there can be a greater degree of targeting.

The aim of the site should be to add value to the campaign by such means as:

- providing more detailed information than the advertising could carry
- reporting on progress towards the goals of the campaign
- providing a transaction that facilitates users' response to the call to action for the campaign.

An important aim of design will be to make it plain that the site ties in with the look and feel of the campaign. Users should be in no doubt they have come to the campaign's site. The content and transactions on the site must reinforce the value of the brand.

Campaign sites should be revised as the campaign changes or be taken down once the campaign ends.

1.5.1.1 Who is the information for?

Departments and agencies should be aware of who the core and non-core audiences are for their sites. It is very likely that the audiences for different parts of the site, or for different sites within a single department's web estate, will vary considerably.

You should be aware if parts of your sites are aimed at younger or older audiences, or if the information is pertinent to users whose first language is not English.

Do you have information written and designed for your audiences? It may be the case that you have policy documents available. Policy documents are not intended to communicate with the public. Does your site also provide information written for the public on those same subjects?

If you are targeting information at particular audiences, you should consider doing some market research or at least consultation with audiences. It might be helpful if the web team views sites alongside members of their core audience.

See **section 2.4** Building in universal accessibility.

1.5.1.2 Language

Writers for conventional media have an easier job than writers for the web.

In the first place conventional writers can assume that the leaflet or advertisement is being seen mostly by the target audience. They can use all their skill to deal with the concerns of that audience its own language.

In the second place, most people including professional audiences avoid reading onscreen. Instead they scan quickly for information relevant to them. If they don't find it, they move on.

Research carried out by John Morkes and Jacob Nielsen has shown that the following practices dramatically increase comprehension by users.
- Text should be at least 50 per cent shorter than the equivalent text in print
- Text should be in plain English
- Text should be broken up into easily scanned bullet-point lists
- Text should be broken up with unambiguous headings and subheadings.
- Hyperbole or puff creates an extra degree of impatience and incomprehension on the web

Other recommendations include:

- Cute, funny, gimmicky headlines may be listed on search engine results and may make no sense out of context
- Every page should be written as if the user has not seen the rest of the site (they may not have).
- Care should be taken to avoid too much duplication – this can be damaging.
- Text should be written, like a newspaper article, with the key information (who, what, why, where, when and how) in the opening paragraphs.

Visit the research report at ***http://www.useit.com/papers/webwriting/writing.html.***

1.5.1.3 Technical aspects of marketing

In general government sites aim at a broader audience than commercial sites. We must ensure that the disabled can use our online information. Our audiences also include as a matter of policy the socially excluded. Our audience includes people on especially secure systems (such as the rest of government and some businesses). We tend to have more professionals or policy experts interested in our information -- and so end up publishing far more long detailed documents than many commercial sites.

This means that the technical aspects of government sites will differ from the typical audience for many commercial websites. Government users may sit behind firewalls that strip out scripting. Corporate and business users probably work on networks whose system administrators do not allow them to download software… so there is no point offering them free downloads of plug-ins. Socially excluded users may be accessing on older equipment. Some of our audiences are international, and for them speed of access (as well as other content issues) may be a priority.

This means that to reach these audiences effectively, the technical aspects of the site must match the needs of our audiences. Mandatory compliance with the W3C Web Accessibility Initiative recommendations will help ensure this. Here are some other considerations.

- What standard of modem speed is the target audience likely to have?
- What standard of colour display will the user's computer have?
- What are the issues of compatibility with older browsers?
- Are graphic files small or will they add to the download time for the site?
- Are graphic links really necessary for the site?
- Will the audience require any plug-ins to download information? Do you offer alternatives so that the site will work without them? Remember many users cannot download free plug-ins.

Although the main part of any website will be constructed using HTML, the target audience for the website will help decide the format that should be chosen for storing subsidiary documents. There is no reason why several formats could not be employed at the same time to ensure maximum usability. In particular our professional or policy audiences may want documents provided primarily to be printed out.

See **section 2.4** Building in universal accessibility
See **section 2.5** Browser compatibility
See **section 4.1** HTML pages, and **section 4.2** Non-HTML file formats

1.5.2 Customer relationship management (CRM and eCRM)

At the simplest level, customer relationship management (CRM) means the attraction and retention of visitors by operating a user-focused strategy.

1.5.2.1 Audience attraction

Audience attraction involves offering the information and services on your website that your user base requires. To do that there must be an understanding of your audiences and their needs if you are to understand what information and services to offer. You will also need to decide if that offering will be identical for each audience segment or whether you will differentiate (making the right offering to the right customer segment). See **section 1.7** Getting users to your site.

1.5.2.2 Audience retention

Audience retention involves acquiring and continuously updating knowledge about visitor needs, motivation and behaviour. Applying this knowledge through a process of learning from your successes and failures will ensure that your website is better managed around the user. The aim is to understand, anticipate and manage the needs of current and potential visitors in terms of what is offered and how it is offered.

Relationship management looks at a continuing series of transactions, rather than an individual transaction. This includes supporting your users online and offline, and satisfying them by responding to their requests for information and assistance as soon as possible.

The user-centric strategy allows the integration of people, processes, and technology systems to support the delivery of user requirements. The organisation's whole team will need to be in the business of building customer relationships, both online and offline.

1.5.2.3 Electronic CRM

With the 'all-electronic' version of CRM, customer relationships become more dynamic and interactive. The creation of a channel and product strategy will define how your organisation delivers its products and services effectively, making sure the right message gets out at the right time and through the right channel. Relevant information can be collected more easily, uploaded automatically and used more effectively.

For example, your department might build a database about its users that described relationships in sufficient detail so that those providing the service can match user needs with products, remind them of the available services and information, and even know what other online and offline transactions a visitor had used. This would provide a web manager with the information necessary to know their users, understand their needs, and effectively build relationships with them.

However, web-based CRM can mean that huge volumes of user information are retrieved, stored, processed and delivered electronically. The IT platforms used must be flexible, adaptive, and scalable. They must also be completely dependable and secure to provide the credibility that will encourage the use of online transactions and resources.

1.6 Discussion groups

A discussion group opens up a form of communication between the organisation and the user. It allows the user to initiate new topics of conversation or respond to existing topics by submitting an electronic form.

A discussion group can be difficult medium to control, while it does open communication with the general public; it can also be abused. It should be moderated and seriously considered before use. It should not be seen as a shortcut to being interactive.

A discussion can be as free or as structured as is required. However, a moderator should always control the content.

Use each checklist to ensure that your web pages comply with these guidelines

1.6.1 Checklist and summary	*Core guidance*
Checklist	❑ Decide whether a discussion group is to be open or closed ❑ If the discussion group is to be closed, carefully control the distribution of passwords ❑ Publish an Acceptable Use Policy alongside the discussion group ❑ The group must be continually moderated ❑ The focus of the discussion group should be decided on before being implemented
Summary	Discussion groups can be delivered by many sources. Your website hosting service may well be in a position to offer this service, or you may have to use a separate service managed by another service provider. Discussion groups can be volatile. However the service is delivered, it will have to be managed and moderated particularly well, especially if it is an open site available to all web users.

1.6.2 Implementation

Discussion group systems are sometimes referred to as *message boards* or *bulletin boards*. These are not the same as *live chat* systems.

Discussion group software typically organises user's contributions into *threads*. Many threads of discussion can be running simultaneously. Users can start up new threads and take part in any number of discussion threads. There is no limit to the number of follow-on messages that expand on these themes.

1.6.2.1 Purpose

Why do you want to run a discussion group? Be careful if the purpose is to:

- keep in touch with public or stakeholder opinion, or
- do something exciting with your website.

If you give people a space to tell you what they think, they will expect their views to have a tangible impact. By encouraging general opinion, you will probably receive very political contributions and there is little value in this. The real value of discussion groups lies in their potential to consult stakeholders on the practical implementation of policy.

1.6.2.2 Communicate your objectives to participants

Once you are clear about your goals, make sure you communicate them to interested parties, especially what it is that you want from participants, and what they will get in return.

This need not imply a commitment to act on the findings. However, you should at least publish a summary of the discussion and consider an official response explaining what (if any) action you plan to take, and why. This is already required under the Cabinet Office Code of Practice on Written Consultations.

1.6.2.3 Editorial and moderation policy

Liability for comments rests with the publisher, not with the individual user. To ensure that contributions stay legal and inclusive, it is important to establish some clear ground rules.

An Acceptable Use Policy (sometimes called Terms of Use) will vary between discussion groups, but broadly there are some themes that most forbid:

- Insulting, threatening or provoking language.
- Inciting hatred on the basis of race, religion, gender, nationality or sexuality or other personal characteristics.
- Swearing, using hate-speech or making obscene or vulgar comments.
- Libel, condoning illegal activity, contempt of court, and breach of copyright.
- Spamming, ie, adding the same comment repeatedly or across different groups.
- Advertising.
- Impersonating or falsely claiming to represent a person or organisation.
- Posting in a language other than English or Welsh.

- Invading people's privacy.
- Posting off-topic comments.

1.6.2.4 Technology

Single versus multi-threaded discussions

Multi-threaded discussions encourage both deep and broad debate because participants can reply to replies as well as the initial comment. However, you may find people squabbling with one another or going off on unnecessary tangents.

A single-threaded facility, such as BBC Talking Point, might be more appropriate if you want more control over the scope of the discussion. Respondents address only an initial question or proposition.

Open versus closed versus read-only

An **open** discussion is one that allows anyone to take part. Access to a **closed** group is by invitation only. Participation in **closed but read-only** groups is by invitation only, but everyone can read the contributions.

Post versus pre-moderation

Unfortunately, some users may behave inappropriately. You will need to plan in advance about how to deal with this. As the publisher, you will be responsible for all material. Furthermore, government discussions groups have a particular duty to promote an inclusive atmosphere.

Post moderation means checking comments after they have been published. Depending on how frequently you review new material, this risks inappropriate material sitting in your group, possibly for hours, or even over a weekend. However, it also allows the group to be fast moving – a long thread can develop in a matter of hours. It is also less of a drain on resources.

Pre-moderation means checking comments before they are published.

Strengths:
- reduces the risk of publishing offensive comments,
- allows a more selective publishing policy, eg, you might decide that you only want to publish comments that genuinely add something to the debate or stay firmly 'on-topic'.

Weaknesses:
- potential drain on resources, eg, you may need to employ a moderator full-time unless you are prepared to make participants wait a long time to see their comments appear, particularly during silent hours and at weekends.

1.6.2.5 Checklist

The following checklist may help you to predict whether or not your forum is likely to attract difficult material:

Subject matter

If it concerns race, gender, age or sexuality, expect people to be racist, sexist, ageist or homophobic. Some topics may also be more prone to libellous comments, eg, standards in public life.

Audience

Will you be dealing with a professional audience or members of the general public?

Anonymity

If you allow people to contribute anonymously, some might behave irresponsibly, although anonymity can also encourage honesty.

See **section 1.2.6** Developing educational content

IMPORTANT

An Acceptable Use Policy must be established and published alongside the discussion group.

1.6.2   Acceptable Use Policy, example of

The following is an example of an Acceptable Use Policy that may be used for an organisation's Discussion Group. It should be clearly visible to all users. Organisations may use the following as a template, making changes where necessary.

It would be preferable for any new user to have to pass through a page with this information before being able to input data on the discussion group itself.

This Acceptable Use Policy is intended to help create an atmosphere in which freedom of speech is balanced by self-discipline and a mature attitude to discussion. We encourage people to join these discussions and it would therefore be very surprising if exchanges did not occasionally become a little heated!

For this reason, we have compiled a Guidance section of useful tips for those who are new to the etiquette of online discussion. Discussion Moderators are available to help you to get the most out of participating in online discussions and to ensure that these rules are observed.

By virtue of your participation in this discussion, you are deemed to have agreed to abide by the rules. Although the Moderator cannot take responsibility for monitoring every message that is sent to the website, we must reserve the right to remove items submitted from anyone who repeatedly ignores these rules.

1. Personal Identification
All messages sent to a discussion must include your name and email address. Do not represent yourself as another person. Anonymous contributions will not be accepted.

2. Use of Language
Messages should not be malicious or designed to offend. In particular, the use of swear-words or undue profanity is discouraged. By participating in any discussion, you undertake to indemnify us and our employees and subcontractors against any liability arising from any obscene, defamatory, seditious, blasphemous or other actionable statement published by you on this site and against all damages, losses, claims and costs (including, without limitation, fines and expenses arising out of or incurred in conducting or defending any proceedings) arising from any such actionable statements.

3. Conduct of Discussion
Your message should be within the scope of the subject under discussion. If you make a contribution that is inappropriate to the subject under discussion, you may be directed by the Moderator not to raise the matter further or to raise it within a separate discussion group.

Reference should *not* be made to the personality of other participants in a discussion nor should attacks be made on an individual's character unless the person concerned has already chosen to bring his or her personality into the issue under discussion.

One to one arguments, disagreements and disputes of a personal nature must be conducted through private Email and not through public discussion.

You should remember that you are legally responsible for what you write. By participating in a discussion, you undertake to indemnify us and our employees and subcontractors against any liability arising from any breach of confidentiality, copyright or other intellectual property right published by you on this site and against all damages, losses, claims and costs (including, without limitation, all expenses incurred in conducting or defending any proceedings) arising from any such publication. You must not make statements that are libellous, obscene, seek to incite racial hatred or otherwise break the laws of the United Kingdom.

4. Private Email
If a person has sent you a private Email you may not forward it to a public discussion group without the prior consent of the person who sent it. This does not prevent you forwarding private Email to the Discussion Administrator *[include email address]* should you consider this appropriate.

5. Advertising and Research
No advertising is allowed except where it is for an event, publication or similar items that has direct relevance to the subject of discussion.

Information about locating and sharing knowledge and expertise is welcomed, but within the specific discussion category provided.

6. Complaints about a Breach of these Rules
Complaints about a breach of these Rules should ONLY be made by private Email to the Discussion Administrator *[include email address]*

The **Discussion Administrator** will take timely and appropriate action with regard to the complaint.

Please note:
By virtue of your participation in this discussion, you are deemed to have agreed to abide by these rules.

1.7 Getting users to your site: metadata, search engines and promotion

An important aspect of publishing information and offering services on the Internet is to ensure that people can find it. Experience on the web illustrates that this is not always easy, with search facilities returning hundreds, if not thousands of options, in response to a specific enquiry. General research shows that two out of three searchers give up before finding what they want.

Search engines and directory services are the primary tools that enable users to locate information on the Internet. Search engines and directory services technologies are evolving rapidly. Consequently, it can be quite difficult to predict how specific technical features on a website and the way its content is structured will affect its ranking in response to searches made in different search engines.

To improve the likelihood that web pages will rank highly in the results of users' searches for the information they contain, it is essential that websites incorporate additional descriptive information designed to be processed by government and third-party search and directory systems. This *internal* descriptive data, intended to be read by computer systems rather than by humans, is referred to as *metadata.*

Government policy on the use of metadata in Internet publications is laid down in the e-Government Interoperability Framework available at: http://www.govtalk.gov.uk/interoperability/egif.asp?order=title

This mandates the use of metadata in government websites. It requires that metadata conforms to the e-Government Metadata Standard (e-GMS). e-GMS is based on the *Dublin Core* model produced by the Dublin Core Metadata Initiative (DCMI) -- *http://dublincore.org/.* Contact *ukgovtalk@e-envoy.gov.uk* for more details.

Use each checklist to ensure that your web pages comply with these guidelines

1.7.1 Checklist and summary	Core guidance
Checklist	❑ Metadata must be added to the top of an HTML file ❑ Metadata must conform to the standards laid down in the e-Government Metadata Standard (e-GMS) ❑ The description of the page must be relevant to the published information ❑ Register your site with search engines and directory services.
Summary	Search engines and directory services are the primary tools for locating information on the Internet. Metadata is key to categorising the information on your website: essentially it is data about data. Authors must insert e-GMS metadata markup elements at the top of an HTML document in order to categorise and describe the information contained within it

1.7.2 Implementation of metadata

A web browser does not display metadata, but the machines accessing the page can assess and efficiently record data from it. Web crawlers, indexing agents, search facilities and web browsers can all interpret this information and use it to collate concise and relevant data on each page in the site.

Metadata may also be added for administrative purposes, for example it is possible to add a 'date for review' indicating the date on which the information on a page is likely to require updating. Web administrators can then quickly and easily locate all pages that need reviewing at a given time, and ensure none of them are redundant or in need of updating.

Examples of pages using Dublin Core metadata include the e-Envoy website at ***www.e-envoy.gov.uk.***

Those responsible for the web strategy should consider creating a thesaurus of keywords and other terms for the same concepts. This will help
• content owners choose the consistent keywords for metadata
• and experienced users find keywords for their searches.

The international standard for the creation of a thesaurus is ISO 2788/BS 5723.

> **IMPORTANT**
>
> *The organisation's library service will be the best internal resource for establishing a set of keywords for any specific area of publication. Their expertise in cataloguing and the use of thesauri will be invaluable.*

The electronic cataloguing of web documents is undertaken chiefly to facilitate the finding of information. The greater the number of metadata elements used, the greater the chance of locating it.

> **e-Government Metadata Standard** (referred to in the **e-Government Interoperability Framework**)
> *http://www.e-envoy.gov.uk*

1.7.3 Getting your site listed on search engines and directories

The burgeoning number of Internet search engines and directories adopt a range of approaches for establishing their entries for the websites they catalogue. This may involve their using software (often referred to as *crawlers* or *spiders*) to scan either the text or the metadata (or both) contained within the pages of the site. It may involve having a human visit the site to catalogue it manually. Or it may involve both automated and human processes.

It is well worth consulting the Search Engine Report website to find out what criteria are used by the most widely used Internet search systems to create catalogue entries for the websites on which they hold information. It is sometimes the case that rearranging page content or restructuring your HTML markup will make a difference to a website's search engine rankings.

Almost every Internet search engine and directory has a web page on which web managers can submit their website's URL for inclusion in that search system's catalogue. Some search and directory systems have a facility for the web manager to provide information about their site as a part of the submission process. The latter effectively constitutes another source of metadata (although only for the specific search or directory system to which the site URL is being submitted) and so the same care should be taken with the precision of any information entered in this way as with the creation of Dublin Core metadata.

Search engine and directory registration (or *submission*) can be done in one of two ways:

- The organisation undertakes the registering process.
- The organisation's web design company/agency undertakes the registering process.

There are many different search facilities on the web and registering can be laborious and repetitive, so it is often advisable to have an external organisation to take responsibility for this task.

It can take anything up to several months from the time of submitting your website's URL to a search engine or directory and the site appearing in that system's catalogue.

Care should be taken with the use of automated services that offer to submit website URLs to multiple search engines. The operators of some search engines decline to accept registrations from such services. Some other purported such services are just an out-and-out scam.

Remember that not everyone uses the same search facility. The more services that the organisation is registered with, the better the chances are of reaching the largest audience. For websites containing content aimed at a specialist audience, it is often worth searching for directory services designed to serve the specialism at issue and registering your content with them.

The registration page URL of many popular search engine and directory sites is shown in the **Checklist: Search engine registration**.

If your organisation changes its operating name, website URL or its structure, it will be necessary to repeat the entire registration process again. Otherwise, it is likely the result of a search will be a broken link.

The Search Engine Report
http://searchenginewatch.com/

1.7.4 Example of metadata

The order that these elements are placed on the page is unimportant but their location on the page is. Here is an example of how metadata details should be implemented within an HTML document:

```
<html>
<head>
<title>Department X Home Page</title>

<meta name="DC.Title" lang="en" content="Office of the e-Envoy -
Home Page">
<meta name="DC.Coverage" lang="en" content="UK; United Kingdom">
<meta name=" DC.Creator" lang="en" content="UK Government Cabinet
Office, Office of the e-Envoy, Stockley House, 130 Wilton Road,
London SW1V 1LQ, UK.  info@e-envoy.gsi.gov.uk">
<meta name="DC.Date.created" scheme="ISO8601" content="2001-04-
25">
<meta name="DC.Date.modified" scheme="ISO8601" content="2001-10-
31"> <meta name=" DC.Description" lang="en" content="Part of the
UK Cabinet Office, the OeE leads the drive to ensure that the
country, its citizens and its businesses derive maximum benefit
from the knowledge economy. It has responsibilities across the
whole e-agenda, notably e-commerce and e-government.">
<meta name="DC.Format" scheme="IMT" content="text/html">
```

```
<meta name="DC.Identifier" scheme="URI" content="http://www.e-
envoy.gov.uk/">
<meta name="DC.language" scheme="ISO 639 2" content="eng">
<meta name="DC.Publisher" lang="en" content="e-Envoy Media">
<meta name="DC.Rights" lang="en" content="
http://www.hmso.gov.uk/docs/copynote.htm">
<meta name="DC.Subject" lang="en" content="OeE; Office of the e-
Envoy; e-commerce; e-business; e-government; e-communications; e-
objectives; business strategy; UK government policy">
<meta name="DC-GOV.Subject.Category" lang="en" content="e-
government">
<meta name="DC.Type.category" lang="en" content="home page">
<meta name="keywords" content=""="UK Public Sector, UK online,
Websites, Defence, Civil Service">
<meta name="description" content="The Office of the e-Envoy, as
part of the Cabinet Office is tasked with delivering the UK
Government's e-agenda">

</head>
```

This example shows that the metadata is inserted in the HTML page directly following the end tag for the `<title>` element and within the `<head>` element.

The example data uses content values for illustrative purposes only.

Dublin Core *http://dublincore.org*

Keywords and descriptions can also be included during the creation of PDF files. This is covered in **section 4.4** on the use of Adobe Acrobat Files.

1.7.4.1 PICS rating

Government websites should also contain additional metadata markup indicating the site contents Platform for Internet Content Selection (PICS) rating. The purpose of PICS ratings metadata is different to that of Dublin Core metadata in that it categories Internet content according to its suitability for viewing by a number of specific audience groups. PIC has been incorporated within the e-Government Metadata Standard.

This area is covered in specific detail in **section 1.8** Platform for Internet Content Selection.

1.7.5 Promoting your website

Your organisation should consider the following additional techniques to draw visitors to the website:

- Provide the URL on all stationery and business cards;
- Printed versions of document should carry your appropriate URL;

- Printed versions of documents should record the URLs of documents on your website;
- Media advertising for information campaigns should carry an appropriate URL;
- Links should be exchanged with other sites in related subjects.

Your organisation should also consider the following:

- How to launch new websites, eg, a press release;
- Getting the site reviewed in technology, ICT supplements and other journals;
- Advertising the site in conventional media likely to be seen or read by your target audience;
- Advertising on other key websites (see **section 1.3.3** The buying of advertising space on other websites).

Checklist: search engine registration

This checklist should be used by web managers and developers to ensure that their website or an individual document is promoted as widely as possible on the Internet. There are two mechanisms for searching the web – search engines and directories. A search engine uses software variously referred to as – robots or spiders – to visit and collect information from new and updated websites and to maintain searchable databases of web resources. Directories are structured lists of categories maintained by human editors. However, the distinction between search engines and directories is not always clear-cut. Many services (for example Yahoo! and Google) combine the features of both search engines and directories.

Regular search engine registration is important and your search engine entries need to be checked on a regular basis. To keep informed of developments in the search engine community consider subscribing to the Search Engine Report at *http://searchenginewatch.com/*

There are also many commercial services that will undertake managing search engine and directory submissions on your behalf. They usually refer to their activities as *website promotion* so there is some scope for confusion. If you are considering employing such a commercial service, care should be taken to establish exactly what it is they are proposing to do for you.

Examples of search facilities (submission pages)	
AltaVista	*http://www.altavista.com/addurl/*
Excite	*http://www.excite.com/info/add_url*
Google	*http://www.google.com/addurl.html*
Go	*http://www.go.com/AddUrl?pg=SubmitUrl.html&svx=HP_addurl*
HotBot	*http://www.hotbot.com*
Infoseek	*http://www.infoseek.com*
Lycos	*http://www.lycos.co.uk/service/addasite.html*
Metacrawler	*http://www.metacrawler.com*
Northern Light	*http://www.nlsearch.com*
Search UK	*http://url.searchengine.com/index.cgi?&cu=uk&cl=english&d=2&w=0&y=1&z=0&g=0&related=0*

Webcrawler	*http://www.webcrawler.com/info/add_url/*

Examples of directory listing facilities (submission pages)	
Infohiway	*http://www.webzone.com/isn/addurl.html*
Lycos	*http://www.lycos.co.uk/*
Magellan	*http://www.magellan.com*
UKPlus	*http://www.ukplus.co.uk/ukplus/SilverStream/Pages/pgUKPlusNewSite.html*
Yahoo! UK & Ireland	*http://uk.docs.yahoo.com/info/include.html*
Yell	*http://www.yellowpages.co.uk/Aboutus*

The Open Directory also provides a mechanism to list your site on many of the search engines. Consider submitting your website to the Open Directory's UK Government category – *http://dmoz.org/Regional/Europe/United_Kingdom/Government/*

1.8 Platform for Internet Content Selection (PICS)

The W3C Platform for Internet Content Selection (PICS) specification allows web managers to set a certification rating for the content of their sites. This is very similar to the ratings system that exists for films shown in cinemas.

A filter configured to use the PICS ratings system will read the classification contained within the data and displays the page only if it meets the user-defined specifications.

Use each checklist to ensure that your web pages comply with these guidelines

1.8.1 Checklist and summary   *Core guidance*

Checklist	❑ Web managers should register their website with at least the ICRA PICS service ❑ Metatags covering your whole site should be placed in the head element of the default page, eg, index.htm or default.htm ❑ Check that all web pages meet the defined rating. Additional metatags can be placed in the home page of directories to rate pages within that directory, and where necessary can be applied to individual web pages
Summary	The ICRA system allows the author of a page or site, through the use of a specific metatag, to identify content of the website or document in each of the following categories: • Nudity and Sexual material • Violence • Language • Other topics (ie tobacco or gambling advertising) • Chat The rating system uses a neutral binary system. A particular element within each category, such as, 'mild expletives' in the language section is either present or absent from the website.

1.8.2 Implementation

There are a number of varieties of PICS ratings systems on the Internet but the most commonly used is the ICRA system managed by the Internet Content Rating Association. Microsoft Internet Explorer and a growing number of filtering products support this.

> **IMPORTANT**
>
> *A rating can be chosen to cover the entire site, which can be added to the site's homepage. If desired, each individual page can be separately certified. The usual practice is to certify only the site as a whole.*

It would be expected that the majority of UK public sector web information sites would have a *none of the above* rating for each of the categories in the ICRA system.

There are two basic steps to using this system. First, the content manager will obtain a rating label (a metatag) for the site and will then add that to the source data of the default page in the domain. This is usually called index.htm and may be a frameset. Second, the user's web browser or filter can be configured to read that PICS certification.

Once turned on, the PICS rating and filtering system can be a very strong tool in restricting the websites that are accessible. If a page has a higher rating than that set by the owner of the browser, the user is requested to insert a password. Only the correct password will allow the page to be downloaded and displayed.

W3C PICS standard
http://www.w3.org/PICS/

1.8.3 Gaining a label

To gain an ICRA label for your site you must visit the following URI:

http://www.icra.org

- Once at the site select the 'Label your website here' button.
- You now have the ability to certify a single page, a directory or an entire website. Select the option that is most suitable.

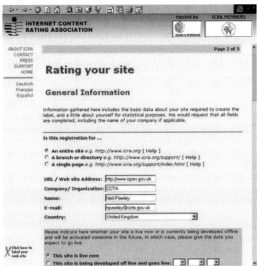

- You will now need to complete the Registration document.

- On this page you will be asked to identify the content of your website or the web page descriptors in each of the ICRA categories. When this section is completed click on the 'Submit' button at the bottom of the page.
- You will now need to confirm or change any of the entered data in the 'Input Verification' page. When completed click the 'Input correct' button.
- Finally the user must agree to the ICRA Terms and Conditions document by selecting the button at the bottom of the page.
- Once completed the ICRA rating will be displayed with instructions on how to incorporate the metatag into your chosen pages. The site includes extra support information should it be needed and runs a free email technical support service.

Key points about labelling:
- A filter will read and cache labels it finds. It will not 'search the site' for labels. Therefore if there are commonly used entry points to the site other than the home page; these too should carry a copy of the label.
- Pages always accessed through links from within the site do not need to be labelled separately as the cached label will be used.
- ICRA's support pages include a flow diagram of how labels are read and interpreted by filtering software.

1.8.4 Example of a PICS metatag

The following is an example of the standard PICS metatag generated from the ICRA site. The URL in bold will need to reflect the page in which the metatag is to be inserted, not the example department URL as is illustrated here.

```
<META http-equiv="PICS-Label" content='(PICS-1.1
"http://www.icra.org/ratingsv02.html" l gen true for "
http://www.departmentx.gov.uk " r (cz 1 lz 1 nz 1 oz 1 vz 1)
"http://www.rsac.org/ratingsv01.html" l gen true for
"http://www.departmentx.gov.uk" r (n 0 s 0 v 0 1 0))'>
```

In this example, the rating (defined in the parentheses) is 'none of the above' in all categories – the website contains neither sex nor violence, etc. The tag includes elements for backward compatibility with ICRA's forerunner – RSACi.

Once this rating has been achieved the website can display the ICRA logo on the homepage to illustrate that the procedure has been completed. This is optional and a range of different colours is available.

More complex example to show flexibility

```
<META http-equiv="PICS-Label" content='(PICS-1.1
"http://www.icra.org/ratingsv02.html" l r (cz 1 lz 0 nz 1 oz 1
vz 1) "http://www.rsac.org/ratingsv01.html" l r (n 0 s 0 v 0 1
0))'>
```

This metatag does not specify the page or site to which it applies. Such a PICS label will be applied *only* to the page it is on. Furthermore, note that the lz 1 term (which is ICRA code for "none of the above" in the language category) has been set to lz 0. This means that the label does not make a positive declaration that there is no potentially offensive material on this page. Such a label might be useful, for example, for pages which carry quoted speech including swear words but which most readers would not deem "offensive" in the context given. You can make analogous changes in other categories.

Labels may be edited at will -- but watch the syntax! ICRA does not need to be informed about every change made and has other tools available that may be useful.

---

e-Government Interoperability Framework
http://www.e-envoy.gov.uk/publications/frameworks_index.htm

1.9 Domain name registration

Web managers are encouraged to develop a domain name strategy and to keep the management of their namespace(s) under review. These .gov.uk guidelines apply to all new requests for registration. It is recommended that you always check the website for the latest guidance – *www.e-envoy.gov.uk/domain.htm*.

1.9.1 Structure of a web address

The address of a web page is known as the Uniform Resource Locator (URL) and is structured like this. Although at first glance this can seem complex, the address can be broken down in the following fashion:

Internet protocol
The first element of the URL is the protocol; it is the http:// prefix that designates the address as a World Wide Web page rather than an FTP site or email address.

Domain name
The second element, is the fully qualified domain name of a server. By convention, the name usually starts with the prefix www if the machine identified is a web server. But this is not a requirement. Users may also see the prefix ftp (where the machine is also an FTP server). In some cases there will be no prefix to the domain name at all. For example, the UKonline web server may be reached at ukonline.gov.uk as well as www.ukonline.gov.uk.

The prefix www, which is generally interpreted, as an integral part of a domain name is in practice a sub-domain representing the server hosting your website. The actual domain name, such as e-envoy.gov.uk, is registered by the organisation through a naming authority (eg, Nominet.UK) and generally reflects that organisation's name, acronym or a specialist subject area the website is to represent.

The fully qualified domain name is the identifier of the entire website and bears no relationship whatsoever to the organisation hosting the service. This means that the department can move the domain name, at any time, to another service provider without causing problems for the end user.

See **section 2.1.2.1** An explanation of the Internet Domain Name Service

Directory and file name
This third section is completely under the control of the organisation's Web manager and is a direct reflection of the site architecture that is decided on.

The use of different levels of directories and sub-directories in the construction of the website will result in this URL becoming longer or shorter. For example, if there were a sub-directory within 'webguidelines' called 'frames' the URL would look like this:

http://www.e-envoy.gov.uk/webguidelines/frames/index.htm

1.9.2 Develop a domain name strategy

An organisation with or planning to have an Internet presence should adopt and exercise a centralised approach on planning the acquisition, management and use of appropriate domain names.

A domain name is intellectual property and accordingly may have both financial and strategic value.

The registration of a .gov.uk domain is undertaken within clearly detailed guidelines. An individual department or agency may wish, as part of a defensive strategy, to consider acquiring other, closely related host names, eg, in the .org, info, .com Top Level Domains. This may reduce the risk of confusingly similar domain names being registered by third parties, thereby leading to confusion amongst Web users. This also reduces the genuine risk of third parties acquiring name for vexatious purposes.

When registering any name you should be aware of the need to avoid infringing existing trademarks and third party business names.

Web managers also should be aware of 'cybersquatting'. This is a practice of buying up domain names reflecting the names of existing organisations with the intention of selling the names back to you or for using them for 'bad faith' purposes, such as, passing off.

See **section 1.2.6** Management documentation.

> **IMPORTANT**
>
> *When you register any departmental, organisational or campaign website that is functionally outside the .gov.uk domain consider its prompt inclusion in the UK Government search engine index and/or the A to Z directories on www.ukonline.gov.uk. Please email brief details to:*
>
> **qfteam@e-envoy.gsi.gov.uk**

1.9.3 Managing your namespace

A small number of three and four letter acronyms may be considered as 'household names', eg, HSE, OFTEL. However, to the broad majority of user acronyms are meaningless. Web managers should encourage a 'user focused' approach and register accordingly. For example, host names like education.gov.uk, environment.gov.uk and defence.gov.uk may be considered intuitive and unambiguous to a general user.

The naming of directories should also be carefully considered. For example, your top-level directories may reflect organisational brands, projects or the editorial focus of the website. They should also be unambiguous when spoken and easy to type. As with domain names be aware of the need to avoid infringing trademarks and third party business names. Using the names of well-known people may also present difficulties.

The Welsh Language Board advise that Departments providing a service to the public in Wales should, where there is a difference between their English and Wales names, consider registering Welsh language domain names. For example, *www.anglesey.gov.uk* and *www.ynysmon.gov.uk* both lead to Anglesey Country Council's website.

1.9.4   Eligibility guidelines for a name within .gov.uk domain

The Internet Corporation for Assigned Names and Numbers (ICANN) is responsible for the assigning of globally unique identifiers including Internet domain names. Country codes such as, .uk are known as top level domains (ccTLDs) and management of these is delegated to individual country managers. In the UK this is managed by the non-for-profit company NOMINET.UK. The design of the naming structure under a country code rests with the country manager.

The Office of the e-Envoy (OeE) is responsible for the policy governing the **.gov.uk** domain and for its rules and guidelines. UKERNA administers the .gov.uk domain on behalf of OeE, in providing the name submission, name modification, approval and registration systems for the domain.

These guidelines apply to all new requests for registration of **.gov.uk** names. Some domain names were registered before the guidelines were laid down. Such names should be regarded as exceptional, and **not** as setting a precedent.

The registration of **.gov.uk** names is limited to UK government departments and agencies, local government bodies (including town and parish councils), and other associated and non-departmental public sector organisations and projects. **It is not for use by individuals, or by associations representing public sector staff, or by public sector pension funds.**

Projects and local authority departments should generally be treated as sub-domains of the parent body eg. *housing*.authority.gov.uk or *project*.department.gov.uk.

The acceptance of a name is conditional on that name being used specifically and exclusively for the organisation on whose behalf it is registered. The committee expect that the use of an approved domain name on a web server will lead directly to the home page for that organisation and not to that of its ISP/hosting service or any other agent. Abuse of this principle will result in the name being withdrawn.

Any application for a .gov.uk domain name should be submitted to Janet Customer Services at UKERNA, using the appropriate templates. These are available online at:

http://www.ja.net/documents/naming/gov.uk-naming-procedure.html

1.9.5 Guidelines for a choice of .gov.uk domain name

The principles for determining what name an organisation may adopt shall be:

- No two character names.
- The name requested shall reflect the legal name or trading name of the organisation.
- The chosen name shall minimise the risk of confusion with other similarly named organisation and avoid the risk of inadvertent masquerading.
- Local authority bodies should avoid using initials wherever possible, as these are generally reserved for central government.
- Three and four letter abbreviations or acronyms (TLAs/FLAs) will be considered **only** if:
  - the customer is a central Department of State (eg FCO); or
  - the customer is a central government body such that it is generally known by that TLA/FLA within government and to the wider public; or
  - there is no reasonable and meaningful alternative.
- The Domain Naming Approvals Committee will be the final arbiter of what is considered to be an acceptable TLA/FLA.
- Project names may be registered where they are pan-departmental or of national significance, eg to facilitate 'joined-up government'.
- Generic names should be avoided for local or intradepartmental initiatives, and used only for genuinely pan-governmental activities sponsored by the Office of the e-Envoy or the Prime Minister's Office.

1.9.6 .gov.uk naming conventions

Requests for registration stand a greater chance of quick acceptance if they follow the following conventions:

- Civil Service departments in Northern Ireland, because they mirror departments in Whitehall, are required to use the **suffix** '-ni'.

- Local authorities may generally use the format "area.gov.uk", unless there is the possibility of confusion with another authority (eg city and county).

- The following optional suffixes may be used (with or without the hyphen):

  - '-bc' Borough Council
  - '-cc' County Council
  - '-dc' District Council
  - '-mbc' Metropolitan Borough Council
  - '-ra' Regional Assembly
  - '-tc' Town Council

- Parish Councils – unless the full title 'parishcouncil' is used the following suffix is *required* with the hyphen '-pc'.

- Where towns or districts have the same name a county/geographic identifier should be used eg town-county.gov.uk

- Certain types of public sector organisations are *required* to use a suffix

- Associations of Local Councils   '-alc'
- Area Child Protection Committees   '-acpc'
- Educational networks   '-edunet'
- Embassies   '-emb'
- Excellence in Cities initiatives   'eic-'   (*prefix* rather than suffix)
- Fire services   '-fire'
- Government Regional Offices   'GO-'   (*prefix* rather than suffix)
- Housing Authority Trusts   '-hat'
- Joint Services Units   '-jsu'
- Learning and Skills Centres   'lsc-'   (*prefix* rather than suffix)
- Library and Education Boards (Northern Ireland only) '-leb'
- Local Education Authorities   '-lea'
- Local Government Associations   '-lga'
- Magistrates Court Committees   '-mcc'
- Magistrates Court Services   '-mcs'
- Museums   '-mus' or museum or museums
- National Park Authorities   '-npa'
- National Trails   '-way'
- Passenger Transport Authorities   '-pta'
- Passenger Transport Executives   '-pte'
- Police Authorities   '-pa'
- Prisons   'hmp-   (*prefix* followed by name)
- Probation Services   '-probation'
- Record Offices   '-ro'
- Sea Fisheries Committees   '-sfe' or '-seafish'
- Street Works Registers   '-swr'
- Valuation Joint Boards   '-vjb'
- Waste Disposal Authorities   'wda'

1.9.7   Additional information required when applying for a .gov.uk registration

A number of requests for registration have been initially rejected with advice because the applicant has supplied misleading or inadequate information.

The name requested must be linked to the organisation it is **for**, rather than the one hosting the service.

Applications should make clear how the status of the organisation qualifies it to be in the UK government domain. For example:

- the status of the organisation, eg, central government executive agency, borough council;
- the role and objective of the organisation
- the status of the staff (eg, civil servants, local government officials);
- the source of funding;
- to whom the body is accountable.

Any questions about these guidelines, or specific candidate names, can be directed to *naming@e-envoy.gsi.gov.uk*. Applications must not be sent to this email address.

address.

> **IMPORTANT**
>
> *If you are considering registering a domain name, it should be clearly understood who is undertaking this registration. If it is an agency doing so on your behalf then ensure that the name is to be handed over to your department/agency. Clarify what will happen to domain name renewal notices. Failure to clarify these lines could leave you vulnerable to an outside agency and possible failure to renew.*
>
> ***Prior to your website going live or a redirect page being published it is important to avoid a domain name holding page being used as a promotional outlet, eg, by your registration agency or website developer.***

1.9.8 'Pseudo domains' – a cautionary note

A number of domains have been registered which, at first sight, might be mistaken for officially delegated country top-level domains. These domains are often referred to as 'pseudo-domains'. The registrants of these domains typically resell subdomain names that also may be mistaken for officially delegated domains. The most common examples include: uk.com, uk.net, gb.com and gb.net.

1.9.9 Nominet.UK

.uk Top Level Domain rules
http://www.nominet.org.uk/rules.html

.uk Top Level Domain Disputes Resolution Service
http://www.nominet.org.uk/ref/drs.html

For a full technical description of a URL see RFC 2616
http://www.w3.org/Protocols/rfs2626/rfc2616.html

Always check the website for the latest guidance on how to register a .gov.uk domain name:
http://www.e-envoy.gov.uk/domain.htm

1.10 Legal issues

The general perception is that legal issues do not apply to the Internet. This section provides summary information on core issues. Web managers are advised that when there is any doubt then legal advice should be sought.

1.10.1 Basic principles

1.10.1.1 Content disclaimers

Public sector websites should not automatically contain disclaimers about content. There is no more reason to include a general disclaimer on a website than there would be to do so with respect to equivalent hard-copy material. On the other hand, the much-increased accessibility of material published on a website might in some instances more readily suggest that a disclaimer is appropriate. An assessment of whether a content disclaimer is needed can only really be made on a case-by-case basis. The department or other public body needs to consider the accuracy of the material, the source of the material and the projected use of and reliance on the material.

Disclaimers could well be relevant where information originating from outside government is made available on a public sector website. In such circumstances, bearing in mind the potential for defamation and inadvertent infringement of third-party copyright, it might be prudent to include some form of disclaimer along the following lines:

> The following information [specific document, etc] is provided for convenience as part of the service we offer at this website. However, the [XYZ Department/Agency (etc)] cannot accept any liability for its accuracy or content. Visitors who rely on this information do so at their own risk.

See **section 1.10.8** Specimen terms and conditions.

1.10.1.2 Legitimate expectation

Information published on a website can create a legitimate expectation as to procedure or substantive policy, just as can the hard-copy equivalents. This also means that any mistake in the course of publication on the Internet could have serious consequences in light of the sheer speed of dispersal of information and the numbers of hits that the more popular websites receive each day.

1.10.1.3 Defamation

The risk of defamation is not diminished by virtue of electronic publication. Anything on the website that looks like it could injure a person's reputation should be scrutinised thoroughly and legal advice sought when in doubt. This applies whether the material was authored by civil servants (or other public sector employees) for the website or originates elsewhere. Even in situations where a public sector website is merely a transient host, such as for a discussion group or question and answer session, defamation will still be an issue.

When the manager of a website first learns that there may be defamatory material on the site, it is vital that swift action is taken to assess the situation. Such action can help to preserve available defences such as innocent dissemination. Where there is any doubt at all, it may be best to remove the offending material from the site until a properly informed decision can be reached.

Some public sector bodies may wish to publish material covered by the *Parliamentary Papers Act 1840* on their website. In the ordinary course, the publication of material coming within that Act (that is, published by or under the authority of either House of Parliament) has the benefit of absolute privilege from defamation actions. However, it has been suggested that publication on the Internet does not attract the protection of the 1840 Act, no doubt because such a medium of publication was not contemplated.

1.10.2 Data Protection Act

The Data Protection Act 1988 contains eight data protection principles which taken together define the standards that must be met when processing personal data. The principles are necessarily at a fairly high level. They are nonetheless at the heart of the Act and the Information Commissioner has powers of enforcement in cases of contravention. Web managers are advised that if there be any doubt legal opinion should be sought.

1.10.2.1 Introduction to the Act

The purpose of the Data Protection Act is to 'make provision for the regulation of the processing of information relating to individuals, including the obtaining, holding, use or disclosure of such information'. Information relating to individuals that is either published on websites or is collected from individuals who visit those sites thus falls within the scope of the Act.

The key features of the Act are:

- the system of notification (replacing registration under the 1984 Act);
- the data protection principles;
- the creation of rights for individuals, including the right to obtain copies of personal data held about them;
- independent enforcement by the Information Commissioner.

The principles and individuals' rights are probably the most significant parts of the Act. Data controllers should be mindful of the right of individuals to seek compensation through the courts for any damage and associated distress suffered as a result of breaches of the Act.

Further guidance and advice is available from the Information Commissioner's website
http://www.dataprotection.gov.uk

The following should be borne in mind:

1.10.2.2 Notification

Data controllers (ie. persons such as a Secretary of State who determine the purposes for which personal data is processed) must notify to the Information Commissioner the purposes for which they process personal data and for each purpose must provide a description of data subjects, data classes, disclosures and transfers of data outside the European Economic Area. This information is placed on the public register. While the operation of a website is unlikely to involve the processing of personal data for new purposes, occasionally this may be the case, and it is certainly possible that new categories of data may be processed for the first time.

Data controllers operating websites should be aware that this might result in a transfer of personal data overseas and such a transfer must be described in the data controller's notification. Please see s.3.1.12 of the *Commissioner's Notification*

Handbook – this is available at ***http://www.dpr.gov.uk***, as is comprehensive advice about notification under the Act.

1.10.2.3 1ˢᵗ Data Protection Principle

'Personal data shall be processed fairly and lawfully and, in particular, shall not be processed unless –

a) *at least one of the conditions in Schedule 2 is met, and*

b) *In the case of sensitive personal data, at least one of the conditions in Schedule 3 is also met.'*

'Processing' includes the collection of information. In order to collect information fairly the data subject should be informed of the identity of the data controller and of the purposes of processing (unless they already have the information) together with 'any further information that is necessary ... to enable the processing ... to be fair'. Among the other information that it may be necessary to provide may be details of any disclosures of data, rights to object to particular uses of data, and information as to which information requested on an electronic form is mandatory and which optional.

If personal data gathered by one department is to be passed to another, the fact that there is an intention to disclose should be made clear before the disclosure takes place, and any necessary consent for the disclosure should be obtained at that point. There may well be individuals who are willing to provide certain information to one department but not to another. Departments disclosing information to another department should be mindful of issues such as duties of confidentiality owed to the data subject, purpose limitation, further disclosure, etc, i.e. the discloser should make it clear to the 'disclosee' why the disclosure is taking place and how the disclosed personal data may be processed. It should be remembered that how personal data obtained by one organisation may be subsequently processed by another essentially depends on how the data was obtained originally.

Controllers should not assume that those from whom they are seeking information would under understand how personal data is used. *Fair obtaining notices* should be designed with the intended audience in mind. For example, a website aimed specifically at members of a particular ethnic group should be intelligible to that group through the use of the appropriate language or terminology. Special safeguards should be introduced when requesting information from a child or a person who is not mentally competent, eg, request the intervention of a parent/guardian of carer. It is always worthwhile piloting a *fair obtaining notice* with a group of typical users.

Where there is a link to another site operated by another data controller, people should be clearly advised as to who may be collecting any information they provide on electronic forms.

Care should be taken to ensure that information is not collected of which the subject is unaware, for instance through use of cookies or the capture of 'clickstream' data. In particular, contracts should specify that ISPs/hosting services are not permitted to collect or make independent use of such data.

When people are invited to leave their email addresses the uses that will be made of these should be explained if there is any room for doubt. It should be a condition of membership of a chat room that members do not make use of others' email addresses for unrelated purposes. Consideration should be given as to whether it is necessary to monitor compliance with this condition, for instance through 'seeding' email address lists.

Fair obtaining notices should be clearly worded and positioned. While it is acceptable for privacy statements or codes of practice to be accessed via a link, *fair obtaining notices* should have sufficient prominence on the relevant forms.

Web managers should be mindful of the restriction that the Data Protection Act 1998 places on the processing of sensitive personal data. In some cases, this means that the individual's explicit consent for the processing may need to be obtained.

The Office of the Information Commissioner is of the view that when there is an intention to develop a chat room the system should be designed in such a way that participation may take place anonymously. Alternatively in a manner where individuals are given a clear choice as to whether their email addresses will be made available to other participants or to observers of the chat room.

1.10.2.4 2nd Data Protection Principle

Personal data shall be obtained only for one or more specified and lawful purposes, and shall not be further processed in any manner incompatible with that purpose or those purposes.

The effect of this principle is to reinforce the first principle by restricting the further processing of personal data, including processing by any recipient of that data, to purposes which are compatible with those for which the data was first obtained.

1.10.2.5 3rd Data Protection Principle

Personal data shall be adequate, relevant and not excessive in relation to the purpose or purposes for which it is processed.

Forms should be designed so that only the necessary amount of information is collected. Care should be taken not to seek information, for instance dates of birth, where there is no operational need for this information. At the same time it is important to collect sufficient information. It should be possible to design forms that have a mandatory area into which certain information must be entered and a clearly marked voluntary area into which other information can be entered. When individuals are being asked to provide information for reasons other than operational necessity, it should be explained to them what the extra information will be used for, eg, research, profiling.

1.10.2.6 4th Data Protection Principle

Personal data shall be accurate and, where necessary, kept up-to-date.

Controllers can normally assume that the information provided by data subjects is accurate. Some sites, however, may attract 'nuisance' visitors who leave information relating to other people. If controllers become aware of such problems then they may have to take steps to verify the identity of visitors and to validate the accuracy of data. In some cases the most appropriate course of action might be to delete the problematic data and to request that other do the same in cases where this data have been disclosed.

1.10.2.7 5th Data Protection Principle

Personal data processed for any purpose or purposes shall not be kept for longer than is necessary for that purpose or those purposes.

The Act does not specify particular retention periods. Data collected on electronic forms should be retained for the same period as similar data collected by traditional means. Web managers are encouraged to keep information that is in a personally identifiable form for as short a period as is operationally necessary. For example, personal data that is collected in the course of the visit to a site, for instance temporary chat rooms, should be deleted once the session has ended.

1.10.2.8 6th Data Protection Principle

Personal data shall be processed in accordance with the rights of data subjects under this Act.

The rights of data subjects are:

- to request a copy of personal data (subject access);
- to prevent processing likely to cause substantial damage or distress;
- to prevent processing for direct marketing purposes;
- not to be subject to automated decision taking.

Subject access requests must be made in writing. Before responding, controllers should be satisfied as to the identity of the person making the request. Responses should not be made to requests made via email unless the controller is able to verify identity, for instance through an electronic signature.

Data subjects have an absolute right to request that their data is not used for direct marketing purposes. There is unlikely to be any issue with advertisements that are displayed to all visitors to a site. It has been suggested that it may be possible to make use of a user profile in order to decide which advertisement to display to which visitor. Use of such techniques should be described to data subjects (1st principle) and there must be a mechanism to suppress the display of advertisements on request.

The Office of the Information Commissioner is of the view that in the future web developers should be able to build features that allow individuals to gain subject access online. This would enable individuals to call up records relating to themselves, without having to make a formal subject access request. Such online subject access will certainly be advantageous to both individuals and data controllers. However, this must be subject to the appropriate security and identify verification procedures.

1.10.2.9 7th Data Protection Principle

Appropriate technical and organisational measures shall be taken against unauthorised or unlawful processing of personal data and against accidental loss or destruction of, or damage to, personal data.

The Act directs controllers to adopt a risk-based approach to security matters. The need to use encryption, electronic signatures and other security features thus increases with the sensitivity of the data that it is proposed to transmit electronically.

Reasonable steps should be taken to monitor the use of any personal data which may be downloaded from websites, for instance by 'seeding lists of email addressed and checking for instances of use for unauthorised purposes.

1.10.2.10 8th Data Protection Principle

Personal data shall not be transferred to a country or territory outside the European Economic Area unless that country or territory ensures an adequate level of protection for the rights and freedoms of data subjects in relation to the processing of personal data.

The recording of personal data on a website or its publication on a site is tantamount to allowing the worldwide transfer of data. Although the principle suggests that data may never be transferred to countries without an adequate level of protection, in fact there are exceptions, which are set out in Schedule 4 of the Act. In many cases the issue will be whether or not it is necessary to have the consent of the data subject to transfer their data outside the European Economic Area. As a general rule, if the personal data in question would in any event be placed in the public domain, for instance data relating to Ministers or senior civil servants, then it would be hard to argue that there was an increased risk to the privacy of those individuals by placing their details on a website. In other cases, it may be appropriate to seek consent.

1.10.2.11 Personal data in the 'public domain'

Even though information about Ministers and senior officials may well be in the 'public domain' already, it is recommended that Web managers implement the following safeguards when posting personal data about individuals on a website:

- The individual should be made aware of the intention to post information about him or her on the Internet before the posting takes place, so that any specific concerns, eg, about security, can be addressed; and

- measures should be taken to prevent the wholesale downloading of the contents of such documents as online versions of professional registers.

1.10.2.12 Use of cookies and privacy statements

The following is an example of a website privacy statement where you do not make use of cookies:

If you are *a user with general public and anonymous access* the *[department/agency name]* website does not store or capture personal information, but merely logs the user's IP address that is automatically recognised by the web server.

We do not use cookies for collecting user information and we will not collect any information about you except that required for system administration of our web server.

This privacy statement only covers the *[department/agency name]* website at *http://www.[put in URI]*. This statement does not cover links within this site to other websites.

See **section 1.10.7**: Specimen terms and conditions for websites.

IMPORTANT
Government websites should not use cookies covertly.

Office of the Information Commissioner
http://www.dataprotection.gov.uk

Notification under the Data Protection Act 1998 and the Data Protection Register
http://www.dpr.gov.uk

1.10.3 Copyright and the notices for government websites

Copyright does not protect ideas or facts. It only protects the manner in which an idea or fact is recorded, whether in writing, on audio tape, placed on a website, on CD-ROM or in any other tangible way. Web managers are advised that when there is any doubt then legal advice should be sought.

1.10.3.1 Copyright

Copyright is a type of intellectual property rights (IPR), but unlike all other forms of IPR, copyright is not something that the creator needs to register or declare. In the UK copyright protection automatically arises when an original work is fixed in a tangible medium or expression. Copyright does not protect ideas or facts. It only protects the manner in which an idea or fact is recorded, whether in writing, placed on your website or in any other tangible way.

1.10.3.2 Who owns the Copyright?

The general rule is that the author is the first owner of copyright in any literary, artistic, dramatic or musical work. The main exception is where such a work is made in the course of employment, in which case the employer owns the copyright.

Government departments and agencies commission a wide range of works by individuals and non-Crown organisations. Unless specific provision is made in the commissioning contract for the copyright in such commissioned works to be assigned or transferred to the Crown, the copyright will continue to rest with the author. Like physical property, it cannot usually be used without the owner's permission.

1.10.3.3 Implications

Commissioning a work does not automatically confer copyright ownership. Indeed it does not even give the commissioning department an automatic right to reproduce or publish the work itself, unless such use is specifically agreed under the terms of the commissioning contract.

Any copyright owner is able to exercise full rights and control the ways in which the work may be exploited. This includes the right to publish, disseminate and copy. Only the copyright owner can transfer or sell (assign) or authorise (licence) its use.

1.10.3.4 Electronic rights

If you are commissioning material to publish electronically, eg on your website, it is advisable to own the copyright and you must have **all world rights** or alternatively specifically **all digital rights**.

1.10.3.5 Infringement of copyright

Anyone one who violates any of the 'restricted acts' of a copyright owner has infringed copyright law. Copyright owners have both civil and criminal remedies to protect their rights. They can recover damages from an infringement and obtain orders (injunctions) to prevent or restrain infringements.

In principle, anything, which is an infringement of copyright, if done in a non-electronic manner, or by non-electronic means, is also an infringement if done by electronic means. The electronic storage, retrieval, duplication, transmission and performance of a copyright-protection work are all potential infringements, however, transient they are. For example, such simple acts as the display of a work on a computer screen may involve infringing action.

1.10.3.6 Moral rights

Under UK law an author or creator (except an employee) of certain copyright material has additional rights:

- the right of *paternity* – an author's right to be acknowledge as the author or creator,
- the right of *integrity* – not to have their work subject to derogatory treatment,
- the rights to *privacy* of photographs and films, and
- the right to *object* to their name being attributed to material they did not create.

Moral rights are not automatic, unlike copyright, they have to be asserted in writing by the author. However, they do transcend economic rights and can not be assigned. They can be waived in a commissioning contract.

1.10.3.7 Working in the electronic environment

In the absence of a copyright notice or statement to the contrary, it is recommended that web managers assume that all material (textural, graphical, audio and video) on the Internet is copyright. Be aware of statements that do permit use but place conditions on that use. The omission of a copyright notice does not imply that you have unrestricted us of the material

In the e-environment it is extremely easy when down loading material to omit an author's name or to cut and paste material in a manner that could be considered derogatory. It may be legal to do something from a copyright point-of-view but that action may well infringe Moral Rights. For example:

- Inserting a number of hyperlinks into the text to link to other relevant articles – the author may well consider such links as derogatory.

- Cutting and pasting in a short extract from a text or graphic may not infringe copyright or you have permission to make the copy. You could, however, be infringing Moral Rights by failing to acknowledge the author/creator or because the short extract may be considered derogatory.

There are several situations in which these rights do not apply:

- Computer programs.
- Where material is used in newspapers or magazines.
- Reference works, such as, encyclopaedias and dictionaries.

1.10.3.8 Database right *(sui generis)*

The database right is very similar to copyright, for example, it is an automatic right and commences as soon as the material exists in a recorded form. There are some differences between database right and copyright:

- The terms of protection is for 15 years from making but, if published during this time, then the term is 15 years from publication.
- The activities that a right holder can control and which are, infringed, if undertaken without the right holder's permission, are different. The rights concern control over the extraction and re-use of the content of the database.
- Activities that a user can undertake without the permission of the right holder that do not infringe the right does not, in particular, extend to fair dealing for the purpose of research or private study for a commercial purpose

For copyright protection to apply to a database it must have originality in the selection or arrangement of the content.

Intellectual Property Rights portal
http://www.intellectual-property.gov.uk

See **Copyright, Designs and Patents Act 1988** (CPDA88)

1.10.3.9 Crown Copyright and HMSO

HMSO Guidance Note 13 – Notices on Government websites *http://www.hmso.gov.uk/g note13.htm* advises government departments on suitable copyright notices for use on departmental and agency websites.

As part of the evolving policy of opening up access to official information, copyright in certain categories of official material is waived to allow it to be freely reproduced (The Future Management of Crown Copyright – *http://www.hmso.gov.uk/document/copywp.htm*). Government documents featured on official departmental and agency websites come into one of the categories of material identified as being subject to waiver conditions. It follows that **unless departments and agencies specify otherwise**, material featured on their sites can be reproduced free of charge and without requiring a formal copyright licence. It is therefore important that the copyright status of material on websites must be clear and set out in a form that can be easily understood.

Inclusion of full and accurate notices is important because:

- it is made evident to visitors to the site that the site has official status;
- it sets out the arrangements for reproducing the material contained on the site;
- it encourages users to create links to the official site;
- It identifies any copyright material that is owned by third parties.

1.10.3.10 Which notices should be featured on your website?

HMSO advises that the following notices should be clearly featured on departmental and agency websites:

- a general copyright statement covering the site; and
- details of how the material may be reproduced and where to apply if a licence is required.

It is also important to make the copyright position clear in terms of the individual documents featured on the website, including acknowledgements of any copyrights that are not owned by the Crown. For a detailed explanation, see the following website.

> **HMSO Guidance Note 12 – Copyright and Publishing Notices**
> *http://www.hmso.gov.uk/g-note12.htm*

A. Copyright statement

On the assumption that a department or agency, or contractor acting on behalf of the department or agency manages the information, it is appropriate to claim the site as being Crown copyright, even if some of the individual documents are not Crown copyright. Accordingly, the site should show the following statement on the homepage or introductory pages on each departmental or agency website:

> © Crown copyright *[followed by year in which the site was established or last amended]*.

B. Statements on departmental or agency websites

Departments and agencies should consider the range of material contained on the site and whether it may be copied without restriction. Set out below are three model statements which can be tailored to meet specific circumstances.

> **Option 1**
> **Where Crown copyright material can be reused with no restrictions**
>
> © Crown copyright *[followed by year in which the website was established or last amended]*
>
> The material featured on this site is subject to Crown copyright protection unless otherwise indicated. The Crown copyright protected material (other than the Royal Arms and departmental or agency logos) may be reproduced free of charge in any format or medium provided it is reproduced accurately and not used in a misleading context. Where any of the Crown copyright items on this site are being republished or copied to others, the source of the material must be identified and the copyright status acknowledged.
>
> The permission to reproduce Crown protected material does not extend to any material on this site that is identified as being the copyright of a third party. Authorisation to reproduce such material must be obtained from the copyright holders concerned.
>
> The *[name of the department or agency]* encourages users to establish hypertext links to this site.
>
> For further information on Crown copyright policy and licensing arrangements, see the guidance featured on HMSO's website at:
> *http://www.hmso.gov.uk/guides.htm*

Option 2
Where Crown copyright material can be reused for research, private study or internal circulation within an organisation

© Crown copyright *[followed by year in which the website was established or was last substantially amended]*

The material featured on this site is subject to Crown copyright protection unless otherwise indicated. The Crown copyright protected material (other than the Royal Arms and departmental or agency logos) may be reproduced free of charge in any format or medium for research, private study or for internal circulation within an organisation. This is subject to the material being reproduced accurately and not used in a misleading context. Where any of the Crown copyright items on this site are being republished or copied to others, the source of the material must be identified and the copyright status acknowledged.

Any other proposed use of the material will be subject to a copyright licence available from HMSO, The Licensing Division, St Clements House, 2–16 Colegate, Norwich NR3 1BQ, Fax: 01603 723000 or email: licensing@hmso.gov.uk

The permission to reproduce Crown protected material does not extend to any material on this site which is identified as being the copyright of a third party. Authorisation to reproduce such material must be obtained from the copyright holders concerned.

The *[name of department or agency]* encourages users to establish hypertext links to the site.

For further information on Crown copyright policy and licensing arrangements, see the guidance featured on HMSO's website at
http://www.hmso.gov.uk/guides.htm

Option 3
Where the reuse of Crown copyright material is subject to licensing arrangements

© Crown copyright *[followed by year in which the website was established or was last substantially amended]*

The material featured on this site is subject to Crown copyright protection unless otherwise indicated. The material may be downloaded to file or printer for the purposes of research and private study. Any other proposed use of the material is subject to a copyright licence available from HMSO in accordance with standard Crown copyright licensing policy. Copyright licences can be obtained from HMSO, The Licensing Division, St Clements House, 2–16 Colegate, Norwich NR3 1BQ, Fax: 01603 723000 or email: *licensing@hmso.gov.uk*

The permission to reproduce Crown protected material does not extend to any material on this site which is identified as being the copyright of a third party. Authorisation to reproduce such material must be obtained from the copyright holders concerned.

The *[name of department or agency]* encourages users to establish hypertext links to this site.

For further information on Crown copyright policy and licensing arrangements, see the guidance featured on HMSO's website at:
http://www.hmso.gov.uk/guides.htm

1.10.3.11 Conclusion to Copyright notices

The copyright status of the material contained on each site and how that material can be used must be made clearly available to all visitors to departmental and agency websites. Departments and agencies should, therefore, provide notices which can be easily understood and which encourage the widest use of the material. If you have any queries or problems, contact *licensing@hmso.gov.uk.*

1.10.4 Disability Discrimination Act

Government policy is to encourage departments and agencies to make their services as accessible to disabled people as is reasonably possible. Overall these guidelines have been developed with this aim in mind. Web managers are advised that when there is any doubt then legal advice should be sought.

1.10.4.1 Details of the Disability Discrimination Act

Part III of the Disability Discrimination Act (DDA) makes it unlawful for a service provider to treat disabled people less favourably for a reason related to their disability. Service providers must also consider making reasonable adjustments to the way that they deliver their services where disabled people find these impossible or unreasonably difficult to access.

There are provisions in the DDA (section 19(3)) that state that 'access to and use of means of communication' and 'access to and use of information services' are both examples of services which would be covered by Part III.

However, it would be for a court to decide whether it would have been reasonable for a particular service provider to make a particular adjustment to enable access for a disabled person, taking into consideration all the circumstances of the case.

Code of Practice. On 26 February 2002, the Disability Rights Commission published a new, revised Code of Practice on rights of access to goods, facilities, services and premises for disabled people. This statutory Code, agreed by Parliament, provides detailed advice on the way the law should work. It also provides practical examples and tips. The status of the Code is that it must be referred to for guidance in court when deciding on Part III DDA cases.

The Code of Practice makes express reference to websites in:

- Chapter 2. What does the Act say about providing services – paragraphs 2.14 and 2.17, and
- Chapter 5. Reasonable adjustments in practice – Provision for people with a hearing disability and for people with a visual impairment – paragraphs 5.23 and 5.26.

The Code is available from:
http://www.drc.org.uk/drc/InformationAndLegislation/Page331a.asp

The **Special Educational Needs and Disability Act 2001**confers similar rights upon disabled students as those available to disabled people under the DDA Part III.

Disability Discrimination Act website
http://www.disability.gov.uk/dda/index

Disability Discrimination Act 1995
http://www.legislation.hmso.gov.uk/acts/acts1995/Ukpga_19950050_en_1.htm

Code of Practice on Rights of Access to Goods, Facilities, Services and Premises
http://www.drc.org.uk/drc/InformationAndLegislation/Page331a.asp

Disability Rights Commission
http://www.drc-gb.org

Helpline email
enquiry@drc-gb.org

Special Educational Needs and Disability Act 2001
http://www.legislation.hmso.gov.uk/acts/acts2001/20010010.htm

1.10.5 Public Records Act

In order to manage their records effectively and fulfil their obligations under the Public Records Acts, departments need to maintain inventories of their electronic and other records, and subject the records to disposal schedules based on the administrative and permanent value of the websites. The Public Records Act 1958 requires that every person responsible for public records of any description shall make arrangements for the selection of records for permanent preservation and for their safe keeping. Web managers are advised that when there is any doubt then legal advice should be sought.

1.10.5.1 Details of the Public Records Act

Public records selected for permanent preservation must be transferred to the Public Record Office not later than thirty years after their creation (except with the approval by the Lord Chancellor in certain defined circumstances). In order to ensure that websites (or parts of websites) can be preserved as long as necessary for the conduct of public business, and if selected for permanent preservation, can be preserved permanently by the Public Record Office, proper electronic records management procedures must be followed to safeguard copies of different versions against loss, interference, or electronic degradation.

Electronic records management needs to take into account that a website may contain materials that could influence the actions of a member of the public. It is also the case that the context in which the material is presented on the site may influence such actions, and that some sites may contain information collected from real-time transactions. It is therefore the responsibility of departments and agencies to assess whether or not copies of complete websites or discrete documents on websites should be preserved in order that they can be produced as authentic records of the information and advice supplied by that organisation.

Departments and agencies need to conduct an exposure analysis of their sites and determine whether it is sufficient to retain copies of individual documents on the website, or whether they should take copies of the entire site. If the former approach is taken, departments and agencies should develop procedures to ensure that record copies of website documents are in fact consistently captured and securely stored as corporate records. If the latter approach is adopted, the analysis should also determine the frequency with which the copies should be taken. Further information may be found at the following website:

Public Records Office
http://www.pro.gov.uk/recordsmanagement/eros/guidelines/procedures3.htm

1.10.6 Welsh Language Act

Ministers have committed government departments and agencies to introducing Welsh language schemes under the Welsh Language Act 1993. Many agencies and departments have already done so, and others are in the process of introducing a scheme. The schemes set out how departments and agencies will use Welsh in the delivery of their services to the public in Wales. Web managers are advised that when there is any doubt then legal advice should be sought.

1.10.6.1 Details of the Welsh Language Act

Departments and agencies should apply the principles of their language schemes (or the schemes they are preparing) to their Internet sites. The aim should be that the public has access to information in both English and Welsh in line with the commitments in schemes. This relates to aspects such as presentation, general information and publicity material as well as placing materials produced in hard copy in Welsh or dual-language on the Internet alongside the English content. The Welsh content should be as easy for the public to access as the English content. Examples of how this can be set out can be found on the websites below.

Anybody wanting further advice on the above should contact the Welsh Language Board.

National Assembly for Wales
http://www.wales.gov.uk

Welsh Language Board
http://www.bwrdd-yr-iaith.org.uk
Email ymholiadau@bwrdd-yr-iaith.org.uk or telephone: 029 2087 8000

1.10.7 Human Rights Act 1998

The Government's commitment to incorporate the European Convention on Human Rights into UK law has led to the introduction of the Human rights Act 1998. Web managers are advised that when there is any doubt then legal advice should be sought.

1.10.7.1 Introduction to the Human Rights Act

Under the Human Rights Act 1998 a British citizen is able to assert their rights under the European Convention on Human Rights through the national courts without having to take their case to the European Court of Human Rights.

Human Rights Unit
http://www.lcd.gov.uk/hract/hramenu.htm

1.10.8 Specimen terms and conditions (including hyperlinking and privacy)

The following specimen information could be used within the terms and conditions on organisation's website. Terms and conditions, and in particular, privacy statements must be clearly visible to all users.

It is important that user's of government websites clearly understand when a hyperlink is taking them out of your webspace. An example hyperlink disclaimer is included. Web managers are advised that when there is any doubt then legal advice should be sought.

1.10.8.1 Using our website – specimen paragraph

Using our website.
The *[department/agency name]* website is maintained for your personal use and viewing. Access and use by you of this site constitutes acceptance by you of these Terms and Conditions that take effect from the date of first use.

1.10.8.1   Intellectual property – specimen paragraphs

Intellectual property
The names, images and logos identifying the *[department/agency name],* are proprietary marks of the *[Crown/agency name].* Copying or our logos and/or any other third party logos accessed via this website is not permitted without prior approval from the relevant copyright owner.

Requests for permission to use our logo should be directed to *[name of an individual inside your department/agency].* Telephone *000 0000 0000*; Fax *000 0000 0000*; email <mailto> xxxx@xxx.gov.uk. Tell us how and why your wish to use our logo(s). Please include your contact details name, address, telephone number, fax number and email.

[bring in the relevant Crown Copyright clause]

1.10.8.2   Copyright clauses on government websites

HMSO Guidance Note 13 – Notices on Government Websites advises government departments on suitable copyright notices for use on departmental and agency websites. See **section 1.10.3** of these Guidelines or refer to
http://www.hmso.gov.uk/g-note13.htm

1.10.8.3 Hyperlinking policy – specimen paragraphs

Hyperlinking to us at the *[department/agency name]*
You do not have to ask permission to link directly to pages hosted on this site. We do not object to you linking directly to the information that is hosted on our site.

However, we do not permit our pages to be loaded into frames on your site. The *[department/agency name]* pages must load into the user's entire window.

Hyperlinking by us at the *[department/agency name]*
It is our policy to obtain permission to link to other websites. We are not responsible for the content or reliability of the linked websites. Listing should not be taken as endorsement of any kind. We cannot guarantee that these links will work all of the time and we have no control over the availability of linked pages.

1.10.8.4 Virus protection awareness – specimen paragraph

Virus protection
We make every effort to check and test material at all stages of production. It is always wise for you to run an anti-virus program on all material downloaded from the Internet. We cannot accept any responsibility for any loss, disruption or damage to your data or your computer system which may occur whilst using material derived from this website.

1.10.8.5 Website disclaimer – specimen paragraphs

Disclaimer
The *[department/agency name]* website and material relating to Government information, products and services (or to third party information, products and services), is provided 'as is', without any representation or endorsement made and without warranty of any kind whether express or implied, including but not limited to the implied warranties of satisfactory quality, fitness for a particular purpose, non-infringement, compatibility, security and accuracy.

We do not warrant that the functions contained in the material contained in this site will be uninterrupted or error free, that defects will be corrected, or that this site or the server that makes it available are free of viruses or represent the full functionality, accuracy, reliability of the materials. In no event will we be liable for any loss or damage including, without limitation, indirect or consequential loss or damage, or any loss or damages whatsoever arising from use or loss of use of, data or profits arising out of or in connection with the use of the *[department/agency name]* website.

These Terms and Conditions shall be governed by and construed in accordance with the laws of England and Wales. Any dispute arising under these Terms and Conditions shall be subject to the exclusive jurisdiction of the courts of England and Wales.

1.10.8.6 Examples of privacy statements

Privacy statement
If you are *a user with general public and anonymous access* the *[department/agency name]* website does not store or capture personal information, but merely logs the user's IP address that is automatically recognised by the web server.

We do not use cookies for collecting user information and we will not collect any information about you except that required for system administration of our web server.

This privacy statement only covers the *[department/agency name]* website at **http://www.** *[put in URI]*. This statement does not cover links within this site to other websites.

1.10.8.6.1 Optional paragraph if you provide personalised or a listserver facility

The system will record your email address and other information if volunteered to us by you. This shall be treated as proprietary and confidential. It may be used for internal review and to notify you about updates to *[department/agency name]* website.

1.10.8.7   Hyperlinking to third party website – specimen disclaimer

It is important that user's of your website clearly understand if a hyperlink on a web page will take them away from your site to a non-government webspace. The following is an example of a statement that could be used on such pages:

> The *[department/agency name]* is not responsible for the contents or reliability of the linked web sites and does not necessarily endorse the views expressed within them. Listing should not be taken as endorsement of any kind. We cannot guarantee that these links will work all of the time and we have no control over the availability of the linked pages.

1.11 Backgrounder on securing websites

It is essential that government websites are secure. Senior officials have a duty of care of the information that citizens and businesses provide to the public sector. The Data Protection Act, Human Rights Act and other legislation require that privacy is respected. Beyond this, Government websites must be secure to build trust and maintain the reputation of electronic government. This will be seriously damaged if websites are defaced, services are unavailable or sensitive information is released to the wrong people.

Web management teams must consult with their Departmental Security Officers or equivalent responsible officer because the security of websites must happen within the context of your security policies.

If your website is managed by an Internet Service Provider (ISP)/hosting service, you should ensure as far that the ISP/host has procedures, eg, ISO17799, in place to comply with your corporate website security. It is recommended that the application and maintenance of those procedures is checked on a regular basis by qualified security consultants such as those accredited under the CHECK service.

The Office of the e-Envoy will answer enquires about security issues. Contact *security@e-envoy.gov.uk*.

1.11.1 What is a security policy?

A security policy is an organisation's to and the setting out of the approach to managing information security, such as, ISO17799. From this cascades all the procedures and practices for day-to-day dealing with information.

A security policy specifically for the website and the services provided through it may be:

- An overview to information security being taken by the Web management team possibly after a risk assessment has been undertaken.
- Rules, both technical and legal, by which an individual who is given access to a government website must abide.
- Procedures and practices for dealing with information from those transacting with your website. See **section 1.10.2** Data Protection Act.
- Procedures and practices for password generation and use.

1.11.2 What is the purpose of secure website management?

The purpose of secure website management is the establishment and maintenance of procedures for staff and outside contractors to use, which minimises the risk to security in the management of an organisation's website. For example:

- to ensure the *integrity* and *availability* of your website's production and infrastructure,

- to ensure the correct and secure operation of your website, such as, access control to your server and not leaving your content management system unattended,
- to ensure the integrity of information published on your website,
- to protect the integrity of software and information, and
- to prevent damage to assets and interruption to your business activities.

1.11.3 The security of your website

It needs to be stressed that most successful breaches of integrity on websites are made possible by misconfiguration of the web server and failure to install relevant security patches. The information in this section aims to raise awareness on correct configuration and patch application.

The security of a website is determined by the security of the following:

- the web server application;
- the operating system of the web server computer;
- the local area network of the web server computer;
- 'backend' (eg database) applications supporting the web server;
- the authoritative domain name server for the web server network,
- remote web server administration, eg, use of FTP, use of server extensions (not addressed here), and
- physical and personnel measures in place to ensure that the web server environment is secure, but these are beyond the scope of this guidance.

In the sections below each area of security will be considered in turn with recommendations for each. All of the recommendations should be followed if good website security is to be achieved.

This guidance presupposes that the web server is open to an untrusted user community and does not address the possibility of trusted users accessing or maintaining the website remotely. Most web servers provide remote file and directory authentication for such purposes, although the types and use of such authentication are beyond the scope of this guidance.

1.11.4 The security of the web server application

A website is hosted by a web server. A web server is an application that accepts requests from client web browsers in the Hypertext Transfer Protocols (http and https) and responds by sending web pages and other content to the client web browsers.

A web page designer can manually generate these web pages or they can be automatically generated. Automatically generated pages may use interpreted scripting languages, such as Perl to produce the web pages by common gateway interface (CGI), or they may use proprietary server-side programming extensions such as Microsoft's Active Server Pages (ASP). Web server security therefore splits into two further areas:

- The security of the web server application itself;
- The security of any CGI scripts or server extensions.

For the security of the web server itself, the following steps are recommended:

a.   As with any application, ensure that you monitor briefings from your CERT and commercial sites such as bugtraq *http://www.securityfocus.com* on a regular and frequent basis and install any security patches relevant to the version of the web server that you are using and that address problems that the server is susceptible to. The website vendor's website should also be able to provide instructions on installing the patches and their coverage of vulnerabilities.

b.   When configuring the web server, ensure that any access controls that can be set within the web server application are set appropriately on all directories under and including the root directory of the web as follows:

- Ensure that no web directories or files within the web directory structure are modifiable or writable by anyone other than the web server administrator.

- Access to web pages should be read-only for users, although a web user will need permission to execute scripts or programs used to generate web pages dynamically.

- Web users should not be able to list the contents of directories, unless there is a clearly identified requirement.

- No access should be granted to other directories or programs in the web directory structure unless there is an explicit need.

- No access should be granted to the web server executable or to the web server configuration files.

- No access should be granted above the root of the web server directory structure.

c.   Do not assign access control override privileges to the user as these can be abused by attackers to turn off access control.

d.   Enable logging on the web server so that all server activity is logged. This should be analysed on a regular and frequent basis by the organisation's IT security officer for events indicative of an attack, for instance attempts to run non-existent scripts. The web server log should also contain all attempted and established connections, error messages, remote authentication attempts, all scripts run and any access control violations for files and directories under access control of the web server. This can be a complex and expensive activity so it may be considered more practical to use an Intrusion Detection System and analysis of these logs.

For the security of CGI scripts and server extensions, the following steps are recommended:

a.   Remove all sample scripts installed with the server.

b.   Disable any server directives or extensions that enable scripts to run operating system level commands on the web server, for example, in a Unix environment, Server Side Includes.

c.   In conjunction with your Departmental Security Officer or equivalent responsible officer ensure that a suitably qualified professional, external to your website development, checks all scripts that are used on the web server to ensure that they validate input to allow only expected types and lengths of input data and produce error messages otherwise. Care should be taken that special characters and empty values are treated adequately. Escapes to an operating command shell should never be permitted.

d.   If possible, store all scripts in the same directory and forbid execution of scripts outside this directory.

1.11.5 The security of the operating system of the web server computer

The security of the web server is only as good as the security of its environment. If the operating system is configured securely, the damage that a malicious user could do will be restricted to what can be obtained with the web user privileges.

For the security of the operating system of the web server computer, the following steps are recommended:

a.   When selecting an operating system, a high level of security will be obtained by:

- selecting an operating system that has been evaluated against a security standard for discretionary access control, recognised by the UK government, which includes an independent check of the security-enforcing source code (eg ITSEC E3 F-C2 or Common Criteria EAL4 with the Controlled Access Protection Profile); and

- configuring the operating system to run in its evaluated configuration, for example:

    Microsoft Windows NT 4.0 Service Pack 6a meets this standard using the NTFS file system, as do a number of Unix operating systems. For details see the IT Security Evaluation and Certification Scheme website at *http://www.itsec.gov.uk*. The use of a certified operating system providing mandatory access control (ITSEC F-B1 or Common Criteria Labelled Access Protection Profile) that separates the user file and process space into levels or compartments will provide even greater security in the web server environment if the web server is run as an unprivileged user in its own compartment.

b.   As in the case of the web server, ensure that you monitor briefings from your CERT and commercial sites such as bugtraq *http://www.securityfocus.com* on a regular and frequent basis and install any approved and necessary security patches relevant to the version of the operating system that you are using. The operating system vendor's website should also be able to provide instructions on installing the patches and their coverage of vulnerabilities.

c.   Ensure that the web server runs with the least privilege needed. The web server should not run as an administrator (including the web server administrator) or superuser (if applicable). In a Unix environment, if superuser privileges are needed to bind to the HTTP port, the binding should be run as the superuser using a set user ID process and all subsequent processes should be run as an unprivileged web user.

d.   Do not assign discretionary access control or mandatory access control override privileges to the web user as these can be abused by attackers who manage to gain web user privilege.

e.   To ensure that the web server is an unprivileged user, restrict access for the web server user to files and directories relevant to the web server application (which may be the directory structure under the web server root). Check the permissions on all other files and directories on the web server to ensure that the user cannot gain access to any executables or data files that are not needed.

f.   If the web server directory structure is not virtual (ie the directories exist within the operating system environment), ensure that access controls are set appropriately on all files and directories relevant to the web server application:

•   Ensure that no web directories or files are modifiable or writable by anyone other than the web server administrator.

•   Access to web pages should be read-only for web users, although the web user will need permission to execute scripts or programs used to generate web pages dynamically.

•   Web users should not be able to list the contents of directories, unless there is a clearly identified requirement.

•   No access should be granted to other directories or programs relevant to the web server application unless there is an explicit need.

•   No access should be granted to the web server executable or to the web server configuration files.

g.   In a Unix environment, it may be beneficial to security to run the web server with a redefined root directory using the 'chroot' command. In this case do not have any symbolic links to files outside the directory structure that includes directories under the redefined root directory.

e.   Enable logging on the operating system so that security-relevant activity is logged. This should be analysed on a regular and frequent basis by organisation's IT security officer for events indicative of an attack, for instance attempts to access files without the correct permissions. All error messages, application startup and shutdown, attempted remote application logins, and changes in file permissions should also be logged. This can be a complex and expensive activity so it may be considered more practical to use an Intrusion Detection System and analysis of these logs.

h.   The web server should be run as a dedicated web server. To decrease the risk of misconfiguration remove all unnecessary executables (including compilers and utility programs) and network services from the web server computer.

i.   Remove all unnecessary user accounts from the server and implement
      passwords for the remaining accounts that are hard to guess and accord with
      organisation's security policy for password generation and use.

1.11.6 The security of the local area network of the web server computer

The web server environment extends from the web server computer to its local area
network and to the Internet or Intranet environment.

For the security of the local area network of the web server computer, the following
steps are recommended:

a.   Install a firewall between the web server computer's local area network and the
      Internet to handle all traffic to and from the Internet. For web traffic the firewall
      should deny all unnecessary incoming services and should offer HTTP and
      possibly HTTPS (X.509 digital certificate compliant Secure Socket Layer over
      HTTP) for commercial standard IP encryption of web traffic as uninitiated
      incoming connections. HTTP should be proxied to provide initial validation of
      the web page request. DNS may be allowed outbound on an unprivileged port
      to request DNS lookups and should listen on that port for responses. It is
      recommended that a certified firewall be used. For details of certified firewalls
      see the IT Security Evaluation and Certification Scheme website
      http://www.itsec.gov.uk.

b.   Isolate the web server computer on its own network segment. This may be as a
      standalone network or on a DeMilitarised Zone (DMZ) that has restricted
      access to the internal network and in particular to any database server that is
      used to store sensitive information. If a company does not have a DMZ, the use
      of a non-routable IP protocol between the web server and the internal network
      could be considered.

c.   Enable logging on the firewall so that security-relevant activity is logged. This
      should be analysed on a regular basis by the organisation's IT security officer
      for events indicative of an attack, for instance, attempts to access services with
      known vulnerabilities, successful/denied connections, error messages multiple
      access attempts and access to insecure ports.

1.11.7 The security of the 'backend' applications supporting the web server

Any supporting 'backend' applications (eg databases) should be stored on another
computer. Care needs to be taken that the web user account can only perform a
specified set of actions on the 'backend' applications so that the security of those
applications is not unduly compromised. For example, if a database application is
used as a read-only source to web users, the web user account should have read
only access, while if the database is updated by the web user account via web forms,
the web user should be restricted to database update queries. This could be
performed by a database application that provides access control by query type and
data object (such as database and table) within the database application.

1.11.8 The security of the authoritative domain name server for the web server network

It is possible to change the IP address associated with a website address (URL). When this is done maliciously it is known as domain name server (DNS) poisoning.

To prevent DNS poisoning, the web address registration authority should if possible upgrade the DNS version to the latest version and apply all relevant security patches. DNS server administrators should also if possible configure their servers to check DNS records obtained from an authoritative DNS server by comparing them with those taken from another authoritative server. Authoritative master primary DNS servers should be protected by a firewall. Zone transfers should be restricted from master primary DNS servers to designated slave DNS servers, which preferably should be within the perimeter protected by a firewall. It is recommended that the web server administrator confirm with the administrator of the authoritative DNS server that the protective measures identified above have been taken.

It is also possible for DNS poisoning to be performed manually, in which case the basic security issues are as follows. The web address registration authority for the domain that includes your web server may receive bogus requests to alter the IP address associated with the website URL, by email for example. The organisation's security officer should satisfy himself or herself that the registration authority has adequate security measures in place to ensure the authenticity of any changes to the IP addresses in their domain. Examples of reasonably secure authentication schemes are digitally signed emails, challenge-response password authentication over the telephone and a recognised signature on official company notepaper that can be verified against 'signatures held for comparision'.

1.11.9 Resources

The IT Security Evaluation and Certification Scheme
http://www.itsec.gov.uk

Framework for Information Age Government Security is available at:
http://www.e-envoy.gov.uk/publications/frameworks/security/security.htm
This document sets security objectives for Information Age government. It assumes that the Internet and other channels such as interactive Digital Television and call centres will be important vehicles of delivery of government services. It reviews the security issues for both internal networks and public systems involved in digital communications.

ISO17799 (BS7799)
This is an international standard that presents a code of practice and requirements specifications for establishing, implementing and documenting the security of information management systems. It is government policy to move to ISO17799 compliance. Further information can be found at:
http://www.bsi-global.com/Information+Security+Homepage/index.xalter

To place.

Computer Emergency Response Team
An organisation can join or create, depending on its size, a Computer Emergency Response Team (CERT). A CERT will provide briefings and emergency alerts. More information about them can be found at:
http://www.cert.org

UNIRAS
The Unified Incident Reporting and Alert Scheme (UNIRAS) is the CERT for UK Government and trusted suppliers. You can access information about UNIRAS on the Web at:
http://www.uniras.gov.uk/ or from GSI at: *http://www.uniras.gsi.gov.uk/*

bugtraq
http://www.securityfocus.com

1.12 Procurement

This section provides advice on the main issues that should be taken into account in procuring services for the design and hosting of websites. This advice should be read in conjunction with wider guidance on government procurement, e-Government Interoperability Framework and your Departmental security policy. Refer to section 1.11.

1.12.1 Procurement of web design services

Contracts should distinguish clearly between the roles of the supplier and the purchaser regarding:

- design – structure and look and feel;
- content provision;
- project management;
- maintenance including updating the site;
- warranties;
- site promotion.

Contracts should specify that copyright for those aspects of design that are not open source reside with the Crown (the purchaser) and not the supplying designer/agency. Where it is agreed that the supplier is retaining the intellectual property source code then a full licence must be provided for the use of the object code with the purpose of the licence, the duration of the licence and any geographical limitations. for example, do you need an non-exclusive, indefinite, world-wide, royalty-free licence?
Your supplier may be using contractors and freelancers and therefore must ensure that all third-party rights have also been assigned and moral rights waived.

Purchasing officers should consider very carefully whether to accept implementation of proprietary code by suppliers where there is an open-source alternative. You may not have the right to amend proprietary code when you need to, and you may have to back to the original supplier to have this done.

In competitive tendering exercises, adherence to these guidelines should be a prerequisite of an acceptable bid.

1.12.1.1 Maintenance and redesigns

Contracts for maintenance should specify service levels, including:

- length of contract;
- number, timing and promptness of updates;
- number of templates to be provided by the contractor;
- potential cost of additional design work outside that specified in the contract;
- programme of work for ensuring effective registration with search engines and other forms of publicity.

Site redesigns should not be part of a maintenance contract. Redesigns should be carried out as new work (a separate project). However, the contract should specify the distinction between maintenance and new work, that is, work that exceeds a certain financial, timescale or scope threshold will be considered as new work under a separate project.

1.12.1.2 Other channels

In contracting for website design, departments and agencies should consider the emerging requirement for information and services to be provided via other channels. However, interactive digital TV is a very different medium and there are several platforms. It is, therefore, not practical to simply delivery the same website for access via PC and iDTV. Web managers need a multi-channel strategy and that appropriate solutions will need to be developed for each channel.

1.12.2 Procurement of hosting services

1.12.2.1 Hosting services

Choosing the correct hosting service with the right level of services requires careful planning. Broadly there are three types of hosting:

- Virtual hosting – this is renting space on an offsite web server that is shared by other users. You manage the day-to-day content of your site.
- Dedicated hosting – this takes your complete web function, including the provision of hardware, connectivity, firewalls, reporting services and other management services. You manage the day-to-day content of your site.
- Co-location hosting – this service offers a secure physical location for web servers and equipment owned by you. The hosting service will also offer the connectivity. You manage the day-to-day content of your site and it needs to be clear who is responsible for your firewall and infrastructure management.

1.12.2.2 Connection guarantees

The level of connectivity (availability) assurance should be agreed with the Internet Service Provider (ISP)/hosting service, as should compensation arrangements if they are not met. It is for the business to decide whether 100 per cent connectivity needs to be guaranteed. If it does, it should be borne in mind that 100 per cent connection can only be guaranteed when connectivity is provided by more than one telecommunications operator. Where web servers are guaranteed 100 per cent uptime, purchasers must be aware that this is only likely when the website is hosted on two servers in different locations. Contracts should specify levels of availability and compensation arrangements if they are not met. Purchasers must be aware of compensation claim procedures, and whether connection and uptime guarantees are calculated annually, quarterly or monthly and whether these are on a fixed or rolling basis.

1.12.2.3 Protection

No information appearing on a public website should be classified (protectively marked). The level of protection provided by the ISP/hosting service site should be sufficient to ensure the continued integrity and availability of your website. The service provider should agree to regular and independent penetration testing to confirm the quality of the protection measures. Guidelines for access control and physical security should be sought through your Departmental Security Officer or equivalent responsible officer and checked against the ISP's procedures.

Refer to **section 1.11** Backgrounder on securing websites.

1.12.2.4 Backup

The ISP/hosting service should perform backup procedures to the client's predetermined schedule. They should guarantee these procedures and the maximum time to site restoration in the event of a failure.

1.12.2.5 Database integration

If the purchaser wishes to implement a database-driven site, either immediately or in the future, they must be aware of any technical limitations and cost implications imposed by the supplier.

1.12.2.6 CGI bin and scripting

Refer to section **1.11.2** The security of the web server application.

1.12.2.7 HTML editor extension provision

Where the purchaser wishes to use WYSIWYG software to produce content for the site, they must be aware of any extensions required by the server, and whether the supplier can support this. There are two potential difficulties with the use of WYSIWYG HTML tools:

- They are renowned for producing non-standard HTML or at least 'bulky pages'. In additions many introduce vendor-specific functionality. This may produce unnecessary overheads to achieve the required HTML validation.
- WYSIWYG tools that rely on server-side extensions for some of their functionality have been the cause of security difficulties. In all cases, the same server-side functionality can be achieved in a more secure fashion.

1.12.2.8 Web server statistics

The contract should specify whether the supplier will provide web server statistical reports, as described in **section 1.4**, or provide the raw log files for reports to be generated as part of another service.

1.12.2.9 Bandwidth

It should be the role of the service provider to ensure that adequate bandwidth is available to you. However, it can be useful for purchasers to estimate growth in the requirement for bandwidth over the course of a contract.

For some websites, bursting connection is desirable (typically useful for websites that receive seasonal or occasional growth in traffic). Unfortunately, it becomes very difficult to predict the overall cost of bandwidth over the year. The alternative is to purchase fixed bandwidth. In this situation, high bandwidth (to cope with bursts of traffic) will be expensive, whereas low bandwidth will result in users being unable to reach the site.

Contracts should include pricing for higher and lower bandwidths than those initially purchased and conditions for changes in bandwidth requirements, including periods of notice. It is not, however, uncommon for bandwidth charges to be based on actual usage.

1.12.2.10 Technical support

You should consider if you need 24x7 telephone technical support from your supplier.

1.12.2.11 Pricing

Pricing should be transparent. Purchasers must be aware of potential 'hidden' costs, such as:

- additional bandwidth;
- additional disc space;
- additional software;
- surcharges on quarterly as opposed to annual payments;
- maintenance of any hardware provided as part of the contract.

1.12.3 Disaster recovery

Ensure that you have written into your contract a range of information covering protective actions, such as:

- the frequency of backup of your complete website;
- the safeguarding of the backed-up copies, eg onsite and/or offsite;
- the suppliers responsibilities and action in the event of 'denial of service' by internal or external intervention;
- the suppliers responsibilities and action if the service is compromised, eg, by power loss, flood or structural or similar damage to their location(s).

1.12.4 Hosting offshore

If it is proposed to host your website outside the UK then it is important that the correct procurement procedures have been used, eg, comply with EU/WTO. As with any ISP/hosting service ensure that you are satisfied, in writing, that they are:

- technically sound, and
- administratively sound and
- can successfully host your domain.

The contractual terms and conditions that may be applied by a supplier hosting outside the UK may not complement the terms and conditions expected to be applied to a UK Government website. You are advised to seek specialist procurement and legal advice.

The security clearance of personnel is an important part of a security policy. It may be difficult for a supplier abroad to meet your security standards. You are advised to seek advice from your security officer.

See checklist : Choosing an Internet Service Provider/hosting service

---

IMPORTANT

1. Your briefing document should focus on the business case and objectives for the project – what your website needs to achieve.

2. Make sure that your supplier confirms that your server or the proposed system solution supports all their proposals and that these proposals will be part of the delivered final product. You should also ensure that their proposals work within your declared privacy policy.

3. Brief in your needs for documentation, staff training and content management and updating. Companies do go out of business, consider safeguarding against this by using an escrow agent – an independent third party that will store a copy of the source code, so that developers can use it in the future.

4. When buying design services it is inadequate for the designer to simply present colour visuals or mock-ups of the look and feel. It is important that they guarantee that these can be closely reproduced on screen and that their HTML markup meets the W3C recommendations. When you buy web design you are also buying the source coding that will render the visual onto computer screens and the standard of this is the backbone in achieving HTML validation and meeting the WAI requirements. It is important that the successful bidder is asked to present a specimen to you as HTML markup.

DOMAIN NAME REGISTRATION (Refer to **section 1.9**)

If you are considering registering a domain name, it should be clearly understood who is undertaking this registration. If it is an agency doing so on your behalf then ensure that the name is to be handed over to your department/agency. Clarify what will happen to domain name renewal notices. Failure to clarify these lines could leave you vulnerable to an outside agency and possible failure to renew.

---

e-Government interoperability framework
http://www.govtalk.gov.uk/

Checklist: Choosing an ISP/hosting service

This checklist appended to section 1.12 is intended to assist you when choosing an Internet service provider (ISP) or supplier for your web hosting and Internet facilities. It is important that the supplier provides the answers in writing and that they are written into your service level agreement.

Questions

Done	Description
	Transfer your existing domain names and your content?
	How much is it going to **cost**?
	Are you getting **virtual space** or **dedicated space**?
	What **type of server/operating system** are you getting? (Mac, UNIX, Linux)? Performance, eg, how fast? Do you want MS FrontPage extension support or to use an ASP database?
	What type of **environment** is the server in, eg, secure and resilient data centre – physically secure, dedicated power, cooling, etc? What time standards are maintained by the server, eg, NTP synchronised?
	How much **server space** are you being offered (eg 5 Gb)?
	Support – is it effective and helpful, on 7x24, on local call rates/email? How many work in the support centre at any given time? Do you have a named individual responsible for support? Are you providing a named individual for support contact? Have you a detailed server/OS maintenance procedure?
	What **access speeds** can you expect, is it a 64 kbs pipe?
	Scalability : How quick could the **bandwidth be expanded** to support an identified or anticipated rise in traffic? How quickly can they **expand your server space** and at what cost?
	Provision of a statement of redundancy and a disaster recovery plan, eg if your site goes down how quickly will your hosting service switch connection? Do they have multiple connections and/or site mirroring arrangements? If their physical location is flooded?
	Security – provision of a security statement is essential. This must cover username/password protection and management policy; virus protection; what standards do they apply and how often are they updated. Do they conduct pentesting?
	Incident responses – including, who has the authority to decide action? Who will decide if police/investigation authority is to be called in? Who will answer press enquiries?
	How often will they **back-up your site** and what physical security is provided for the back up?
	How quick can they register and/or renew Domain on your behalf? How quickly can they add a **new** and **additional domain name**?
	Are **server log files/traffic analysis reports** provided weekly/monthly? Are they made available server-side?
	Will they **support scripting** and do you have access to your CGI bin?
	Site update procedures, eg, FTP access – for controlled uploading/downloading? Do you unlimited 24 hour authenticated (SSH/SSL) access?

	Do you want an **FTP server** to provide an anonymous FTP downloading facility? Will the FTP environment have the option of SSL or SSH connection?
	Do they provide any **streaming** facilities? If so please detail type and number.
	Do you have an option for an **SSL/TLS** (Secure Sockets) server connection?
	Do they provide email accounts and **listserver facilities**?
	Can **databases** be integrated into your facility?
	Do they provide facilities to host closed/open **discussion groups**? (refer to **section 1.6**)
	What are your integrity and availability requirements? Does the service supplier have or working to achieve ISO17799 compliance?
	How much is it going to **cost**? Have this broken down into details, including buying, leasing, licences etc
	Privacy Are you using **cookies**? Do the hosting arrangements fully comply with your published **privacy statement**?

2.1 Basic website structure

One of the first steps to be taken when an organisation is planning a website is to decide the underlying structure. It must be flexible and organised in such a way as to make the day-to-day housekeeping and long-term maintenance straightforward and efficient.

Use each checklist to ensure that your web pages comply with these guidelines

2.1.1 Checklist and Summary   *Core Guidance*

Checklist	❑ Use a hierarchical rather than flat structure for directories ❑ Individual files should have easily identifiable names ❑ Once a file-name and its location are established it should not be changed ❑ The web manager should keep an exact and up-to-date local copy of the entire website
Summary	A website should make effective use of a hierarchical directory structure to separate and organise the files contained within it. Some departmental websites will only contain a small number of files and will require only a simple structure. Others will be large and will therefore require a more sophisticated structure, which will need detailed advance planning and to be supported by appropriate management processes. However large or small, each website will still have to adhere to certain conventions to ensure that all information is as accessible as possible for the duration of its lifespan.

2.1.2 How the Web fits into the Internet

The Internet fundamentally comprises a huge number of interconnected local- and wide-area networks (LANs and WANs). A basic level of intercommunication between all computers attached to the Internet is guaranteed because all of them use the TCP/IP (Transmission Control Protocol/Internet Protocol) protocol suite (set of signalling rules). Computers running TCP/IP and that have a connection to the Internet are referred to as 'Internet hosts' (or simply 'hosts'). A host's connection to the Internet may be permanent (for example via an Ethernet LAN connection) or intermittent (typically via a telephone modem dial-up connection).

TCP/IP provides the basic level of communication between hosts necessary for the implementation of 'high-level' protocols (sometimes referred to as 'application protocols'). Examples of high-level protocols are email, file transfer protocol (FTP) and the Hypertext Transport Protocol (HTTP) that is used to request and deliver World Wide Web ('web') pages and other content.

Many Internet high-level protocols use a software engineering technique named client/server programming (or simply client/server). Client software running on one computer issues a request to matching server software (typically running on another computer) for it to perform a service such as conducting a database transaction, or sending a web page. Client software that makes server requests directly at the behest of a human computer user and that displays the results of the requests to the user is known as a 'user agent'. In the case of the Web, user agent software is usually referred to as a 'browser'.

Internet Service Providers (ISPs)
Organisations that provide connections to the Internet network infrastructure for their customers are known as Internet Service Providers (ISPs). ISPs that rent out capacity on servers attached to or close to the Internet's high-speed backbone networks are termed 'hosting providers'. Hosting providers that rent out computer room space with backbone class connections in which customers can set up their own servers are sometimes known as 'co-location' providers.

Internet hosts running HTTP server software are now normally referred to as 'webservers'. The term World Wide Web refers to the huge mesh of information stored on the millions of webservers around the world. Web browsers allow access to this information and enable users to 'navigate' the hyperlinks between different sections of it regardless of whether the destination of a link is on the same server as its source or on another webserver anywhere else in the world.

Specifying Internet resources: Uniform Resource Locator (URL)
Each resource (for example a web page, image file, PDF file or animation file) on the web is identified by its network 'address' called its Uniform Resource Locator (URL). A web client fetches a resource by issuing an HTTP request for its URL to the webserver on which the resource is stored.

An example of a URL is:

http://www.ukonline.gov.uk/explanation/example.htm

URLs comprise three parts:

- The URL system extends beyond the web to encompass Internet resources that are accessed using other high-level protocols. The first part, 'http' in this example, is called the 'scheme'. In this example, the 'http' scheme indicates that this is the URL for a world wide web resource.

- The second part 'www.ukonline.gov.uk' identifies the Internet host on which the resource is stored and from which it is to be fetched. 'www.ukonline.gov.uk' is the Internet DNS name of the webserver. See **section 2.1.2.1** An explanation of the Internet Domain Name Service.

- All the rest is called the 'URL path'. It is used by the webserver to identify the resource being requested. The form of the URL path is specific to the webserver. Most commonly it will identify the location in the webserver's disk filesystem where the resource is stored. Alternatively it may be a 'virtual path' that is translated by the webserver software into the actual location on disk where the resource is stored. Other examples of what the URL path might represent include the details of a database query whose result comprises the resource to be served or an instruction to run another computer program on the server that will generate the resource to be served.

See **section 1.9** Domain name registration

Pages of text intended for display in web browsers are each stored in a separate file on the webserver. (Note that a 'web page' may actually extend to more than a single page when printed out on paper.) Web pages are 'marked-up' with instructions to the browser telling it, for example, how to organise the text for display, where in the page image resources are to be inserted, and which page elements are to act as 'hyperlinks' to other web pages. The markup language used in web pages is named HyperText Markup Language (HTML).

The time required to fetch a web page across the Internet is an important consideration. A web page that seems to display instantaneously over a corporate high-speed Internet link may take a frustratingly long time to load over a low-speed modem dial-up connection. A slow-loading page is likely to interrupt a user's train of thought and if the document does not immediately confirm their reason for having accessed it in the first place, it will be glanced at and ignored. It is most important to consider how documents should be structured for web publication in order to have it display as quickly as possible over the speed of Internet connections typically available to the intended audience.

2.1.2.1 An explanation of the Internet Domain Name Service

Each computer attached to the Internet is assigned an 'IP (Internet Protocol) number' (sometimes referred to as an IP address). An IP number is a string of four numbers separated by full points, for example, 62.43.124.67. (Each number is always in the range 0 to 255.) Computers such as web servers and email relays that are permanently connected to the Internet have a permanent or 'static' IP number. Computers that are intermittently attached to the Internet, for example by way of dial-up telephone connections, are typically assigned an IP number for the duration of their connection from a pool of numbers managed by their ISP.

An IP number can be imagined to serve an analogous purpose to that of a conventional telephone number: in order for a web browser to connect to a web server, the browser must know the IP number of the server it needs to reach.

The Internet Domain Name Service (DNS) is a solution to the problem that IP numbers are not easily memorable. The DNS associates names (DNS names) such as www.e-envoy.gov.uk, www.bbc.co.uk and the like, with corresponding IP numbers. Following the analogy with the telephone system, the DNS may be thought of as providing a roughly equivalent service to directory enquiries. When given a DNS name, the Domain Name Service will reply with the corresponding IP number.

The Internet DNS is a complex system. It is replicated, meaning there are many computers on the Internet that provide a domain name service (nameservers or DNS servers). The DNS is also distributed; meaning that not every nameserver knows the IP number corresponding to every DNS name that has been issued. However, every nameserver does know to which other nameservers it should refer on lookup requests that it cannot directly answer itself.

In order for computers attached to the Internet to be able to consult the DNS, they must first be instructed how to contact the DNS. (The telephone system analogy is that you must first know directory enquiries' telephone number before you can get though to have them look up other peoples' numbers for you.) The IP number of one or more (topologically) local nameservers usually has to be supplied as a part of the initial set-up details for a computer that is to be connected to the Internet.

When a web address (URL) is typed into a web browser, the browser has first to contact and consult its local DNS server(s) to convert the DNS name portion of the URL into an IP number to which it can subsequently send the web page request. Issuing a request for a web page is therefore normally a two-stage process on the part of the browser: determining the IP number corresponding to the DNS name component of the URL, followed by sending the URL request to the web server's IP number. Both stages have to work properly in order for web pages and other content to be fetched across the Internet. The progress of the different stages is usually reported in the status bar at the bottom left of Web browser windows. Whenever a web page fails to load, checking the progress messages in the status bar will usually reveal whether the problem is with the nameservice, or whether it lies elsewhere.

2.1.3 Basic options for website structure

The design of a website covers many different areas. Decisions need to be made on how it is going to look; how a user should navigate through the information contained within it and what content should (and should not) be published on it.

As important as all of these areas are, the underlying organisation of the HTML files and other resources that comprise the website should be considered early in the project. This is neither a difficult concept nor a specifically technical issue so there is no real requirement for decision-makers to have detailed understanding of the way webservers or the Internet work.

A website has to be stored within the directory and file structuring system (the 'filesystem') provided by the webserver computer. There are two basic options. One is to construct the website in a flat (linear) fashion. The other is to use the more structured hierarchical approach. Whichever method is employed, careful consideration needs to be given to file names and their relationships to each other.

Whichever arrangement is chosen at the beginning will, in all probability, be the one you will have to manage during the entire lifespan of the project. It is difficult to change at a later date.

2.1.3.1 Flat (linear) construction

This method of organising files requires little initial planning. A root directory is named (for example 'root') and every file is placed within this one directory. All files – HTML, PDF, text, GIF and JPEG – sit side-by- side, at the same level in the filesystem hierarchy.

This is the simplest arrangement, although it is likely to turn out to be the least effective way of organising information in the long run if the website grows beyond the smallest of sizes.

In a flat construction scheme, linking between files is a simple matter of specifying the name of the target file. The Web manager always knows where to find a file, as they are all contained in the same directory.

The important issue when using this form of file management is to ensure that all file names are descriptive and meaningful. When a website contains only 50 documents and 30 graphic files, finding the correct file for editing is relatively easy, but once the website has grown and contains hundreds of files the process becomes very much more difficult.

2.1.3.2 Hierarchical construction

This is by far the preferred option for the majority of websites. It is flexible, expandable and easier to manage on a day-to-day basis.

Hierarchical organisation uses a number of sub-directories stored at the next level down from the website's root directory. Connected files, grouped either by their file type (for example GIF, PDF) or by their relevance to each other (eg business plan 2001), are stored together in their own directory.

index.htm
- contact.htm
- help.htm
- links.htm
- organisation.htm
- sitemap.htm
- whatsnew.htm
- images
- frames
- library
  - html
  - pdf
  - rtf
  - txt
- css

On the left is an example of a simple architecture for a website. The root file (index.htm) is the homepage that is automatically served when the user requests a web URL containing only the website's DNS name.

The files listed underneath the homepage's title are also stored in the root directory but are accessed by links from other pages.

In the example, other directories have been set up to contain related files. Within the library directory, there are a number of sub-directories for HTML, PDF, RTF and plain-text documents.

All images for the website have been grouped together. Within this directory could be many sub-directories for specific areas within the website.

It is a good idea to establish a section of the directory structure as a central images repository to ensure that images used through the website are only saved once. Such images could include the organisation's logo graphic, navigational button images, and so on.

These guidelines recommend that government websites should use Cascading Style Sheets (CSS) to control aspects of the graphical and typographical design specifications for the website. Storing CSS files in their own directory ensures that access to them can be managed and that they cannot be mistakenly amended or deleted.

2.1.4 Do not change names when moving files

Whenever a website is redesigned there is invariably a wish to reorganise and reconstruct the existing files into a structure that better reflects the department.

File names and their placement within the website architecture, should, where at all possible, not be changed, for a number of reasons:

External links
Over time, an increasing number of external websites will link to certain pages controlled by a department. Web managers will rarely be aware of how many links out on the web depend on pages under their control because external organisations may well not have asked for permission to establish a link in. If a page is peremptorily relocated it will break links in from other websites.

Search facilities
Search facilities use unattended 'robot' applications to visit websites in order to compile their catalogue entries for them. These automated visits to a department's website are likely to be sporadic, as there are many websites to scan. Any change that is made between visits will not be reflected in their search service, which can result in potential visitors getting 'Error 404', document not found' messages on their first visit to a department's web presence.

Personal bookmarks
Over time users will have bookmarked pages for personal use. Suddenly finding that a useful resource has disappeared can have a negative effect on the perception of your department's web presence.

Any file or collection of files that has to be relocated must have redirects put in place to ensure that previous visitors who have bookmarked the old location will still be able to access the files in their new location. Departments should not use metadata redirects for this purpose: as discussed in **section 4.1.5**, some web browsers do not support this feature and this will result in users being unable to access the required information.

Multiple server redirects can be very difficult to maintain over a long period of time. If server redirects are employed, a short message should be available to visitors indicated that the information now has a new address and that they should replace any existing bookmark with the new URL.

See **Annex K** Redirect page.

2.2 What content should be on your website?

Effective communication on the web is the product of good content and quality of presentation. Departments and agencies should develop websites that are rich in authoritative and up-to-date content that is well written, caters to the needs of a wide range of audiences and is easily accessible. Publication on the Internet should generally be simultaneous with publication in other media.

2.2.1 Introduction

This section states minimum requirements for the content of websites. It aims to establish what users should expect in homepages, and it sets out for the benefit of web teams a list of the minimum requirements with which they should comply. Together with material in section 2.4 it contributes to the establishment of an authoritative look and feel for government websites. Within these general parameters, it is for departments to determine how best to organise content with their own audiences in mind.

Departments and agencies should be aware of who the core and non-core audiences are for their websites. It is very likely that the audiences for different parts of the website, or for different websites within a single department's estate, will vary considerably. It is very desirable that, in planning websites, departments should carry out market research or other consultation with core and non-core audiences and that this should be repeated subsequently. It is especially desirable that designers and website managers should view sites alongside members of their core audience and be responsive to their comments.

Departments should apply the same principles of plain language and inclusive language to their websites as they are expected to do to printed documents.

2.2.2 Minimum website requirements

Departments should, where appropriate, publish the following information and documents online:

- list of Ministers and their responsibilities
- CEO/management board responsibilities
- organisation's aims and objectives
- all public sector organisations should provide in an easily accessible form (although not necessarily on each of their websites), their organisation's structure
- postal address(es),fax and telephone numbers, email address(es) – refer to **section 2.2.4**
- responsibilities, aims and objectives of units and divisions
- membership and terms of reference of advisory groups
- names and telephone numbers or email addresses of contacts for further information on specific policies or services (note that these need not be named individuals)
- complaints procedures
- public service agreements
- complaints procedures

- Command Papers – refer to **section 2.3.3**
- for Bills before Parliament, a link to
  www.publications.parliament.uk/pa/bills.htm
- legislation for which the department has the lead, or a link to the Official
  legislation website – refer to **section 2.3.7**
- press notices or a link to the relevant section of the Central Office of
  Information website
- consultation documents – refer to **section 2.3.4**
- research reports and statistical information
- forms published by the department and guidance for their completion
- recruitment policies, procedures and information – refer to **section 2.3.2**
- frequently asked questions (FAQs)
- Inforoute – refer to **section 2.3.5**

2.2.3 Minimum homepage requirements

The following is a checklist of items that must be included on your web homepage:

- the organisation's full name
- the organisation's logo
- email contact address.

It should also, where appropriate, contain links to the following:

- UK online at the URL ***http://www.ukonline.gov.uk*** – refer to **section 2.3.8**
- contact addresses – refer to **section 2.2.4**
- complaints procedure
- organisation's statement of purpose
- organisation's structure, including agencies, directorates etc
- 'What's New' section
- terms and conditions (to include privacy statement, copyright statement,
  disclaimers and hyperlinking policy) – refer to **section 1.10**
- feedback page
- FAQs (frequently asked questions)
- help facility
- search facility
- language anchor pages – refer to **section 2.7**
- ***http://www.info4local.gov.uk*** – refer to **section 2.3.6**

2.2.4 Contact addresses

A full postal address must be provided as well as an email address.

Generic or team email addresses should be used, depending on the strategy of your
organisation, eg, webguidelines@e-envoy.gsi.gov.uk. This allows for portability of
email addresses during personnel changes.

Personal email addresses must not be used; for example, richard@hotmail.com
should not be used instead of richard@e-envoy.gov.uk.

When email addresses are to be included within an HTML page they should be displayed using the universally understood email format.

A team or individual name alone is not sufficient because:

- a new web user may not realise that they can establish contact if just the name is displayed, and
- some users may have changed the default settings of their web browser. They may have underlining of links turned off and some may have all links displayed in the same colour as standard text.

GENERIC EMAIL ADDRESSES

Examples of the good use of generic or team email addresses are the 'enquiry email addresses' employed on the following sites:

http://www.odpm.gov.uk/about/email.htm and

http://www.dft.gov.uk/about/email.htm

2.2.5 Department location

Although not essential for all, it is always a good idea to include maps and direction instructions to assist people visiting your department.

The map should be presented either as a web graphic such as, a JPG or GIF, or a downloadable PDF file. Whichever format is chosen there should also be a text version covering directions by rail, road, bus and underground.

2.2.6 Version control of website publications

Please refer to **section 3.2.8**.

2.3 Cross-government requirements

There are a number of requirements for sites to comply with central guidance on policy and administrative issues. Some of these apply to all sites, others to sites within specific areas of business. In each case, lead responsibility for the relevant policy area lies with a particular department or agency. The purpose of these guidelines is to ensure that departments are aware of the list of requirements and of the links to sites including UK online.

2.3.1 Parliamentary answers referring to the Internet

Departments should comply with the following guidance when referring Members of Parliament to material on the Internet:

- Electronic publishing should not be used as the sole form of reference for documents likely to be in heavy demand from Members. In such cases a hard copy must also be provided. If a document proves to be unexpectedly popular the Library of the House must be entitled to request three printed copies from the department in line with the existing arrangements for deposited papers, and the department should supply these copies within 24 hours.
- Members, or the Library on their behalf, should not be expected to download and print documents of more than 20 pages. Documents which are longer than this should be supplied to the Library in hard copy.
- Internet references should take the Member or the Library staff as precisely as possible to the specific information that has been requested. They should not just reference departmental homepages.
- References to the Internet should only be given if the department is confident that the document is going to remain on the Internet at the same URL. (The Library keeps permanently all the papers that are 'deposited' but there have been examples of consultation documents published only on the Internet and then removed at the end of the consultation period.)

2.3.2 Recruitment

The *Modernising Government White Paper* commits the Government to making it easier for people who want to join the civil service to find out about opportunities and to apply for them.

Under the Modernising Government Action Plan, the Cabinet Office is responsible for providing a recruitment gateway to the civil service using websites. In the short term, notified vacancies will be posted on the central civil service careers site. However, departments should include recruitment pages on their own websites, to which the central site can link. Vacancy information can then be updated more quickly. These pages can then be linked where appropriate to individual recruitment units around the country.

The Civil Service Recruitment Gateway is at *http://www.civilservice.gov.uk/jobs/*

A message that a department is not recruiting is almost as important to applicants as vacancy information, and can reduce the number of general enquiries about opportunities.

2.3.3 Publication of Command Papers on the Internet

It is now common practice that, apart from the most routine documents, the full text of all Command Papers is published on the Internet. The Stationery Office Limited (TSO) will, unless otherwise advised, undertake the task of putting Command Papers on the Internet simultaneously with the preparation and publication of the print version. TSO will make a charge for the conversion and mounting on the Internet, but this can be minimised with early liaison and consultation.

TSO also archives Command Papers and will include the URL for all Command Papers in the official bibliographic record (UKOP). Details of the URL should also be included in the printed version within the text, if appropriate, or on the reverse of the title page.

To ensure effective archiving of Command Papers, TSO builds in pointers or links from the TSO site to departmental sites. In turn, departments are encouraged to put pointers from their site to the TSO site. This allows feedback and facilitates ordering of the print version direct from TSO.

Where TSO undertakes the task of publication on the Internet they have adopted the following convention for naming and locating Command Papers on the Official Documents website:

www.official-documents.co.uk/document/cmxx/nnnn/nnnn.htm

where xx is the first two digits of the Command Paper and nnnn is the full Command Paper number. The URL can then be added automatically to UKOP, and departments can quote the URL in the printed version (and elsewhere).

An example of a URL is as follows:

Cm 4764 – Intelligence and Security Committee: The Mitrokhin Inquiry Report http://www.official-documents.co.uk/document/cm47/4764/4764.htm

Although TSO can undertake the work required to enable a Command Paper to be published on the Internet, departments retain the right themselves or through a third party to license a Paper for free distribution via the Internet. Departments should, however, remember that the TSO-contracted printer might be the only source of the final electronic version of the Command Paper. Appropriate arrangements will need to be made with TSO to ensure that this is available in good time for the necessary work to be undertaken to enable simultaneous Internet publication.

When departments do opt to use alternative means for publication on the Internet and the print version of the Paper is published by TSO they should:

- include a statement on the document homepage that TSO is the publisher of the printed version and give the Command Paper number, ISBN, price and, to facilitate ordering of the print version, a link to TSO's ordering address;
- notify TSO of the URL the department assigns before the Paper goes on the web;

- notify TSO of any change in the URL over time;
- adhere to the same standards described above for keeping links live and monitoring them;
- provide TSO with corrections to changed hyperlinks; and
- if the Paper is moved, ensure redirection of users to the new location.

In order to assist searching, departments should consider placing Command Papers in directories named after an individual Command Paper's number. An example of such a URL may be:

> Cm 4764 – Intelligence and Security Committee: The Mitrokhin Inquiry Report
> http://www.department.gov.uk/publications/cm4764/...htm

When publication on the Internet is intended, care needs to be taken that the text cannot be accessed before the Paper has been laid before Parliament and published in its printed format. Where TSO is undertaking publication on the Internet they will, unless otherwise advised by the department, assume that access to the Internet version is to be allowed at the same time the Paper is formally published.

It should be noted that all Command Papers published as a response to a Select Committee Report should be published on the Internet and the URL advised to the Clerk of the relevant committee. This enables the committees' web page to link to responses and so tell the whole story of a committees' inquiries.

2.3.4 Consultation papers

> **Code of practice on written consultation**
> *http://www.cabinet-office.gov.uk/servicefirst/2000/consult/code/ConsultationCode.htm*

> **Register of consultations** (within CitizenSpace)
> *http://www.ukonline.gov.uk*

All UK government departments and agencies who conduct any public consultation should have arrangements in place to ensure that their own consultation web page(s) and the central Register of Consultations are absolutely up to date.

NDPBs (non-departmental public bodies) are encouraged to follow the Consultation Code and contribute to the Register. The devolved administrations are free to adopt the Code.

2.3.5 Inforoute

Inforoute is a new gateway to information held by UK government departments and it provides direct access to the government's **Information Asset Register** (IAR). An IAR is a database of an organisation's information assets. The government's IAR is an amalgamation of the IARs being created by each government department and agency.

Individual departments have primary responsibility for putting in place their own IARs, which they will maintain on their own websites. Her Majesty's Stationery Office (HMSO) has overall responsibility for IAR formats and standards, and for maintaining the Inforoute website. Inforoute will regularly check departmental IARs and index all of the entries so that users can search all of the records for items which cover the particular topic in which they have an interest.

In order that the Inforoute website can index all entries included in the government's IAR it is essential that the individual IAR records can be identified. This can be done by enabling 'directory listing' wherever the records are held on your web server.

Where security or other considerations prevent 'directory listing' being enabled then a separate 'index file' needs to be created, otherwise the IAR search engine will not know what records need to be indexed. In this case an HTML file needs to be created. This file should be named as <index.htm>. It will need to contain a hyperlink to each file that needs to be indexed. When new files are added or other files removed from the IAR the index file will need to be amended accordingly.

Enquiries about linking to Inforoute should be addressed to HMSO email : inforoute@hmso.gov.uk.

Inforoute
http://www.inforoute.hmso.gov.uk/

Inforoute enquiries should be addressed to
Inforoute@hmso.gov.uk

HMSO
http://www.hmso.gov.uk/

2.3.6   Gateway for local authorities – info4local.gov

http://www.info4local.gov.uk provides a one-stop gateway for local authorities to get quick and easy access to local government-related information on the websites of departments and agencies. The site is run by a group of five departments, with the Department of Transport Local Government and the Regions (DTLR) in the lead. Its main features include:

- a 'What's New' section with summaries of the latest publications and guidance from departments, with a direct link to them on departments' own websites;
- an at-a-glance guide under subject headings such as best value, education, housing, and planning and built environment to what information is available across key departments;
- easy access to news releases from departments and agencies; and
- an email alert service to let people know at their desktops about new information on the site.

If you do publish information for local authorities you should contribute to this joined-up e-project. Email Anne.Scott@odpm.gsi.gov.uk for further information.

Information for local government from central government
http://www.info4local.gov.uk

2.3.7 Official legislation websites

UK legislation (Acts of the UK Parliament and Statutory Instruments) –
http://www.legislation.hmso.gov.uk
Scottish legislation – *http://www.legislation.oqps.gov.uk*
Northern Ireland legislation – *http://www.northernireland-legislation.hmso.gov.uk*
National Assembly for Wales legislation –
http://www.wales-legislation.hmso.gov.uk

2.3.8 UK online – toolbar integration on government websites

UK online is a partnership between government, industry, the voluntary sector, trades unions and consumer groups to make the UK one of the world's leading knowledge economies and ensure universal access to the Internet.

2.3.8.1 Overview

It is a requirement that all government departments should support the remote integration of a toolbar into their websites so that the current and appropriate information from central government can be easily accessed by the users of Government websites.

The toolbar
- Brands your site as being part of government
- Maintains the cross-government UK online brand consistently across government
- Helps join up government sites by linking other important sites or new online publications.

It is designed to fit in with most browser toolbars and to keep design of your own home page distinct and whole. The toolbar should only be integrated with your homepage and with the main page of your major subdomains.

This is achieved by means of a *frameset* that calls both the toolbar and the current homepage into the same browser window. The toolbar should only be applied to the home page of your site and not to the entire site.

Use of this toolbar by non-UK and non-public sector websites is not permitted without the specific written permission of the Editor of www.ukonline.gov.uk.

2.3.8.2 Instructions: *if your site does not currently use frames*

If your site already uses frames refer to **section 2.3.8.3.**

The following code defines the frameset that splits the window into toolbar and content areas. The frameset page becomes the replacement default page for your web site. So if your current homepage is <index.htm>, we would recommend that the existing page is renamed <index2.htm> and a new file created based on the following code to and saved as <index.htm>.

```
<html>
<head>
```

```
<title>The    title    of    your    government    department    or
initiative</title>
</head>

<frameset    rows="40,*"    framespacing="0"    framemargin="0"
frameborder="0" border="no" noresize>

<frame name="ukonline_toolbar"
title="This  frame  provides  links  to  the  UK  online  Citizen
Portal, and to the latest news stories in Government"
src="http://toolbar.e-envoy.gov.uk/standard-toolbar.htm"
marginwidth="0"           marginheight="0"           scrolling="no"
frameborder="0" noresize>

<frame name="website_content"
title="This  frame  contains  the  home  page  of  the  department  you
are visiting"
src="index2.htm"
marginwidth="0" marginheight="0" frameborder="0" noresize>

</frameset>

<!-- no frames alternative -->
<!-- please  add  your  department  name  to  the  intro  text  and
change links where appropriate - ->

<noframes>
<body>
```

Insert text here that provides a textual description of your site, eg, `Welcome to`
`the Department of XYZ website.`

```
<a href="index2.htm">Enter the site</a><br>
```

`This link will take you to the UK online Citizen Portal,`
`<a href="http://www.ukonline.gov.uk">www.ukonline.gov.uk </a>.`

```
</body>
</noframes>
</html>
```

Changes to your existing homepage
This toolbar need only be displayed on the homepage of your site. So when this is
applied you will have to make some small changes to the code of the page.

All links in the homepage need to be changed as follows. A link like:

`<a href = "next_page.htm">Link</a> to the next page`

needs to be re-written as:

`<a href = "next_page.htm" target="_top">Link</a> to the next`
`page`

If you do not do this the toolbar will appear on the new page too.

Any links you have in your site to the home page should remain unchanged so that when they are clicked on, the new home page, including the toolbar, is displayed.

2.3.8.3 Instructions: *if your homepage already uses frames*

If your site already uses frames on the homepage or across the site, a more complicated solution is needed. As an example, if your existing homepage frameset is something like:

```
<frameset cols = "200, *">
<frame name="sidebar" src="sidenav.htm">
<frame name="content" src="homepage.htm">
</frameset>
```

then the code needs to be modified so that your existing frameset is nested within the new one:

```
<frameset rows="40,*" framespacing="0" framemargin="0"
frameborder="0" border="no" noresize>

<frame name="ukonline_toolbar"
title="This frame provides links to the UK online Citizen
Portal, and to the latest news stories in Government"
src="http://toolbar.e-envoy.gov.uk/standard-toolbar.htm"
marginwidth="0" marginheight="0" scrolling="no"
frameborder="0" noresize>

<frameset cols = "200, *">
<frame name="sidebar" src="sidenav.htm">
<frame name="content" src="homepage.htm">
</frameset>

</frameset>
```

Be aware that the UK online toolbar will remain visible for the duration of the user's visit to the site unless the Web manager undertakes extensive reworking of the site. Decisions on whether or not this is an issue will lie with the Web manager.

2.3.8.4 Support

Should you have any questions regarding to this document, please send them to Paul Cronk at the Office of the e-Envoy -- ***paul.cronk@e-envoy.gsi.gov.uk*** telephone 020 7276 3024.

UK online
http://www.ukonline.gov.uk

2.4 Building in universal accessibility

This section ensures that a UK government website is developed to serve the largest possible audience using the broadest range of systems (hardware and software platforms) and that the needs of users with disabilities are considered.

We cannot count on our users having standard technology, therefore, to ensure access to our information on the web the onus is on our web managers to deliver the message in a way that allows everyone to benefit.

It is very important that your organisation's website is not only user-centered and usable at the outset but that it maintains that level of accessibility and usability throughout its existence.

Use each checklist to ensure that your web pages comply with these guidelines

2.4.1 Checklist and summary	*Core guidance*

Checklist	❏ Keep pages simple
	❏ Be consistent throughout the website
	❏ Use HTML as the default information format
	❏ Browser-specific HTML or scripting methods should not be used in the website
	❏ Keep the use of images to a minimum – consider the use of thumbnails
	❏ Do not rely on colour to convey information
	❏ Text colour must always contrast with background
	❏ Only use clear, commonly used fonts
	❏ Use HTML to structure the document, not style it
	❏ Use Cascading Style Sheets to format and style basic elements of a website
	❏ Any font sizes defined in the Cascading Style Sheet must be customisable by the end user – do not hard code
	❏ Any colour used must be customisable by the end user
	❏ HTML page should validate against specified version of HTML
	❏ All important images must have an 'alt' attribute and description
	❏ 'alt' descriptions should be meaningful
	❏ A consistent text navigation bar should be used along with a 'skip navigation link'
	❏ Other forms of navigation should be available for users who cannot use pointing devices
	❏ If used, imagemaps should always be in client-side format
	❏ A text alternative must be offered if a client-side imagemap is used
	❏ An alternative text version of any information offered in audio or video format must be supplied
	❏ Any information offered in a format that requires a plug-in must also be offered in HTML
	❏ All web pages must comply to the World Wide Web Consortium's Web Accessibility Initiative (WAI) 'A' standard
	❏ The appropriate WAI logos can be displayed on the organisation's homepage to illustrate compliance with W3C recommendations

Summary

A myth surrounding website development is that building accessible and inclusive pages is expensive, they have to be dull and boring, and they have to be written for the lowest common denominator – this is not the case! It is also not the case that users must view a web page the way the designer intended. With the range of browsers, screen sizes, colour depths and other user preferences it is often not possible to have a web page look the same to all users.

What is important is that users should be able to view a web page the way they wish to view it with the equipment that they have available and avoid those negative experiences that result in losing repeat visits.

Integrating accessibility into your web development process efficiently creates websites that work effectively for more people in more situations – and that means more users. The challenge to your web developers has to be in creating web pages that are both visually appealing and fully accessible to a wide range of users.

We are moving into a world in which managing different versions of your content will become the norm. You will provide different content for different media such as mobile devices. You are likely to design and write content in order to communicate with different audiences as well. The advent of broadband access will mean that more multimedia content will also be appropriate.

Equally, to make a website inclusive, there needs to be alternatives to support people and systems with differing abilities. This is not just an issue for the disabled. Some corporate systems are protected by firewalls that strip out active content. Accessibility is also an issue when communicating with a business audience.

- if frames are used, a valid **noframes** element must be used and each frame within the frameset must have the **title** attribute set – see **section 6.4**.
- **scripts** and **applets** should be supported by a **noscript** element for those users who access via browsers with scripting disabled or via firewalls with scripting blocked out – see **section 4.6**.
- text equivalents, or transcripts must support **non-text elements** –multimedia or graphically presented information.
- Alternative **text-only** pages **should rarely be necessary and are not best practice**. If text-only pages are used it is essential that their content:

  - is as complete and comprehensive as graphic content
  - is updated simultaneously with graphic content

- **colour** alone should not be used to convey information.
- **navigation** – for the visual user overt controls are used to move to and interact with the menu, the toolbar, scroll bars, links etc and this is generally done using the mouse pointer. For obvious reasons, people who are visually or physically impaired may require **keyboard equivalents** for these mouse actions. The latest browsers and HTML standards are adding these keyboard equivalents – see **section 2.4.4**.

Context. The sighted web user gets a good sense of the content and scope of a web document at a glance. The layout and navigation should enable users to quickly find a specific part of the document.

When using screen readers and screen magnifiers only a small part of the screen can be presented at one time. So website users who are dependent upon this technology may have three immediate difficulties:

- obtaining an overview of your web page which includes getting a sense of the structure of the document
- moving to a specific section of the document, and
- obtaining access to graphically presented information.

For example, screen readers only communicate what the browser or operating system renders. This information is revealed by listening to a synthesised voice or Braille display that presents only text and which 'speaks' one piece of information at a time in a serial fashion.

Moving from accessibility to usability. Accessibility means that a broad range of software and audiences can actually receive your content. It is now mandatory that government websites comply with the minimum level of the World Wide Web Consortiums Web Accessibility Initiative.

However, compliance with WAI recommendations alone does not necessarily mean that a website will meet the needs of different users. This is the difference between accessibility and usability. With careful consideration the site can be written and designed so that it works well when browsed through screen readers or screen magnifiers. For example:

- label all graphics with the alt attribute (commonly known as 'alt tag'), remembering that the screen reader software will announce the 'link to' or 'image' depending upon the source coding used;
- limit the number of overall navigation links to 10 on any single string;
- provide 'skip navigation links' link at the top of each page containing the main menu buttons;
- ensure that users of screen magnifiers do not have to scroll sideways to view important content or navigation
- remember that many people cannot use a mouse but must tab through content to get to the options or information they need on a page.

Text only versions. Ideally a website should be both accessible and useable. Some websites rely on a non-graphic, text-only version to make their sites accessible.
But a text-only version may not be useable if, for example, it contains too many links or is confusing when presented through assistive technology. It is essential to ensure that content is complete and up-to-date.

Rather than invest in a text-only version that is not useable, it may be better to clarify the navigation and text to improve usability as well. We would prefer you made the graphic version of your website more usable, taking steps such as reducing numbers of links and clearly describing options and navigation.

Where you are using multimedia or plug-ins, such as Macromedia's Flash, we would prefer that the user accesses *(as the default)* a usable website with an option to choose to use a multimedia alternative rather than being delivered the multimedia version as the default with an option to choose the alternative.

2.4.2 Audiences with special needs

There are many people who find it difficult to interact with computer technologies. One of the ways in which government websites differ from commercial sites is the requirement that the needs of these audiences are part of our website strategies.

2.4.2.1 Key audiences to remember

The inexperienced or technophobic
Electronic devices such as video recorders and microwave ovens cause confusion for some people. Others have little experience of computers. For both audiences, the inherent complexities of a home computer can make retrieving information from the web very difficult.

The socially excluded
A proportion of the public do not have the means to purchase a home computer. Their job may not bring them into contact with IT and a digital TV may be out of the question. A PC with limited capabilities in the local library may be the only resource available to this sector of the population.

Older users
Advancing years can bring one or a combination of the disabilities listed in **section 2.4.2.2** to a user.

Non-English users
Many people in the UK do not use English as their first language. Extra care should be taken to ensure that the English used on a web page is clear and simple to understand.

2.4.2.2 Physical impairments

Recent disability figures for the UK suggest that there are:
- over 8.54 million people registered with one form of disability or another;
- of these over 2 million have a visual impairment;
- eight million people suffer from some form of hearing loss;
- one million people have a form of learning difficulty;
- over seven million people have literacy problems.

It is worthwhile remembering that impairments take a variety of forms and can exist together in combination.

Specific considerations for the common disabilities are as follows;

Visual impairment

The web is superficially seen as a visual medium, but as the majority of information in a website is in text format there are many ways in which this data can be manipulated. Screen reader software reads a web page one line at a time, horizontally across the screen. The text is spoken using a speech synthesiser or alternatively sent to a retractable Braille display or to a fixed single line display. Screen magnification software is used to magnify portions of a screen using a zoom feature. Many people who have visual impairment still have a degree of usable vision. Simply using clear fonts and distinguishable colours may be all that is needed.

Hearing impairment

Many people with auditory disabilities have little difficulty in using websites unless streaming audio and video files are used. This can be overcome simply with the use of text captioning. This also assists those non-native speakers who may find written language easier than spoken.

Motor impairment

Many diseases and physical conditions can cause a person to have a loss or limitation of function in muscle control or movement, which can mean difficulty in using a conventional keyboard or a mouse. Software such as, Sticky Keys can make difficult keystrokes more accessible and WAI offers the ability to assign hotkeys to navigation elements. The use of speech recognition systems allows the user to speak commands to their computer. Other alternative input devices include pointer devices and eye scanning systems controlled by mouth or head movements.

Cognitive disability

Reading difficulties such as dyslexia and limited mental agility can all limit the understanding of information. Users may have problems with memory recall or text recognition; they may also have problems entering information correctly, such as querying a search facility.

Selective disturbance

Flickering and flashing text or images can trigger epileptic seizures in some individuals and do not encourage usability among the visually impaired.

IMPORTANT

A very simple if not comprehensive way of seeing your existing website in a different light is to turn off the graphics capabilities of your web browser. This will give an indication of your site's usefulness without graphics.

2.4.3 Compliance with W3C WAI recommendations

2.4.3.1 W3C Web Accessibility Initiative (WAI)

Many people that use the web have disabilities of one form or another, which could be sensory or motor disabilities. It is very important to ensure that any web page produced by public sector bodies is as available to these users as to any other. Government websites are now expected to comply with the W3C WAI recommendations.

The W3C states that there are basically **ten quick tips** that should be used to produce web pages that can be seen as truly accessible. They are listed as:

Images and animations	Use the 'alt' attribute to describe the function of each visual
Imagemaps	Use client-side imagemaps and text for hotspots
Multimedia	Provide captioning and transcripts of audio and descriptions of video
Hypertext links	Use text that makes sense when read out of context. For example, avoid use of 'click here'
Page organisation	Use headings, lists and consistent structure. Use CSS for layout and style where possible
Graphs and charts	Summarise or use the 'longdesc' attribute
Scripts, applets, and plug-ins	Provide alternative content in case active features are inaccessible or unsupported
Frames	Use <noframes> and meaningful titles
Tables	Make line-by-line reading sensible. Summarise
Check your work, validate	Use tools, checklist and guidelines at *http://www.w3.org/WAI/Resources*

2.4.3.2 The 14 guidelines of the Web Content Accessibility Guidelines 1.0

To ensure that your organisation's website is universally accessible, the following should be considered and implemented.

WCAG 1.0 guideline	Remarks
Provide equivalent alternatives to auditory and visual content	Provide content that, when presented to the your user, conveys essentially the same function or purpose as auditory or visual content, eg, text summaries or transcripts
Do not rely on colour alone	Ensure that your text and graphics are understandable when viewed without colour
Use mark up and style sheets and do so properly	Mark up documents with the proper structural elements; control your presentation with style sheets rather than with HTML presentation elements and attributes
Clarify natural language usage	Use mark up that facilitates pronunciation or interpretation of abbreviated or foreign text, this assists speech synthesisers and Braille devices, it also allows search engines to find keywords in a natural language
Create tables that transform gracefully	Ensure that your tables have necessary mark up to be transformed by accessible browsers and other software

Ensure that pages featuring new technologies transform gracefully	Ensure that pages are accessible even when newer technologies are not supported or are turned off, eg, when style sheets are not supported, when appropriate provide the <noframes> and <noscript> options
Ensure user control of time-sensitive content changes	Ensure that moving, blinking, scrolling, or auto-updating objects or pages may be paused or stopped
Ensure direct accessibility of embedded user interfaces	Ensure that the user interface follows the principles of accessible design: device-independent access to functionality, keyboard operability, eg, do not rely on scripts, applets and plug-ins for essential functions
Design for device-independence	Use features that enable the activation of your page elements via a variety of input devices, eg, if an imagemap is used provide a text alternative
Use interim solutions	Use interim accessibility solutions so that assistive technologies and older browsers will operate correctly

Use W3C technologies and guidelines	Use W3C technologies (according to specification) and follow accessibility guidelines. Where this is not possible or doing so results in material that does not transform gracefully, provide an alternative version of the content that is accessible
Provide context and orientation information	Provide context and orientation information to help your users understand complex pages or elements, eg, complex relationships between parts of a page can be difficult for users with cognitive disabilities and for those with visual impairment
Provide clear navigation mechanisms	Provide clear and consistent navigation mechanisms – orientation information, navigation bars, a site map, etc in order to increase the likelihood that a user will find what they are looking for on your site
Ensure that documents are clear and simple	Ensure that documents are clear and simple so they may be more easily understood, eg, consistent shape and feel, use of plain language, recognisable graphics

2.4.3.3 Implementation of the W3C WAI 'A' rating

A website can be rated at one of three Web Content Accessibility Guidelines conformance levels – A (Priority 1 items), AA (Priority 1 and 2 items) and AAA (Priority 1, 2 and 3 items).

All UK government websites are expected to achieve, as a minimum, and adhere to the single 'A' (Priority 1 items) level. When this has been completed the W3C WAI logo can be displayed on the website home page, if required.

WAI 'A' rating accessibility logo
http://www.w3.org/WAI/WCAG1A-Conformance

If this mark is not achieved, one or more groups will find it difficult to access information on your site. Satisfying this checkpoint is a basic requirement for some groups of the user population to be able to use web documents. The following checklist must be completed before a webpage can be considered to have attained this mark:

In general (the para references are to WCAG 1.0 Priority 1 checkpoints –
http://www.w3.org/TR/WCAG10/full-checklist.html

	1.1 Provide a text equivalent for every non-text element (eg via 'alt', "longdesc"' or in element content). *This includes*: images, graphical representations of text (including symbols), image map regions, animations (eg animated GIFs), applets and programmatic objects, ASCII art, frames, scripts, images used as list bullets, spacers, graphical buttons, sounds (played with or without user interaction), stand-alone audio files, audio tracks and video.
	2.1 Ensure that all information conveyed with colour is also available without colour, for example from context or mark up.
	4.1 Clearly identify changes in the natural language of a document's text and any text equivalents, eg captions.
	6.1 Organise documents so they may be read without style sheets. For example, when an HTML document is rendered without associated style sheets, it must still be possible to read the document.
	6.2 Ensure that equivalents for dynamic content are updated when the dynamic content changes.
	7.1 Until user agents allow users to control flickering, avoid causing the screen to flicker.
	14.1 Use the clearest and simplest language appropriate for a site's content.

...and if you use images and imagemaps

	1.2 Provide redundant text links for each active region of a server-side image map.
	9.1 Provide client-side image maps instead of server-side image maps except where the regions cannot be defined with an available geometric shape.

...and if you use tables

	5.1 For data tables, identify row and column headers.
	5.2 For data tables that have two or more logical levels of row or column headers, use mark up to associate data cells and header cells.

...and if you use frames

12.1	Title each frame to facilitate frame identification and navigation

...and if you use scripts and applets

6.3	Ensure that pages are usable when scripts, applets, or other programmatic objects are turned off or not supported. If this is not possible, provide equivalent information on an alternative accessible page.

...and if you use multimedia

1.3	Until user agents can automatically read aloud the text equivalent of a visual track, provide an auditory description of the important information of the visual track of a multimedia presentation.
1.4	For any time-based multimedia presentation (eg a movie or animation), synchronise equivalent alternatives, (eg captions or auditory descriptions of the visual track) with the presentation.

and if all else fails

11.4	If, after best efforts, you cannot create an accessible page, provide a link to an alternative page that uses W3C technologies, is accessible, has equivalent information (or functionality), and is updated as often as the inaccessible (original) page.

2.4.4 UK Government accesskeys standard

The accesskey attribute, introduced in HTML4.0, is intended to provide keyboard shortcuts in that they provide an alternative form of navigation.

This attribute should be added to the hypertext link element within an HTML page as follows.

```
<a href="whatsnew.htm" accesskey="2"> What's New </a>
```

This addition allows users with limited physical capabilities to navigate the organisation's website more easily. There are some drawbacks, for example:

- functionality depends on the type of operating system you are using,
- the attribute is only supported by MS Internet Explorer 4 and above and by Netscape 6x versions,
- with Windows-based systems the user has to press the 'Alt key' and the accesskey, and
- with the Macintosh system the user has to press the 'Ctrl key' and the accesskey.

In the example above, the organisation's What's New page has a '2' value given which should be used consistently throughout the Website.

When a user visits your department's website for the first time they bring their collective experience gained from all other sites. It is, therefore, important that UK Government Websites adopt a constant accesskeys standard. Variations from this will make it more difficult for users as they have to learn new navigational skills each time.

Listed below is the recommended **UK Government accesskeys standard**:

S	Skip navigation
1	Home page
2	What's New
3	Site map
4	Search
5	Frequently Asked Questions (FAQ)
6	Help
7	Complaints procedure
8	Terms and conditions
9	Feedback form
0	Access key details

When this navigational system is made available, it is important to inform your website users, as soon as they enter. Otherwise, users who are least able to do so will be faced with a mouse-dependent navigational system that could have been bypassed. Each page could display a message, eg,

'UK government accesskeys system'

Web managers can extend this system by attributing any one of the other 25 alphabetic characters to pages within their website but should ensure that the core elements listed above are used. It is important to ensure that the additional keys selected do not compromise shortcut keys used by various browsers, eg, Microsoft Internet Explorer 'alt h' drops down the help menu.

The Tabindex attribute is detailed in **Section 6.5.2.5**.

2.4.5   Other accessibility considerations

2.4.5.1 Download speeds and accessibility

Bandwidth or the capacity to send and receive data is an important consideration when designing an electronic document for distribution over the Internet. It is important that the link to the Internet (from the computer serving the pages to customers) has sufficient capacity to be able to handle the expected load. Otherwise, the response to users will be unsatisfactorily slow.

Most people today connect to the Internet over a phone line, typically using a modem with a speed of 28.8 to 56 kilobits per second (kbit/s). This 'narrowband' communication requires user to wait while a dial-up connection is made before they can access the Internet, and means that Internet use when connected is slow.

Broadband services offer significantly faster data rates, enabling the delivery of services, such as high speed Internet access. These may also be 'always on' connections to the Internet.

However, what looks great and downloads quickly within the confines of the Web manager's high-speed network connection does not necessarily work as well for the average user of the Internet. It is probably best to presume that your user is connected through a 28.8 kbit/s modem. Documents published on the Web need to be kept small, be linked efficiently and contain only the data and graphics that they require.

2.4.5.2 Colour blindness and clarity

Usability for people with visual disabilities difficulties must always be a primary consideration.

When designing a website be aware that complicated background patterns can make it difficult for viewers with low vision and difficulties, such as dyslexia, to interpret foreground information, such as text and hyperlinks.

- If using a coloured background have one that is single and solid, rather than textured or patterned.
- The contrast between the background and the text is very important.
- There are a range of colour combinations that do cause difficulty, for example:
    - Red and green
    - Red and purple
    - Yellow and white/light grey
    - Pink/lavender pastel colours
- White text on a black background will appear thinner than the same weight of font in black on a lighter background. Designers may wish to use a heavier font to compensate for this. White text out of blue is particularly legible.
- If is proposed that a background graphic be used to give a solid background colour it will always be better to use the colour itself, rather than the graphic.

- **Dyslexia** – some users prefer black/dark blue print on a pale blue/yellow background.

- **Flexibility** – ensure that the chosen colour can be overwritten by the viewer's browser settings (see **annex G** changing browser fonts and colours).

- **Printer friendly** – ensure that the text and images are legible when printed out on a standard 300dpi greyscale printer using white A4 size paper.

Simulating colour-blind vision
http://www.vischeck.com

Safe web colours for colour-deficient vision
http://more.btexact.com/people/rigdence/colours/

2.4.5.3 Splash screens and accessibility

Some websites use splash screens to introduce the contents of the entire site or a particular section. Such pages, usually containing an image and a brief line of text, are displayed on screen for a set period of time before automatically redirecting the browser to another more descriptive page.

Although this technique can be appealing it has limited use and can seriously hinder the accessibility of a website. Some browsers are not capable of following this sort of automatic redirection.

It is strongly advised that Web managers do not employ this feature. A W3C recommendation is not to use client-side redirects.

2.4.5.4 Styling pages for accessibility

- All pages in a website must be clearly laid out.
- CSS should be used to format the basic elements of the page.
- CSS should be used to format the text rendering of the page.
- A page must be easily read and understandable if the CSS is disabled.
- Standard HTML markup should be used to structure the document.
- Only specify standard fonts within documents.
- Always specify whether the font is to be sans-serif or serif as the lowest default setting.
- Ensure that text is always clearly distinguishable from the background colours.
- Do not use proprietary extensions for tags.
- Do not rely on plug-ins to deliver information, always offer an HTML alternative.

> **IMPORTANT**
>
> *See how your site looks on a browser that cannot use Cascading Style Sheets by disabling the link to the CSS in the HTML file. Now when it is viewed in the browser you will see the data without the styling.*

2.4.5.5 Accessibility with drop down menus and pop-up windows

Drop down menus:
- Drop-down menus are generally fine but the JavaScript triggering them can cause some problems for users with screen readers and screen magnifiers.
- A <noscript> alternative is necessary.

- The options offered in a drop-down should be repeated as text links on the same page.

Pop-up windows:
- Popup windows do not work in all browsers.
- If they are relying on JavaScript to trigger them then some users will not get them and in some cases they will replace the existing content.
- A <noscript> alternative is required.
- They are disorienting for users who cannot see that a new window has been created, eg, users with a screen reader or screen magnifier, or where the pop-up window covers the original one.
- Provide the user with an alternative.

See **section 2.4.5.13** Scripts and accessibility.

2.4.5.6 Accessible images

- All images that convey data or link to other areas of the website must include an 'alt' attribute and description.
- Avoid the use of invisible images to aid page layout, use CSS attributes and values. Screen readers pick up references to images. The HTML hspace and vspace attributes are deprecated in HTML4 – see **section 2.8.7** Cascading Style sheets.
- Do not use an image when a text link will work just as well.
- If an image is simply for decorative purposes (a horizontal line, a coloured spacer, a transparent spacer or material termed 'screen furniture' or 'eye candy') and is not essential to the understanding of the website, an empty alt=" " should be used, also known as a 'null alt'.
- If the image is a photograph of a named individual or small group of individuals, they should be named within the 'alt' attribute value.
- If an image conveys detailed information, eg a pie chart, that cannot be included within an 'alt' value, link the image to a page that gives the data in textual format.
- If the image is a navigation button then the function it performs should be within the 'alt' attribute value.
- Provide client-side imagemaps, as these do not need to reconnect to the website to work.
- If an imagemap is used, a text navigation alternative should be included to accompany the image.

2.4.5.7 Accessible multimedia

Multimedia content is becoming more common on websites, although the large file sizes and long download times can make this delivery method an unwelcome feature.

When you link to an audio or video file, indicate to the user its format (eg, .wav, .au) and size.
Do not assume that the user has the requisite media-player software so provide clear instructions on how to obtain this software. Beyond the technical difficulties of installing such software, some firewalls may not actually permit the passage of this material.

Auditory content, eg recorded voice or music, may be inaccessible to users who have a hearing impairment and will be inaccessible to those with computers with no audio capability or who do not have, or cannot use (because of a firewall), the plug-ins necessary to do the playback.

- Provide a meaningful descriptive text for the audio link and a text transcription of the audio content.
- Provide visual notification of any sounds that are played automatically.

Video content may be difficult for those users with visual impairment, or who have computers unable to play video. Hearing impaired users will have the same difficulty with a video as they do with pure audio content.

- Provide meaningful audio descriptions of all video clips.
- Provide text transcription of the audio content and consider including the dialogue and a meaningful description of the visual images.
- Provide video clips that include audio with open captions for reading.

2.4.5.8 Accessible text

- Is not easy to read long lines of text, however, the number of words per line will depend upon the font size which the user should be able to control.
- Use upper and lower case type.
- Use standard HTML elements and attributes that convey structure rather than presentation for example <h1>, <em>, <strong>, <blockquote>, <li> etc.
- Do not misuse structural elements and attributes for purposes of layout for example avoid use of <blockquote> to indent a paragraph.
- Avoid blinking or scrolling text. This creates problems for people with visual disabilities; it creates a difficulty for text-reading software; some moving type is browser specific, eg the marquee element; some moving type uses scripting or active content that may also be browser-limited and may not be permitted by some system firewalls.
- Provide an "alt" attribute for horizontal rules.
- Provide expansions of acronyms and abbreviations.

2.4.5.9 Accessible lists

- Ensure that list structures are constructed correctly.
- Do not use images for bullet points. Use the bullet styles available in HTML.
- Keep you content easily understandable, for example, a What's New list should list the most recent documents first.

2.4.5.10 Accessible tables

- Avoid using tables to arrange text documents in columns.
- Provide summary information for a table using the 'summary' attribute.

- Table width should be set using the "%" value rather than a fixed pixel value. The table will then scale to the user's displayable area and avoid left to right scrolling (see **section 6.3**).

2.4.5.11 Accessible links

- Text links to documents should be descriptive and convey meaning rather than using just 'Click here', for example, 'Click here to go to the next page'. It is more meaningful to link on the words 'Go to the next page'.
- Split consecutive links by using, for example, the vertical bar (|) character with a space before and after. This will aid visually impaired readers.
- Provide keyboard shortcuts for standard navigation items – see **section 2.4.4**.
- Links do not have to be in the *de facto* blue.
- For the benefit of viewers with, eg, low vision, or dyslexia, contents links should show which pages have been accessed.
- For the benefit of viewers with low vision or with mobility impairment do consider the size of the hyperlink footprint. A hyperlink to a footnote that uses a superscript figure font, for example, markup such as `'<a href="footnote-1.htm"><sup>1</sup></a>'`, can be difficult for a user with motor disabilities. Consider using a style that avoids subscript or superscript characters and provide a larger footprint, for example, `'<a href="footnote-1.htm">[note 1]</a>'`.

2.4.5.12 Accessible frames

- Ensure that a website using a frames environment is usable with non-frames-capable browsers by using the `<noframes>` option.
- Give each frame a meaningful title.

2.4.5.13 Scripts and accessibility

All browsers do not support client -side scripting (JavaScript, JScript and VBScript). Some users choose to disable it and some firewalls do not permit its passage to the desktop. The use of scripts can be a barrier to accessibility and the viewer should not have to solely rely upon them. For example,

- Where appropriate provide an alternative with equivalent text using the <noscript> element. The non-script supporting browsers will display this element containing HTML information.
- The <noscript> element can also contain a hyperlink to an alternative accessible web page with the same content.

> `<noscript><a href="alternative.htm">`This is a summary of alternative information`.</a></noscript>`

- When using JavaScript to open a popup window from a link, you should not use:

```
<a href="javascript:window.open('logo.htm', 'popup',
'scrollbars, resizable, width=300, height=200')">
```

This link will fail to function when JavaScript is not enabled. The following, for example, should work in all browsers, however, it will take the viewer to a new HTML page and they will have to rely on their browser back button to return to your original page:

```
<a href="logo.htm" onclick="window.open('logo.htm',
'popup', 'scrollbars, resizable, width=300, height=200');
return false">
```

See **section 4.5** Client-side scripting and programming.

2.4.5.14 Easy Access

The Easy Access channel applied on the Portal ***www.ukonline.gov.uk*** addresses accessibility issues. This channel is intended as an option for people who have difficulties using the more graphical channel – whether through lack of experience of using the Internet, or disabilities.

The channel offers enhanced legibility through high contrast, the use of only three colours and minimal use of graphics. The three colours chosen are visible to almost all people with colour blindness. Tab ordering and link indicators aid users of screen reading software. External links do not open a new browser window.

No content is reduced or re-written before it appears in the Easy Access channel – it is taken directly from one database so all content being viewed is the same for all users. Importantly, the channel is not just a text version of a graphical site.

The information displayed is rearranged into a vertical hierarchy. Sections contain enhanced spacing, increased clarity of headings and paragraphs and line separators between different content. Images appear where necessary – such as with the main news article, thus enhancing the experience for people who can see the screen.

This is a method of supporting a 'WAI 'A' site (or an inaccessible website) with an enhanced accessibility channel.

2.4.6 Simple HTML attributes for accessibility

Each of the following examples is simple to implement and takes just a few minutes but can make all the difference to many visitors to your website.

A number of these additions are only available for use when the HTML 4.01 standard is used to construct the page. If HTML 4.01 is to be used, then the author of the document must use the correct DTD, quoted at the very beginning of the HTML file. Further information on this topic is covered in **section 3.2**.

2.4.6.1 Accesskey

This attribute should be added to the hypertext link tag within an HTML page as follows.

```
<a href="whatsnew.htm" accesskey="2"> What's New </a>
```

This addition allows users with limited physical capabilities to navigate the organisation's website more easily. Different browsers work in subtly different ways but most will work if the user holds down the 'alt' key and the accesskey value at the same time.

In the example above, the organisations What's New page has a '2' value given in accordance with the UK Government accesskeys standard. This should be used consistently throughout the website. See **section 2.4.4**.

2.4.6.2 Alt attribute for accessibility

This attribute should be added to the image tag within an HTML page as follows:

```
<img src="logo.gif" alt="Our organisational logo">
```

Keep this attribute short. If used correctly, it will ensure that a meaningful description will be displayed on the browser screen if the link image is unavailable or the browser cannot handle graphics.

Structuring the 'alt' attributes correctly allows differentiation between images within the site. The following 'alt' attributes could all be used to describe different possible purposes of an image of a magnifying glass:

Icon: magnifying glass	An icon graphic
Link: search	The same image that is a link to a search page
Photo: magnifying glass	A photographic image

- All images that convey data or link to other areas of the website must include an 'alt' attribute and description.
- Where possible the 'alt' description should be no longer than 100 characters
- Do not use invisible images to aid page layout, where appropriate, use CSS attributes and values instead. Screen readers pick up references to images. The HTML hspace and vspace attributes are deprecated in HTML4 – see **section 2.8.7** Cascading Style sheets.
- Do not use an image when a text link will work just as well.
- If an image is simply for decorative purposes (a horizontal line, a coloured spacer, a transparent spacer or material termed 'screen furniture' or 'eye candy') and is not essential to the understanding of the website, an empty alt="" attribute description should be used.

- If the image is a photograph of a named individual or small group of individuals, they should be named within the 'alt' attribute description.
- If the image is a navigation button then the function it performs should be within the 'alt' attribute value.
- If an image conveys detailed information, for example a pie chart, that cannot be included within an 'alt' description, link the image to a page that gives the data in textual format.
- Provide client-side imagemaps, as these do not need to reconnect to the website to work.
- If an imagemap is used, a text navigation alternative should be included to accompany the image.
- Where images require a description that is inappropriate by use of the 'alt' attribute consider using the 'longdesc' attribute in the <img> tag. This provides a screen reader user with a link to a separate page that contains this comprehensive description. Browser support is currently poor but we should anticipate wider support in the future. The 'longdesc' page should be accessible and you should consider whether it should contain a repeat of the image being described. When using the 'longdesc' attribute the text value is the URL of the long description. The following example shows support for a 'D-link'.

```
<img border="0" SRC="image/photo.gif" alt="a yacht in
harbour" - see long description "width "250"
height="300" longdesc="aboutyacht.htm">
<a href="aboutyacht.htm"> [D]</a>
```

2.4.6.3 Title attribute for accessibility

This attribute can be added to the HTML href element within an HTML page as follows:

```
<a href="game.htm" title="Rules of the game of
football">Football</a>
```

This word 'Football' may make sense to the user who can see the rest of the page but is not clear in itself. The title assists the user with a more descriptive message.

A screen reader will read out the text contained in this attribute, and there is no way of stopping it. An example of a bad implementation of this attribute would be:

```
<a href="whatsnew.htm" title="This link goes to the What's
New section of our website, listing all items that have
been added to the site in the past seven days">What's New</a>
```

A visually impaired user would have to wait for the entire message in the title attribute to be read and would then have the text element of the page 'What's New' read out as well. This is an example of a link that is self-explanatory and does not require the use of the title attribute

It is extremely important to control the number of times the title attribute is used in a page. It is very useful if used correctly, but can be cumbersome and disruptive if overused and badly implemented.

The title attribute can also be used within the frame tags. A more detailed explanation of this usage is in **section 6.4**.

2.4.6.4 Summary attribute for accessibility

This attribute should be added to the table element within an HTML page as follows:

```
<table border="0" width="100%" summary="Cups of coffee
sold">
```

This attribute must be employed with the same level of control as the title attribute. Correctly used it is helpful and informative. When incorrectly used it will just get in the way.

Be careful to avoid replicating any data already supplied in the `<caption>` tag or in the table heading.

This attribute is discussed in more detail in **section 4.2.4.2**.

2.4.6.5 Acronym attribute for accessibility

This element can be used within an HTML page as follows:

```
<acronym="World Wide Web Consortium"> W3C </acronym>
```

This element can be employed as many times as is necessary in a page. It can be very helpful to users who do not necessarily understand the shorthand language used within an organisation.

The use of this attribute is immediate when a user hovers their pointing device over a displayed acronym. A box will appear displaying the descriptive text of the acronym. This is important, when for example, a user is directed to the middle of an organisation's website by a search facility or link from an external body. The organisation-specific acronyms may well all be new to the user and each will need to be explained.

> **IMPORTANT**
>
> *When buying design services it is inadequate for the designer to simply present colour visuals or mock-ups of the look and feel. It is important these are also presented to you as HTML mark up. When you buy web design you are also buying the source coding that will render the visual onto computer screens and the standard of this is the backbone in achieving HTML validation and meeting the mandatory WAI requirements.*

2.4.7 Validation and testing

Validation is important in ensuring platform independence, but alone is not sufficient. Developers should ensure that web pages are not dependent on a certain resolution, colour depth or font size. They should test and evaluate an early working version (a beta test) of a site with representative users. This is also known as prototyping.

Well-authored HTML is a highly structured and usable mark up language that is backward compatible ensuring that many web browsers can display information contained within a web page and equally providing accessibility at little or no cost. Although the web is often seen as a visual environment, accessible web pages should adjust and remain accessible in any browsing medium and adapt to allow audio and Braille presentations.

Once the page is completed it can be checked for conformity to a specific version of HTML by running it against the World Wide Web Consortium (W3C) automated validator. Cascading Style Sheets should be validated using the W3C automated validator. Tagged Adobe PDF files should be tested using a screen reader. This will demonstrate how your information will actually be presented to user and how the reading order and navigational links will work. Hyperlinks should be carefully checked.

These validators are available online from the following URLs:

HTML validator service
http://validator.w3.org

CSS validation service
http://jigsaw.w3.org/css-validator/

2.4.7.1 Bobby™ testing

It must always be remembered that the W3C WAI is not a standard but a set of guidelines. There is no automatic way in which an organisation can get its website validated against the guidelines.

A page can be compared against the guidelines to raise a Web manager's awareness of certain issues. The well established Bobby™ software tool was developed by The Center for Applied Special Technology's (CAST) and now owned by the Watchfire Corporation.

Individual pages can be run through the Bobby™ service by visiting the site and typing the page URL into a specific box. The service will scan the page and then return an automated report *highlighting areas of concern* and suggesting what could be done to rectify them. A downloadable version of Bobby is available for testing an entire site.

The reports can look extremely daunting at first because of their length and quantity of detail but it is a service worth persevering with. It must be noted that this application has a number of limitations:

- It will highlight areas that need to be looked at, but will not correct the submitted page.
- It also suggests using attributes that are not supported by any web browser at present.
- It does not validate a web page. This should be done using the W3C validator.
- A Bobby approved certification does not necessarily mean it is usable by all.

Bobby™ analysing application
http://bobby.watchfire.com/bobby/html/en/advanced.jsp

> **IMPORTANT**
>
> *Getting validation clearances, a successful 'Bobby Approved' should not be regarded as an endorsement of accessibility – your Bobby report should be interpreted as help in identifying accessibility problems.*

2.4.7.2 The WAVE accessibility test

The Wave accessibility tool, from Pennsylvania's Initiative on Assistive Technology, is an online service that will check your pages and mark it visually with icons that help you understand how assistive technology will read or display the page. Useful features are:

- it will show the order in which elements will appear on the page to, eg, a screen reader;
- it denotes "alt" text of images and applets;
- it marks links that contain JavaScript events, headings, and HTML keyboard shortcuts;
- highlight non-HTML elements and multimedia.

Wave accessibility tool
http://www.wave.webaim.org:8081/wave/index.jsp

2.4.7.3 Page Valet

The Page Valet is an online validator with a range of accessibility testing features based on the W3C's Web Content Accessibility Guidelines. Useful features are:

- support for a range of markup languages
- it will show your source code with any errors annotated and highlighted (provided your browser supports CSS).

Page Valet *http://valet.webthing.com/page/*

2.4.7.4 A-Prompt Toolkit

The University of Toronto's Adaptive Technology Resource Centre (ATRC) and the University of Wisconsin's TRACE Centre have jointly developed the A-Prompt Toolkit. This offline Web accessibility verifier has been designed to check for the three WCAG conformance levels – A (Priority 1 items), AA (Priority 1 and 2 items) and AAA (Priority 1, 2 and 3 items). It also checks for compliance with Section 508 of the US Rehabilitation Act. When accessibility issues are detected the toolkit displays relevant dialog boxes and guides to enable the user to fix a range of problems. Some tasks are semi-automated, such as correcting:

- missing 'alt' attributes,
- missing titles on frames, and
- missing row and column headings on data tables.

The toolkit can be downloaded to a PC (Windows OS).

A-Prompt Toolkit *http://www.aprompt.ca/*

2.4.7.5 LIFT online accessibility and usability checker

LIFT software is available for checking your HTML plus a range of accessibility and usability evaluations with fix suggestions. The LIFT Online free trial will check five pages starting from your specified URL. The test is against a subset of UsableNet's accessibility and usability rules. The report does require the Web manager to interpret the suggested improvements in order to ensure accessibility compliance.

UsableNet offer a free accessibility suite that is an extension to Macromedia Dreamweaver MX. This assists in the testing of web pages against Web Content Accessibility Guidelines 1.0 (Priority 1 and Priority 2).

LIFT Online 5 page free trial *http://www.usablenet.com*

2.4.8 Portable Document Format (PDF) and accessibility

The Portable Document Format (PDF) is widely used in electronic publishing (see **section 4.4**). It is the universal file format that preserves the look and feel of a document, including the fonts, formatting, colours and graphics, regardless of the application and platform used to originate it. Information in PDF is generally considered inaccessible to web users whose disabilities make it difficult to interact with computer technologies.

Adobe PDFs have become the portable document format standard for government on the World Wide Web but PDF documents cannot be considered as accessible. However, Adobe have taken considerable steps to improve the accessibility of both their Acrobat software and the information contained in their PDF files. Their latest specification (PDF1.4) is incorporated in Acrobat 5.0 and features some of the following usability enhancements:

- support for assistive technology such as screen readers and/or refreshable Braille output devices through the Microsoft Active Accessibility (MSAA) application programming interface for the Windows operating system;
- the level of contrast between text and background can make a big difference in the legibility of a page and Acrobat allows user to increase contract by creating custom colour schemes that override the colours specified in a document;
- the ability to zoom in and reflow text on the screen;
- keyboard shortcuts to enable navigation without the use of a mouse.

It is important to understand that your legacy PDF documents: those not originally created using the PDF 1.4 specification will remain inaccessible. To give them a level of accessible you have to either:

- recreate them from their source material into tagged Adobe PDF files using the PDF1.4 specification in Acrobat 5, or
- view your documents using the Acrobat Reader 5 with the Make Accessible plug-in.

2.4.8.1 Make Accessible plug-in

The Acrobat 5.0 Make Accessible plug-in automatically analyses the logical structure of a document and creates a new version of that file that will read more logically with assistive technology. The plug-in allows the users of Acrobat 5.0 for Windows to convert untagged legacy PDF files into tagged Adobe PDF files. A tagged Adobe PDF file is designed to ensure:

- the information is in the correct reading order on the page;
- includes paragraph attributes needed to reflow text correctly;
- the reliable translation of all text into Unicode so that all characters, eg, hyphens and ligatures, can be read correctly by a screen reader.

2.4.8.2 Accessible checker

The Adobe Accessibility Checker is a tool intended to identify common accessibility problems in Adobe PDF documents. This tool will, eg, check a document for missing ALT information on images, and for unrecognisable character encoding. When found they are logged and reported so that you can choose to fix or ignore the identified problem.

> **Adobe online accessibility resource**
> *http:// access.adobe.com*

> ### Practical tip if your are a sighted web manager
> *To get a rough idea how some screen readers interpret information:*
>
> - *Sit away from your computer and make sure you cannot see the screen*
> - *Ask someone to take a rule and lay it horizontally on your computer screen;*
> - *Ask them to read aloud, without pause, from left hand edge of your screen to the right hand edge;*
> - *Ask them where there is an illustration to say the word 'image' and before any hyperlink say the words 'link to';*
> - *Ask them to continue to continue to move the ruler down one line at a time and read without pause.*
>
> *Better yet, invest in a screenreader yourself – or get an auditor to tell you how useable your pages are on assistive technology.*

2.4.9   W3C work in progress

The W3C's Web Content Accessibility Guidelines Working Group (WCAG WG) has released a working draft of the ***Web Content Accessibility Guidelines 2.0***. This shows how more generalised, less HTML-specific) WCAG checkpoints might read. These checkpoints explain how to make web content more accessibly to users with disabilities. Working draft available at ***http://www.w3.org/TR/WCAG20/***

See also the following working drafts:

Requirements for WCAC 2.0 – http://www.w3.org/TR/wcag2-req/

***HTML Techniques for WCAG 2.0 –
http://www.w3.org/WAI/GL/WCAG20/HTML-TECHS/***

***PDF Techniques for Web Content Accessibility Guidelines 1.0 and 2.0 –
http://www.w3.org/WAI/GL/WCAG-PDF-TECHS/***

XML Accessibility Guidelines – W3C has published a working draft at
http://www.w3.org/TR/xmlgl

2.4.10 Further reading and resources

Don't forget that all this is just the beginning of the process of ensuring universal accessibility.

Always test your website with a diverse user group. Discussion with other Web managers will only make the task easier. Over time, experience may show that certain elements that were added with the best intentions do not work and they may make extracting data from a page more difficult rather than easier.

A number of manuals and guidelines published by W3C expand on the major themes outlined here. It is recommended that Web managers familiarise themselves with their content. A great deal can be achieved by reading through the W3C guidance on this topic.

How People with Disabilities use the Web *http://www.w3.org/WAI/EO/Drafts/PWD-Use-Web/Overview.html*

Getting started: Making a web site accessible *http://www.w3.org/WAI/gettingstarted*

Web Content Accessibility Guidelines 1.0 *http://www.w3.org/TR/WCAG10/* or *http://www.w3.org/TR-WAI-WEBCONTENT/* **WCAG1.0 Errata** *http://www.w3.org/WAI/GL/WAI-WEBCONTENT-ERRATA*

Core techniques for Web Content Accessibility Guidelines 1.0 *http://www.w3.org/TR/WCAG10-CORE-TECHS/*

Checklist for Web Content Accessibility Guidelines *http://www.w3.org/TR/WCAG10/full-checklist.html*

Techniques for Web Content Accessibility Guidelines *http://www.w3.org/TR/WCAG10-TECHS/*

HTML Techniques for Web Content Accessibility Guidelines *http://www.w3.org/TR/WCAG10-HTML-TECHS*

HTML 4.0 Accessibility Improvements *http://www.w3.org/WAI/References/HTML4-access*

CSS Techniques for Web Content Accessibility Guidelines *http://www.w3.org/TR/WCAG10-CSS-TECHS/*

Accessibility features of CSS (Cascading Style Sheets) *http://www.w3.org/TR/CSS-access*

Accessibility features of SMIL (Synchronised Multimedia Integration Language)
http://www.w3.org/TR/SMIL-access/

Accessibility features of SVG (Scalable Vector Graphics)
http://www.w3.org/TR/SVG-access/

Disability (Department for Work and Pensions)
http://www.disability.gov.uk

Disability Rights Commission
http://www.drc-gb.org

Disability Discrimination Act
http://www.disability.gov.uk/dda/index.html

Royal National Institute for the Blind
http://www.rnib.org/digital

Royal National Institute for Deaf People
http://www.rnid.org

National Library for the Blind Visionary design
http://visdesign.nlbuk.org/index.php?menu=1

TechDis Web accessibility and Usability resource
http://www.techdis.ac.uk/seven/index.html

British Dyslexia Association
http://www.bda-dyslexia.org.uk

Betsie application
http://www.bbc.co.uk/education/betsie/index.html

{textualise;}
http://codix.net/textualise

Designing a more usable world – for all
http://trace.wisc.edu/world/

Quality Framework for UK government website design
http://www.e-envoy.gov.uk/webguidelines.htm

Guidelines for UK government websites – Framework for local government
http://www.e-envoy.gov.uk/webguidelines.htm

Checklist: Universal usability

This checklist should be used by web producers and managers to ensure that the pages presented on the Internet are as accessible and usable as possible to the largest possible audience and, as a minimum, comply with the Web Content Accessibility Guidelines 1.0 Priority 1 checkpoints for achieving W3C Web Accessibility Initiative rating 'A'.

Basics

Done	Description	
	Keep pages simple and easy to understand	
	Presentation, content and navigation should be consistent throughout the website	
	The page must comply with the WAI 'A' standard. Online guidelines are available from the W3C website at *http://www.w3.org/TR/WCAG10/*	
	No website or single HTML page should be developed for a particular browser	
	Do not rely on colour to convey any information, review needs of colour blind users	
	A consistent text navigation bar should be available at the very top of each page	
	HTML must be the default standard for publishing information on the website	

Text

Done	Description	
	Text colour must always contrast with background colours	
	Use only clear, commonly used fonts	
	Avoid the use of small text	
	Users should have the ability to scale fonts and change background colours within a website	

Images

Done	Description	
	All important images must have an alternative, ie, 'alt' attribute and value	
	All 'alt' attributes should be meaningful and as short as practical	

Styling

Done	Description	
	Use HTML to structure the document, not style it	
	Use Cascading Style Sheets to style objects within a web page	
	The website must be legible and easy to use if Cascading Style Sheets are not available to the end user	

Linking alternatives	
A text alternative must be offered when an imagemap is used	
An alternative text version of any information must be offered in audio or video format	
Any information that is offered in a format that requires a plug-in must also be offered in HTML	
General testing	
The website must be tested for accessibility and usability during its development	
W3C HTML validation report from *http://validator.w3.org*	
If employing CSS then a validation is to be used from *http://jigsaw.w3.org/css-validator*	
Bobby report to be obtained from *http://bobby.watchfire.com/bobby/html/en/advanced.jsp*	
Page Valet report obtained from *http://valet.webthing.com/page/*	
A-Prompt off-line web accessibility verifier used *http://www.aprompt.ca/*	
Each HTML page should be tested against the basic browsers for usability and rendering testing (and you should test using a screen reader)	
Each page within the website must be legible when viewed with only 16 colours	
The website must be easily usable when viewed on a 800 x 600 screen size	
Individual pages must be legible when printed out on standard office/home printers	

2.5 Browser compatibility

Web browsers are computer programs that use the Hypertext Transfer Protocol (HTTP) to access data across the World Wide Web.

They interpret the HTML and CSS formatting instructions contained in documents, and display the information with the appropriate structure (headings, tables, images etc) and presentation (font sizes, styles, colour etc).

Although Microsoft Internet Explorer and Netscape Navigator are the most popular web browsers, there are many more available that have been developed often with particular operating systems or disabilities in mind.

Use each checklist to ensure that your web pages comply with these guidelines

2.5.1 Checklist and summary   *Core Guidance*

Checklist	❑ The document must validate to the appropriate HTML standard
	❑ The document and website should be usable when viewed on an 800 x 600 screen size
	❑ The document should be legible when viewed with only 16 colours
	❑ The site and each page should be tested for legibility and usability on a range of browsers
	❑ The site must be tested for accessibility during its development
	❑ A site or page must not be developed for a particular browser
	❑ Any web page must be able to print out legibly on a standard office printer
Summary	Web content is constructed with any number of authoring tools and viewed on a wide variety of computers running various different browsers on all manner of operating systems.
	Webmasters must ensure that the whole of their web presence is generally available to the widest possible audience. No part of a website should be designed specifically for a particular browser. This will simply disenfranchise users who happen to use other applications software.

2.5.2 What is a web browser?

A web browser is a computer program that allows users to access information across the World Wide Web. The capabilities of different browsers vary and different browsers will typically render a Web page differently according to their capabilities.

Many browsers only partially support the latest revisions of recommended mark-up standards including HTML and CSS. Generally, details of what standards and versions of them are supported by which browsers are not easy to find. See **Annex A** Web browser applications.

Every information resource accessible on the Web has a unique address or URL. The user typically enters the URL of a 'web page' into the browser and the browser locates and fetches the resource. Any other files that are dependent on this file including external script and CSS files, images and other embedded content are also fetched. See **sections 2.1.2** and **2.1.2.1** for more details of how this works.

When the browser receives the file, it interprets the HTML and CSS mark-up within it and uses these to format the file for display and renders it as a 'page' on the screen or other output device.

Every browser has a number of common features that facilitate the retrieval of information from the web by the user:

- There is an address box for entering URLs.
- 'Forward' and 'back' buttons allow the user to move back and forth among the documents previously downloaded in a session.
- A 'print' button allows the user to print the web page that is currently displayed.
- A 'Bookmark' button allows the user to save the URL of a displayed page for easy retrieval at a later date.

2.5.3   Types and versions of browsers

Most government organisations have Microsoft Internet Explorer or Netscape Navigator installed as their standard office web browser used to access their departmental intranet. Typically, the same browser and version of it is installed on all of the desktop computers within the organisation. Because everybody has the same version of the same browser, all users see an identical view of their Intranet content.

Unfortunately these same conditions do not exist on the Internet where a diverse range of browsers of varying vintages are in use. There are many reasons for this. Although the pace of browser development is fierce and competitive between manufacturers, not all users elect to install every new version that is released. Newer releases of browsers tend to work best on contemporaneous versions of their corresponding operating systems and the underlying computer hardware. This may act as a disincentive or even a barrier to updating browsers. Many organisations have deployed a standard platform 'package' of hardware, operating system and applications software suite that have all been tested and verified to work together. The complexity and cost of the package integration and testing work is such that it may not be appropriate to install every new browser release that comes along.

Beyond the world of the MS-Windows PC, there are other computers and devices running different operating systems each with browser development strands that are different to the PC MS-Windows ones. Versions of Internet Explorer and Netscape Navigator are available for other desktop PCs such as Apple Macintosh and the UNIX system family. However, there tend to be subtle and not so subtle differences between the way they render HTML and CSS and in their document object models and scripting environments compared with the MS-Windows counterparts.

Devices such as electronic personal organisers and cellular mobile telephones are also increasingly capable of browsing the web. The display screens on these devices are very small compared with those on desktop computers and their browsers use modified versions of the HTML markup language. Consequently it is necessary to build modified versions of 'standard' websites to work with these devices.

There are a number of special browsers, add-ons to standard browsers and purpose-built computer hardware devices available to enable users with any of a wide range of disabilities to access the web. See **section 2.4** for the implications of the requirement to build in universal accessibility to websites.

Most web users now have access to monitors and display adapters that can display 800 x 600 pixels. Although this can be taken as the default standard it is still important to ensure that your website is legible in the lowest screen size of 480 x 640 pixels.

By the same token, some users still have graphics adapters in their PC that can only display 16 colours. While this should not limit creativity, all pages produced and made public must still be legible and understandable when viewed in this format.

> **IMPORTANT**
>
> *Many PC graphics cards allow users to change their monitor settings down to 16 colours and reduce their viewing capabilities down to 480 x 640 screen size.*
>
> *Doing this will enable you to see what some web users have to endure when visiting your site.*

2.5.4 Example of different browsers

The following screen image captures illustrate the subtle differences in the way a number of browsers display the same web page. The browsers were all running on a Microsoft NT4 operating system with an 800 x 600 pixels screen set in 'True Color' mode. It can be seen that the font sizes, the structure of tables and the rendering of bulleted lists have all rendered slightly differently.

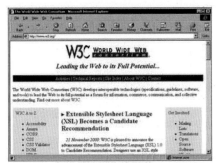

Microsoft Internet Explorer 4

Netscape Communicator 4.6

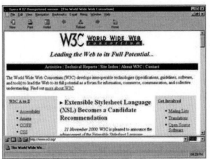

Opera 4.02

Amaya 4.1

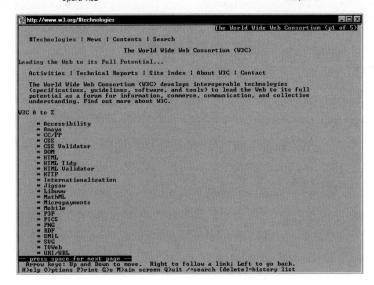

Lynx

2.5.5   Testing with different browsers

The recommendation is that pages on government websites should work with a wide range of browser makes and release versions. HTML version 4 should be used to specify content structure and CSS should be used to specify presentation properties. Client-side scripting (JavaScript) may also be used. However, web sites should degrade gracefully: that is to say they should be usable:

- with browsers that recognise only prior revisions of the HTML markup language;
- with browsers that pre-date the introduction of CSS;
- with all versions of browser scripting environments (Document Object Models);
- with browsers that do not support client-side scripting at all or that have client-side scripting turned off.

In order to be sure that your web site works properly with a wide range of browsers you should consider testing it (or a representative part of it) with a range of browsers. The following are worth considering for testing with:

Netscape Navigator 1 or NCSA Mosaic 1
These very early graphical browsers cannot render frames, which makes them ideal for testing the `noframes` elements of websites that use frames. These browsers also do not support HTML tables.

Netscape Navigator 2
The second version of this browser can render a limited number of the frames attributes. Its inability to deal with any JavaScript scripting will raise awareness of any possible problem areas. It does not support CSS.

Netscape Navigator 3
This was the first graphical browser to support the use of frames and some limited JavaScript capability. If a frames-capable site displays well in this browser you can be fairly confident that it will work in most others. It does not support CSS. This browser is available free of charge.

Microsoft Internet Explorer 3
The capabilities of this browser are broadly similar to those of Netscape Navigator version 3 although there are differences in the way specific HTML elements render. Both the MS-Windows version and the Apple Macintosh contain (differently) partial and buggy implementations of CSS. Both versions also have an implementation of JavaScript that was reverse-engineered by Microsoft from the Netscape Navigator 3 version. Microsoft first used the name 'JScript' to refer to this implementation of JavaScript. As with the CSS implementation, the MS-Windows and Apple Macintosh JScript implementations are quite different. Microsoft released updates to the MS-Windows JScript implementation for the MS-Windows version during the lifetime of this browser.

Netscape Navigator 4
This is a widely installed version of the Netscape browser. An important point to be aware of with regard to ensuring that website implementations are compatible with Netscape Navigator version 4, is that a there was a large number of minor releases each with different capabilities.

Microsoft Internet Explorer 4

This browser was the first to include a comprehensive document object model (DOM) that gave access to every HTML element (and its attributes) and CSS property in displayed pages via the scripting environment. Microsoft referred to this feature as 'Dynamic HTML' (DHTML).

Microsoft Internet Explorer 5

At the time of writing, this is the most commonly used web browser. Any website must render properly on this browser. This browser is available free of charge.

Mozilla

The Mozilla organisation was originally formed by the Netscape Corporation as a way of involving the web software development community in the making a web browser designed for standards compliance, performance and portability. This browser is available free of charge.

Netscape Navigator 6.1 and 6.2

These are the latest versions of the Netscape Navigator browser and is based on the Mozilla organisation's software.

Microsoft Internet Explorer 6

At the time of writing, this browser had recently been released. It is the first browser to include support for the W3C Platform for Privacy Preferences (P3P) recommendation. The user's privacy preferences as set in the browser preferences may interact with a website's published P3P privacy policy in a way that will cause this browser to manipulate cookies served to it. See **section 4.6** Cookies.

Amaya

This is an open-standard web browser designed and distributed by the W3C. It has a number of built-in browsing modes: the same web pages can be displayed in standard graphic mode or in a DOS Lynx emulator mode. Amaya is extremely useful for testing compliance with open standards and accessibility. At the time of writing version 5.2 had been released. This browser and authoring tool is available free of charge.

Opera

This browser not only supports the browsing of pages on the World Wide Web but can also render WAP pages in WML. This browser is available for a free 30-day trial period but further use of the browser requires a licence fee to be paid.

Opera Software has recently released their version 5 browser, which although completely free, has a reduced viewing area and displays advertising all the time.

LYNX

LYNX is a line-mode browser that has been available for many years and is still popular today. It displays pages in a 'DOS format': it displays only unstyled text. It remains popular for a number of reasons including because it renders documents very quickly and also interfaces extremely well with Braille displays.

Many of these browsers are also available for multiple operating systems, such as, Microsoft Windows, Apple Macintosh and members of the UNIX operating system family. Web pages will often render differently in the same browser running on a different operating system platform. You should therefore also give consideration to testing on a selection of different operating system platforms.

2.5.5.1 Useful browser resources

Old version of Netscape browser products may be downloaded from:
http://home.netscape.com/download/archive.html

An overview comparison of the capabilities of different makes and releases of Web browsers can be viewed at: *http://www.webreview.com/browsers/browsers.shtml*

Details of the CSS-1 capability in older browsers can be viewed at:
http://www.webreview.com/style/cs1/charts/mastergrid.shtml

Annex A contains a list of many of the browser applications available.

2.5.6 Special-purpose browsers

Many different browsers are used for viewing information on the web.   The ones mentioned so far in this section are only some of those available.

Some sections of the user community use special-purpose browsers to help overcome a specific disability. It is the webmaster's responsibility to be aware of these browsers and their specific capabilities and to ensure that the organisation's website is accessible through them.

The W3C WAI committee has stated:

> People with visual impairment or reading difficulties rely on speech output, Braille displays or screen magnification; and in many cases use the keyboard instead of the mouse. People who can't use a keyboard depend on voice recognition for spoken commands, or on switch devices which head, mouth or eye movements can control. People whose eyes are busy with another task may need web access using voice-driven systems.

See **section 2.4** Building in universal accessibility.
See **Annex B** contains a list of some of the browser applications used by people with disabilities.

2.6 Information and text

For Departments that provide few services to the public, the website will primarily be a way of providing and exchanging information, most often in the form of text. Even sites concerned with providing services will need to make sure that information about policies and procedures communicates effectively. The basic questions about text are the same for all websites.

Does your site get users to the text content they need quickly?
Once users have decided to read a text page, does it communicate to them effectively?
Is the text marked up in such a way that users can choose or control the format, thus contributing to the accessibility of the content?
Are procedures in place to keep text content up to date and accurate?

Use each checklist to ensure that your web pages comply with these guidelines

2.6.1 Checklist and summary	*Core Guidance*
Checklist	❑ Consistent publishing procedures to ensure that online and offline publications are co-ordinated ❑ Procedures for adapting text content for use on other delivery platforms such as mobile devices ❑ A style guide against which text can be edited ❑ All documents edited for accuracy, consistency, and style ❑ Where necessary, pages written especially for the website and its audiences ❑ All pages, headlines etc make sense out of context ❑ All new documents have metadata, preferably provided by the content owners ❑ Web managers can add or amend pages quickly and simply ❑ Are content owners able to amend their own pages once they are published? ❑ Maintenance of documents, checking of links and archiving of older documents are part of your regular routine ❑ Scan through the text on HTML pages -- short and in plain English ❑ Text is displayed against backgrounds in strongly contrasting tones ❑ CSS stylesheets do not fix font properties not fixed so users can change the size if necessary ❑ Documents designed to be printed are provided in universally accessible formats. PDFs should have RTF or plain text alternatives.
Summary	Much text on the web will be scanned through quickly rather than read in detail. Text must be short and in plain English. Bullet points, lists and subheadings will make text easily scannable. To communicate effectively some text on a site should be written specially for the medium and aimed at key audiences. Text should be displayed so that is universally accessible. This includes documents designed primarily to be printed out. Clear procedures for editing, maintenance and archiving should be routine. Web strategies should be working towards technical solutions that allow content owners to amend or update their own pages.

2.6.2 Website content generation

While information for publication within government is generally created electronically, the primacy given to conventional publishing often means that material does not always reach the web team in electronic format. Where late corrections are made to texts, there is a real risk that there is no authoritative electronic version of documents. If there is to be rapid, accurate and accessible Internet publishing, departments should adopt publishing strategies that establish an authoritative electronic version of documents as a basis for both the electronic and paper versions of texts. The Senior Editor or editorial board has a key role to play in pressing for this practice to be established.

Information for the website should be provided and preferably created in an electronic format that can easily be converted into validated HTML.

Information for the website should be accompanied by a 'display by' date and, where there is one, a 'retire by' date, enabling the web team to ensure that information is up to date.

2.6.3 Online publishing tools

There are many different publishing tools for publication of all sorts of data. Departments and agencies will need to be able to generate text and graphical content for their website in conjunction with any programming, interface design and project management tools required. It is likely that a number of tools will be needed to achieve this.

The typical minimum requirements for site creation and maintenance are:

- **text editor** to generate mark-up in longhand;
- **HTML editor** to generate mark-up more quickly. Many HTML editing software also incorporate some site management tools (see **Annex C**);
- **graphics editor** to produce, manipulate and modify images (see **Annex D**);
- **FTP software** to deliver pages to the web server (see **Annex F**);
- **email software** to receive and reply to website-generated email and forms;
- **site management tools** may be used that provide functions of HTML and text editors, FTP software, link management tools and web statistics packages.

Static data publishing may be the most effective way to publish online simply, but for larger websites or complex data sets **dynamic data publishing** should be considered. The choice is a matter for departmental web teams.

2.6.4 Production timescales and publishing overheads

The processes of publishing documents electronically should be well designed and regularly checked for efficiency.

Publishing data on the website should save on the printing, distribution and storing of printed documents and the wastage caused by overestimated print runs. Users now have the ability to print a selected document or a section of a document at their leisure.

In a well-designed parallel print and web-publishing operation, it should only be necessary to maintain one master copy of a document.   There should be processes in place to ensure that as soon as a changed version is approved, all publication formats can be generated quickly and near simultaneously.

It is important that an electronic master copy is kept of each document published on the website. This makes the creation of new versions in other formats potentially easier. It also provides an archive version for historical purposes.

Note that with web publication, some production costs, such as the cost of paper, toner/ink and production time, may be transferred to the user, who will print out information as needed.

2.6.5 Maintenance

It is important that all documents contained within the website are maintained at all times. Information must be up to date and error free.

Each document should adhere to the site template and all data should be formatted in a consistent way.

A 'What's New' section should be included within the website so that users have a constant and familiar route to new and updated information.

Particular care should be paid to the use of Cascading Style Sheets, which are used to control the formatting of the website.

Finally, the website strategy should be working towards a technical solution and operational procedures that will allow designated content owners outside of the web team to amend and update their own information on already published pages. This will reduce the workload on the web team and the procedures should be designed to help the site keep up to date and accurate.

2.6.6 Text

Much of the information on your website will be presented to the user in text form. It is therefore important that all text is laid out well, is scannable and clearly legible.

- Core information must be provided in plain text or HTML formats.
- Text must be displayed in a contrasting colour to the background colour used.
- Text colours must not be relied upon because users can select their own colours in which the text will be displayed.
- Moving and scrolling text should be avoided. If this is unavoidable then the user must be able to freeze it (for example by positioning their pointing device over it). This does not apply to words that are presented in a graphics format. The HTML marquee and blink elements should be avoided
- All text formatting should be carried out using Cascading Style Sheets (CSS).

For guidance on text communication issues see **section 1.5.1** Focussing on User Needs: Marketplace.

2.6.6.1 Fonts

HTML4.01 recommends that all font formatting should now be effected with CSS. This method potentially centralises and provides more control over the formatting of text. However, it must always be remembered that some browsers still do not support CSS.

A page must always be legible even if CSS markup is disabled.

- Use of the HTML font element is now depreciated in favour of formatting using CSS.
- Specifically, therefore, the font element size attribute should not be used as the way of controlling the size of text.
- Only commonly available fonts should be specified with CSS, eg Arial, Helvetica, Times New Roman. The appropriate generic font family should be included at the end of CSS font specifications as recommended in the W3C CSS specification to cater for the event that the user does not have any of the named font families installed on their computer. The following table gives examples of the fonts that are typically installed on two popular operating systems.

Typeface variation	Popular Windows fonts	Popular Macintosh fonts
Sans-serif	Arial, Verdana*, Trebuchet MS*	Helvetica, Verdana*, Trebuchet MS*
Serif	Times New Roman, Georgia*	Times, Century Schoolbook, Palatino, Garamond
Monospaced (fixed width)	Courier New, Andale Mono*	Courier, Andale Mono*
Images, sorts and icons	Wingdings, Webdings	Zapf Dingbats, Webdings

* denotes a font designed for screen use and that is typically installed as a part of the MS Internet Explorer browser package.

- Font size within the CSS should not be hard coded in, for example, pixels or points. Instead relative units such as ems or percentages should be specified. W3C WAI agree with the use of ems/percentrages
- Sans serif fonts are recommended for body text.
- ALL CAPITALS should not be used.
- Avoid the overuse of italics which can be difficult to read on screens.
- Underlined text should be avoided so as not to cause confusion with hyperlinks. Consider the use of boldface in its place.
- The font colour should be in contrast to the background colour, to aid readability (see **section 2.4.5.2** and **section 2.83**).
- Ensure that your chosen fonts and sizes can be overridden by the viewer's browser settings (see **Annex G** Changing browser fonts and colours).

2.6.6.2 Link management

Government websites should not contain broken hyperlinks.

'Under construction' is a term often employed in websites when an area has not been finished. This can be annoying for users and should not be used on a government website. If a section is not completed it should not be on your site.

All links on the website should go to the expected document. It would be very disorientating for the user to expect one thing and then be given another. This is simple on a small site but rather more difficult on a large one, particularly when there are many different groups of people involved in putting data on the website.

All links that go to organisations outside of the UK government should be clearly labelled as such, stating that the content and technical availability of the linked pages will not be under the control of the website from which the link is made. See **section 1.10** Specimen terms and conditions.

All links to external websites should be tested at regular intervals. As the content at the target of such links is outside the Web manager's control it could be moved or deleted at any time. Users are just as likely to blame the organisation that links to the material, as they are the organisation that has moved the data.

When a department links to an external website efforts should be made to ensure that the targeted website adds a reciprocal link back.

2.6.6.3 Standard of language

People rarely read pages presented on the web word-for-word. They will tend to scan through a page and select individual words and sentences. For this reason and to assist those with reading difficulties and those using assistive technology, it is very important that the information contained in a document is presented correctly. The correct use of bullet points, headings and summary paragraphs throughout a publication will ensure that the maximum number of readers will gain the information you wish to impart.

- Use plain language.
- Minimise punctuation, and avoid using colons and semicolons.
- Always avoid using too many words and overly long words.
- Keep text concise and simple.
- Always include summaries for documents.
- Use short sentences.
- Use single idea sentences.
- Use lists and bullet points whenever possible.
- Include the main idea in the first sentence of the paragraph. Use following sentences to expand the main point.
- Use concepts and terminology consistently throughout the document and website.

It should also be remembered that standards of English that are suitable for printed documents might not necessarily be suitable for the web. Text should be simpler and easier to digest, ensuring that every user can fully understand the information that is being presented.

IMPORTANT

Use a spellchecker as a first defence against mistakes. All documents to be published should also be proof-read by independent staff to ensure that the correct grammar and spelling are used.

It is also good practice to write to a consistent house style that covers the use of upper and lower case lettering, use and definition of abbreviations, etc.

SCREEN FONT

Reading a screen can be difficult for some users under some circumstances and the choice of typeface can make a significant difference to screen legibility.

To improve the legibility of type on screens, the Tiresias Consortium under the direction of the Royal National Institute of the Blind has designed Tiresias PCfont.

http://www.tiresias.org/fonts/about_pc.htm

2.7 Use of other languages

It is important that web managers publish information in all appropriate languages.

This not only ensures that the information is accessible to the widest possible audience but also that members of the public are not being prevented from using the information because of the community from which they originate.

Use each checklist to ensure that your web pages comply with these guidelines

2.7.1 Checklist and summary   *Recommended*

Checklist	<ul><li>Use a language anchor page</li><li>Use the META CHARSET element</li><li>If the page cannot be made to display reliably in HTML then use PDF</li><li>Place the language code in the URI.</li><li>Text should not be presented in graphic format, for example, as GIFs</li></ul>
Summary	Most web content is written in English yet we have a large number of users who read and speak English as a second or third language or indeed not at all. For services provided to the public in Wales, and with due regard to the Welsh Language Act, the Welsh and English languages must be treated on a basis of equality. In Wales, bilingual information is provided to the public as a matter of course. See **section 1.10.6** Welsh Language Act.

2.7.2 Using other languages

Technology is developing to deliver web resources in many written forms, and in audio, and content authors and web managers need to be aware of these.

A number of points should be borne in mind:

- *Flexible design*. All languages are not created equal. A paragraph in English may be 30 per cent longer in German and 40 per cent long in Hindi. Chinese is read from top to bottom, Urdu and Arabic are read from right to left.
- *Know your audience*. There are significant differences between UK English and American English. The same is true in other languages.
- *Identify your audience*. Generally web communities are identified by language not by the subject matter.

2.7.3 Language anchor pages

If your website contains material in any minority languages or in any European Union languages it is essential to provide an index (anchor) page for each language.

Users reading non-English language pages will not be able to find a menu in their language from your home page. The anchor page can be bookmarked so that these users can go direct to a menu in their own language.

This anchor page will form a key element in any future system of portals for users following versions in languages other than English.

Key points to remember:

- A bilingual anchor page (in effect a table of contents) should index all your translated documents and hyperlink directly to each in the translated language and in English.
- It is important that when text cannot be published in standard HTML formats that it be made available as a PDF version.
- The use of text in graphics formats should be avoided. This would not be available if the browser had the graphics was turned off, the exception for graphics being text navigation buttons in scripts, such as Bengali. The 'alt' attribute should be in English (in Welsh on Welsh language pages) and identify the language being used.
- The notification and prompt for obtaining the Adobe Acrobat Reader should also be included on this page and when appropriate in both English and the translated language.
- Navigation on these pages should be in both English and the translated language.
- Consider the value of adding a language code into the file name (URL), eg, /webguidelines/fr-index.htm (index to French language anchor page) or /webguidlelines/urdu-index.htm (index to Urdu language anchor page).

2.7.3.1 Example of a bilingual prompt to download a PDF reader – instruction in English and Welsh

In English:
The following document is available in portable document format for downloading. The Adobe Acrobat Reader® can be freely <bring in URL> downloaded.

Viewers with visual difficulties may find it useful to investigate services provided to improve the accessibility of Acrobat documents – *http://access.adobe.com*

In Welsh:
Mae'r canlynol ar gael ar ffurf Adobe Acrobat. Mae'n bosib llwytho Adobe ® Acrobat *http://access.adobe.com* yma. Efallai y bydd o ddefnydd I ddarllenwyr a chanddynt nam ar y golwg I ymchwillo I'r gwasanaethau sy'n gwneud dogfennau Acrobat yn fwy hygyrch.

2.7.3.2 Examples of a bilingual navigation – in English and Welsh

Previous/Blaenorol | Contents/Cynnwys | Next/Nesaf

Return to: National Assembly for Wales
Yn Ôl i : *Tudalen Gartref Cynulliad Cenedlaethol Cymru*

2.7.3.3   Example of a bilingual anchor page – Bengali and English

Example of a bilingual anchor page (to be built in HTML with supporting graphics and saved as bengali-index.htm)

Page title:	**Bengali**
Document *Text link*	Disability Relief Scheme (a 350kb PDF file) <hyperlink to the Bengali language version>
Graphic link	ডিসএ্যাবিলিটি রিলিফ স্কীম <This image file is to hyperlink to the Bengali language version, ALT attribute "Disability Relief Scheme – in Bengali">
PDF reader prompt	The Bengali language documents accessed from this page are in portable document format for downloading. The Adobe Acrobat Reader® can be freely <bring in URI> downloaded.

2.7.4   HTML Meta Charset element

To facilitate the viewing of multilingual web content Web managers should ensure that the meta HTTP content-type charset attribute is used. This element tells the client's browser what character set to use when rendering the content. For example:

```
<meta http-equiv="Content-Type" content="text/html; charset=iso-
8859-1">
```

Including this element in the header of an HTML page tells the browser that the content was encoded with the ISO 8859-1 (Latin, western European) character set.

```
<meta http-equiv="content-type" content="text/html;
charset=Windows-1251">
```

Including this element in the header of an HTML page tells the browser that the content was encoded with the Windows-1252 (Western) code page that is a superset of the ISO 8859-1 character set.

2.7.5   BSI and other presentational requirements

A British Standard on translation details a number of points that Web managers will find valuable in content management.

The front cover (in the web case, your **homepage**) should contain:

- The title, in the language into which the translation has been made
- The title of the original in English
- Any series title should appear in the language into which the translation has been made and in English

2.7.5.1 Transliteration

Names of organisations or particular initiatives should be translated, or transliterated, at their first occurrence. On pages in languages other then English or Welsh the translation or, where necessary, the transliteration, should appear in the text, followed by the English version in brackets.

On pages in languages other than English or Welsh, the names of organisations, particular initiatives or programmes known by their initials should be treated similarly, with the English initially appearing in brackets. Subsequent references should consist of the translated or transliterated initials only.

2.7.5.2 Addresses

Apart from on pages in Welsh, or bilingual English and Welsh pages, addresses should not be translated, but a brief description of each organisation should appear before its address, if appropriate. In all language versions other than the English, the terms telephone, fax and email should be translated but the numbers and email address should remain as in English (or Welsh) no matter what the language. URIs must remain in English or Welsh.

2.7.5.3 Numbers

All numbers should remain in English (on Welsh language pages, in Welsh, or on bilingual English and Welsh pages, in both languages), together with the units to which they refer, provided these are commonly used units. For example, units of currency.

2.7.5.4 Emphases and hierarchy of headings

All emphases in the English (or Welsh) version, eg, bold should, where possible, be preserved in the translation, as must the hierarchy of headings.

2.7.5.5 Logos

No elements of departmental logos should be translated without approval of the management of the department/agency corporate identity.

2.7.5.6 Copyright and other legal notices

These should appear in both English (and for websites servicing the public in Wales, in Welsh) and in the translated language.

2.7.6 Character sets

When a web page is delivered to your browser, each character pattern (glyph) that is to be rendered is encoded as a numerical value (codepoint). The set of correspondences between codepoints and the glyphs is usually referred to as a **character set** or **code page**. Different languages use different sets of glyphs (scripts) and consequently use different character sets to encode them.

Some web browsers, notably Microsoft Internet Explorer, are able to display a wide range of scripts and their associated writing systems. This capability to display web content in other scripts is independent of the language version of either the browser or the underlying operating system.

In Internet Explorer, character sets are grouped into 'language packs' as follows:

- **ISO Latin-1** – English (American and international), Danish, Dutch, Finnish, French, German, Italian, Norwegian, Portuguese, Spanish and Swedish. This Latin script character set consists of 26 base letter characters (A to Z) in upper and lower case with ten numerals (0 to 9). In addition several languages use ligatures and accent marks. And there are the punctuation marks.
- **ISO Latin-2** – includes Albanian, Belarussian, Croatian, Czech, Greek, Hungarian, Polish, Romanian, Russian, Turkish, Slovak, Slovenian, with Russian, Bulgarian, Serbian being written in Cyrillic script. Greek is rendered in the Greek script.
- **Arabic.**
- **Hebrew.**
- **Chinese Simplified** as written in the People's Republic and in Singapore
- **Chinese Traditional** as written in Hong Kong and Taiwan.
- **Japanese.**
- **Korean.**
- **Indian sub-continent languages** – Bengali, Gujerati, Hindi and Urdu are not readily available in character sets.

2.7.7   Examples

Language	Example of space requirements	Remarks, character set - language code
Arabic	Uses large fonts	"ar"
Bengali	25% more space	Spoken form is Sylheti "bn"
Chinese	Same space as English	Character set Traditional Chinese (Hong Kong). Spoken forms, eg, Cantonese, Mandarin Character set Simplified Chinese (Singapore) "zh"
Farsi	Uses large fonts similar to Arabic	Used in Iran "fa"
Greek	25% more space	Character set Latin 2 "el"
Gujerati	25% more space	"gu"
Hindi	25% more space	Character set Latin 2 "hi"
Turkish	25% more space	"tr"
Urdu	Same space as English	Runs from right to left and from back to front. Urdu typescript does not lend itself to underlining. "ur"
Vietnamese	25% more space	"vi"
Welsh	Slightly more space than English	Character set Latin 1 <lang="cy">

ISO 639-1 Code for the representation of the names of languages
http://www.oasis-open.org/iso639a.html

Codes for the Representation of Names of Languages (Registration Authority)
http://lcweb.loc.gov/standards/iso639-2/langhome.html

2.7.8   Unicode – the future

The complexity associated with handling multiple character sets is intended to be rationalised by the ISO 10646 (Unicode) standard. The universal adoption of Unicode will make dealing with multilingual web content and the Unicode standard has been adopted by the W3C.

Refer to **Section 1.10** for Welsh Language Act
Refer to **Section 4.4** for Portable Document Format

2.7.9   Example of an other languages anchor page used by DWP

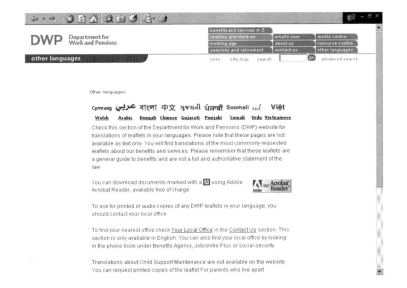

2.8 Web graphics

Images within a website can be used to lend structure and colour; they can also be used for decorative and illustrative purposes. These images can be saved in a number of formats, each of which has its own specific uses.

The use of graphics should be carefully planned and be consistent throughout the site. Their use should be minimal to increase their effectiveness and reduce potential rendering delays for users.

Use each checklist to ensure that your web pages comply with these guidelines

2.8.1 Checklist and summary	Core guidance
Checklist	❑ Website line art and screen furniture elements should normally be stored in GIF format ❑ Photographic images should normally be stored in JPG format ❑ The choice of GIF vs JPEG format is not an exact science and neither is the selection of the various palette and compression options available within each respective format. There is usually a trade-off between the visual quality of an image and its file size. Some experimentation with file format, palette (GIF) and compression level (JPEG) may be necessary in order to determine the optimal visual appearance and file size combination for each graphic ❑ Images that convey data or link to other areas should have an 'alt' attribute and value ❑ An 'alt' reference should be no longer than 100 characters ❑ Images should not be used to convey textual information ❑ All HTML image elements should have values specified for the width and height attributes ❑ Complex images conveying detailed information should be linked to a text description ❑ There should be only one copy of common graphics, such as an organisation's logos, stored in a central images directory ❑ Single images should not be larger than 30kb ❑ Large images should be represented by small thumbnail images, hyperlinked to the full-size image ❑ Animated images should cycle no more than four times ❑ Anti-aliasing should not be used when small text is used in an image
Summary	Images are an integral part of publishing data on the web. Although they are useful and decorative they should be managed properly to ensure that they do not hinder the user's access to information.

2.8.2 Sensible use of graphics

It is important to remember that users are visiting your website to gain information, not to be stunned by the visual imagery that has been included within each section. Organisations will not be thanked for slowing down the loading time of any document just because its display template is rich in graphics.

Sensible use of images will establish an organisation's identity on the web and will help illustrate and clarify sections in a publication. All other images may just be decoration. There is nothing intrinsically wrong with this as long as it is minimal and controlled. A small image can be 3kb in size, equivalent to over 500 words of text in an HTML file.

2.8.3 Web-safe colours

It is important to remember that not every user of the Internet has access to a computer that has the most recent and advanced graphics card installed. What may look colourful and well defined to you may be quite incomprehensible to other users.

The web-safe colour palette should be used for text, hyperlinks and background colours. GIF art should, where possible, be generated using the web-safe palette, explained below.

There must always be a clear contrast between background colours and font colours. Black text on a cream or white-coloured background will always work.

There are two ways an author can specify colour within a page, whether it is for a background, text or use in Cascading Style Sheets: by name or by hexadecimal number.

Colours are preferably specified using their hexadecimal (number base 16) RGB values. A colour is specified by the intensity of the three primary colours red, green, blue each indicated with two hexadecimal digits representing eight binary digits. Each hexadecimal digit can have a value in the range 1 to 16 represented by the numbers 0-9 and the letters a-f, 0 being the lowest and f the highest. Each colour value starts with a # symbol and is then followed by six hexadecimal digits. This is an 'additive' colour specification in which the first two digits represent the intensity of the red component in the final mixed colour, the second two the green and the last two the blue.

This 24bit-colour specification scheme provides a palette of about 64 million colours to choose from, ie, the number 2 raised to the power of 64. However, it is recommended that Web pages should be constructed using only the colours taken from the more restricted palette available on computers fitted with graphics adapters capable of displaying only 256 colours. There is a further technical restriction on many 256 colour computers that result in only 216 rendering properly on-screen. Because these216 colours are common across a wide range of computer systems, they are said to comprise the 'web-safe' palette.

For example, a Web author wishing the background of a page to be white should specify the following CSS property for the page body element:

```
body {background-color: #ffffff}
```

White is generated by the addition of the full intensity of each of red, green and blue, so each of the three two-digit values are set to the maximum value. Using zero intensity for all three primary colours produces black:

```
body {background-color: #000000}
```

The 216 colours of the web safe palette are generated when the value for each of the three primary colour components is restricted to one of the values: 00, 33, 66, 99, AA, CC, FF. So, for example #CC33AA is a web-safe colour, but #6A143B is not.

> **IMPORTANT**
> If a user has hardware that does not have a video card capable of rendering the web-safe colour palette, then the colour in rendered pages may be degraded.
> Where possible test your web pages for legibility and usability on a machine with a 16-colour graphics card.

Web Colour Reference
http://www.webreference.com/html/reference/color//websafe.html#HEAD-3

2.8.4 Text alternatives to graphics

Not all web browsers can display images, and some users, particularly the visually impaired, cannot make use of images even if their browser displays them. It is therefore imperative to ensure that all images within a website have an alternative text message describing the image contents.

The 'alt' attribute should be added to the HTML `img` element, followed by a descriptive value for the image. An example of this is:

```
<img src="logo.gif" alt="logo:Cata logo">
```

For this example a graphic browser would display the logo on the page, a screen reader would just read out the 'organisational logo' message and a non-graphic browser would display 'organisational logo' on screen.

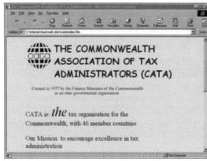

With images

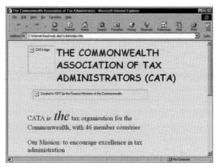

Without images

> **IMPORTANT**
>
> *It may not always be necessary to add text alternatives when solely decorative images are used on a web page. Each 'alt' message will be read by a screen reader so unnecessary messages could actually hinder the use of a page. Use alt=" " see* **section 2.4.5.6**.

2.8.5 Image dimensions

It is important to always specify the dimensions for a graphic. This gives the browser a helping hand in rendering the page with as few screen redraws as possible. The 'width' and 'height' attributes must be specified in pixel values. For example:

```
<img src="logo.gif" alt="logo:department logo" width="154"
height="35">
```

2.8.6 Image alignment

Images can be aligned to the left, centre or right of a page as in this example:

```
<img src="logo.gif" alt="logo:department logo" width="154"
height="35" style="float:right">
```

These are referred to as 'floating images'. Use of this attribute will allow text to flow around the image rather than having the image sit in isolation within a page.

2.8.7 Image spacing

Images can be positioned on a page by using designated spatial margins for each image. The value for each attribute used must be specified only in pixels. For example:

```
<img src="logo.gif" alt="logo:department logo" width="154"
height="35"  style="border-width: 0px; margin: 25px 20px 25px
20px">
```

This example instructs the browser to display the image:

- Border-width indicates the size of the border in pixels to place around the image;
- The margin specification indicates how much empty space in pixels to allow on each edge the image starting from the top edge and moving clockwise around the image;

This is a far better way of controlling space around images than using spacer graphics. These graphics tend to be transparent and only exist on a page to space out other elements. They are neither efficient for loading documents nor user friendly, particularly when using screen readers or when automatic image loading is turned off in a browser.

2.8.8 Imagemaps

Client-side imagemaps, introduced by Netscape in 1996, do not require any interaction between the page and the originator's website once the page has been loaded to the user's browser. They can be used offline because all the co-ordinates of the hot spots are contained within the HTML page.

When an imagemap is used, a text alternative should be supplied alongside the graphic in question. This text must be formatted using CSS and must be legible against the page's background colour.

HTML authors should be aware that some early browsers do not support client-side imagemaps and may wish to include server-side imagemaps as well to cater for them. Browsers that can use client-side imagemaps will use them in preference to server-side ones if both are provided.

2.8.9 Graphic navigation

When graphical buttons are used for navigating a website, the site must always be as easy to use when these graphics cannot be viewed. There must always be a descriptive value to the 'alt' attribute that is given to every navigationally important graphic.

> **IMPORTANT**
>
> *Turn off the automatic graphics download in your browser to give an indication of what your page is like when you cannot see the graphic buttons.*
>
> *Is it still easily usable?*

When graphic buttons are used, values must be specified for both the 'width' and 'height' attributes within the image element. This helps the browser to render the page with the minimum number of screen redraws.

It is important that graphic navigation buttons are not too large. This will help to ensure that the largest area possible is given over to displaying the document whilst also ensuring that the sizes of the graphic file are kept small.

2.8.10 Images containing text

Web managers should always try to avoid using images to convey textual messages. It is far easier to use HTML text and CSS to format the text in a number of ways. If text is used it is important to ensure that it is always legible and that the font colour contrasts with the background colours.

If the text is small in size it may well be better to disable the anti-aliasing feature that most image manipulation software uses when rendering text. This feature adds a slight blurring to the text so that it looks softer and is easier on the eye. This is fine with large fonts, but with very small text this blurring actually makes the information more difficult to read. Without this feature the text will look 'blocky' but will always be legible.

Navigational button	Navigational button
Anti-aliased text graphic	Non anti-aliased text graphic

2.8.11 Image file sizes

The smaller the file size of an image the quicker it can be loaded to a user's browser. The usability of a page will be degraded if users are forced to wait unnecessarily long times for decorative images to load.

- Keep all web images as small as possible.
- Each image should be no larger than 30kb.
- Large images should be shown by using a thumbnail – a small version of the image that then hyperlinks through to the full-size version.

2.8.12 Table alternatives to graphics

Large, complex images such as pie charts and bar charts cannot reasonably be described using the 'alt' attribute. When these are used the image should hyperlink through to an HTML page with the data given in tabular format. This ensures that the data is accessible to the widest possible audience.

2.8.13 Image directories

Placing all of a website's images within one location in the website file structure will make the management and subsequent HTML linking easier for a Web manager. Images distributed all over a site may be easier at the very beginning but can be confusing and make locating specific images difficult at a later date.

It is recommended that consideration should be given to where images will be stored in the websites's directory (folder) hierarchy at the same time as the overall hierarchy is planned. Commonly used schemes include having a sub-directory for images within each document directory, or alternatively, replicating the document directory name and structure scheme from the website root. The former scheme generates image URL paths of the form /foldera/sub-folders/images/ whilst the latter scheme results in image URL paths of the form /images/folders/sub-folderb/.

Some images will be used only once on a site; others, such as logos and graphical navigation elements, will be reused on multiple occasions. A single copy of each reused image is easier to manage, particularly when it needs to be replaced. One change is all that would be needed to effect the change through the entire website. Be cautious, when replacing an image. The replacement should be of identical dimensions to the one it is replacing otherwise the new image will appear distorted to the size on the old image.

2.8.14 Graphic formats

An HTML file stored on a web server does not actually contain the images that appear on the page. HTML img elements in the file instruct graphical browsers to fetch the image resource from the URL specified in the src attribute.

Images that are used several times in a page are only fetched once from the web server. An image used on one page that a user views and that is also used on subsequent pages will likely be retrieved from the browser's memory or disk cache rather than from the web server. A website that reuses graphical elements within pages and across multiple pages will therefore render more efficiently than one that uses a lot of unique images.

Web site imagescan be saved in a variety of formats with the two popular formats currently being Graphics Interchange Format (GIF) and Joint Photographic Experts Group (JPEG) format. Generally GIFs are used for monochrome or colour line art and JPEGs are used for photographs and other continuous tone images. These formats have different features and strengths described below.

File compression
It is important to reduce the size of graphics files. Graphics files tend to be large compared with HTML files and large files demand long loading times. Larger dimensions and colour palettes increase the file sizes. File compression can significantly reduce a file size. The two main categories of compression are **lossy** and **lossless**. Formats that use lossy compression lose some data during compression, degrading image quality, but can achieve high compression ratios. Formats that use lossless compression preserves images fidelity but does not achieve high compression ratios.

Colour information in graphics formats
'Bitmap' format files such as GIF and JPEG store the colour information for each bit or pixel or 'dot' of the image. Uncompressed file sizes increase in proportion to the amount of colour information stored. The amount of colour stored for each pixel is often referred to as an image's 'color depth'.

2.8.14.1 Graphic Interchange Format (GIF)

GIF was the first compressed image format that became widely available and remains one of the most popular used for web graphics. Unisys owns the copyright for the GIF format. Images in this format can be used freely by organisations on the web but image manipulation software manufacturers have to pay a licence fee.

GIF has two standard subformats – 87a and 89a. Both subformats support interlacing, which allows browser to decompress and display alternating pixel rows of an image, instead of decompressing and displaying the image line-by-line. The effect is that the image renders rapidly, apparently at low resolution, with the fine detail being progressively filled in.
The GIF format uses lossless file compression. While this results in high-quality image reproduction, it also means that GIF files are larger in size than the same image would be if it were saved in a format using lossy compression.

A GIF is saved as a bitmap, effectively a series of 'dots' each having a particular colour value. This means that the image cannot be blown up to a larger size without losing definition.

Colour palette – GIF files use a predetermined colour palette. Typically an 8-bit (meaning 256 colour) palette is used although only the 216 so-called 'web-safe' colours are actually used in the image. When colours are sent to video cards that are not able to display them they usually display patterns of available colours that are intended to persuade the human brain to perceive the desired colours. This is called 'dithering' and the process can make images appear grainy.

Transparent GIF files – an advantage of the GIF89a subformat is that it allows a single colour in the palette to be nominated and displayed as transparent. This enables the construction of image 'cut-outs' for use in web pages.

Animated GIFs – an animated GIF is a set of GIF files concatenated and saved as a single file. Animated GIFs work in a similar fashion to a child's flipbook. Multiple images are shown sequentially to give the appearance of movement. Any animated GIF that is used in a website should:

- add value to a page;
- not loop indefinitely, but be limited to a maximum of four cycles;
- be kept to as small a file size as possible;
- not distract attention from the content of the page.

2.8.14.2 Joint Photographic Experts Group (JPEG) format

JPEG format uses a sophisticated lossy file compression algorithm optimised for photographic images in order to produce smaller files than lossless compression formats, such as GIF. Most software that allows images to be saved in JPEG format allow the user to make a trade-off between the lossiness of the compression and the size of the JPEG file that is created. The sharp edges that are used in line art rarely occur in natural photographs and a great deal of detail can be lost from a photograph without making much discernible difference in its appearance.

As with GIF, JPEG images are stored as bitmaps, which results in a loss of definition if the image is enlarged.

Colour palette – This JPEG is a 24-bit colour format that can support over 16 million colours. However, only users whose computer graphics cards support 24-bit colour will be able to see the full range of colours.

Progressive JPEGs – The JPEG format, like GIF, supports interlacing. However, a new JPEG format called ProJPEG (Progressive JPEGs) improves on interlacing by presenting images in stages. The first stage is a greyscale image, the next state has a few colours and the last stage is the full colour. The advantage of this is that the user sees a version of the entire image quickly. ProJPEGs file sizes are larger than regular JPEGs.

2.8.14.3 Portable Network Graphic (PNG)

PNG (Portable Network Graphic) format has been developed by the W3C and is intended ultimately to replace GIF files.

PNG works in a very similar way to GIF in that it uses indexed colour, has a lossless compression algorithm and is interlaced. However, it has a number of additional advantages:

- images can have more than one transparent colour specified;
- the degree of transparency can be controlled;
- its compression ratio is superior to that of GIF by 15 – 30 per cent.

As yet, not all web browsers support this image format, which makes it of limited use for general website usage. Any graphic offered in this format must also be offered in a common format such as GIF.

> **W3C PNG standard**
> *http://www.w3.org/Graphics/PNG/*

2.8.15 Examples of graphic formats

The following image file has been saved in the three most common formats used on the Internet.

Their respective file sizes were:

```
GIF    13kb
JPG    7kb
PNG    4kb
```

2.8.16   Use of thumbnail images

A thumbnail image is a small version of a larger image. As small versions of larger images file they function as fast-loading 'sample' images when placed in web. The use of thumbnails gives users the opportunity to decide whether they wish to see the full-size version of images.

Each individual thumbnail image is linked to its corresponding larger image. A user can view the detail of the larger image by clicking on the thumbnail and waiting for the larger file to load.

There are two ways to link thumbnail images to their larger images:

- Create a direct link to the image file. This displays the image in the upper left of the browser window, and you have no control over the appearance of the background behind the image.   Users have to use the browser's back button in order to return to the original thumbnail page.
- Create a separate HTML document for each large image, this gives you more control over how the image is displayed on the page and enables you to employ your established page navigation system to return to the original thumbnail page.

2.8.17   Scalable Vector Graphics (SVG)

See **section 5.4.4** Extensible Mark-up Language (XML) for **Scalable Vector Graphics (SVG)**.

3.1 File storage and servers

When an organisation's website is planned, the basic levels of file storage and naming conventions have to be considered alongside the design and navigational elements.

Planning for the long-term from the outset will ensure that the file organisation and naming scheme does not hinder the development and expansion of a site and will help authors and users alike.

Whatever decisions are made, full documentation of the site structure, colours, standards of document construction, templates and reasoned arguments for these preferences should be prepared.

Use each checklist to ensure that your web pages comply with these guidelines

3.1.1 Checklist and summary — *Core Guidance*

Checklist	❏ All file names should generally be saved in lower case
	❏ File names should not include spaces
	❏ If file names are to be split, it is generally recommended that the hyphen character (-) rather than the underscore (_) should be used . There should be no other form of punctuation in a manually generated URL file path
	❏ File names should be kept short but should also be descriptive
	❏ A standard should be set for the HTML file extension, which once decided on, should, be adhered to (ie html or htm)
	❏ The site's HTML homepage should be no larger than 40kb in total
	❏ Subsequent HTML pages should be no larger than 120kb in total
Summary	Web managers need to be aware of the different operating systems used for storing and serving information on the web. Each of these systems has different requirements for internal linking and file naming.

3.1.2 Introduction

Web managers must be aware of any specific characteristics of the web server on which their website is hosted that may affect the way their website works.

A number of points should be considered in order to ensure that a website could be served from any web server system. These measures will:

- aid portability if an organisation changes its web hosting service;
- simplify and standardise the file naming strategy, and;
- aid recognition of files.

3.1.3 Web servers

Of all the many different operating systems used for web servers the two most widely used are the Microsoft Windows NT and UNIX families.

There are a number of differences between the two technologies that need to be understood.

3.1.3.1 Microsoft Windows NT Server and files

The current generation of the Windows NT Server operating system family (version 5) is named Windows 2000 Server, although there are three different variants of it available. It is most common to use Microsoft's own Internet Information Server (IIS) as the web server software on Windows NT 4 (IIS4) and Windows 2000 (IIS5). However, a range of third-party alternative web server software is also available.

The Microsoft operating systems allow flexibility in file naming conventions. For example, HTML file names can be of mixed case (for example HomePage.htm) and can include spaces (for example
Home Page.htm).

A principle feature of IIS is that administrators can use ASP (Active Server Pages) to dynamically construct and serve web pages and the high degree of integration with many other Microsoft software products.

3.1.3.2 UNIX and files

The name UNIX is not an acronym: it doesn't actually stand for anything (in fact it's an obscure joke about the name of an earlier operating system named Multics). The name refers to a large number of closely related operating systems that have been developed since 1969.

The development history of UNIX is extraordinarily convoluted, but the name UNIX is currently owned by the Open Group to which many companies that supply UNIX-related operating systems belong.

Specific implementations of UNIX typically have their own product name. UNIX operating systems are supplied, for example, by Sun Microsystems (Solaris), Silicon Graphics (IRIX) and IBM (AIX), typically for their larger, more powerful computers.

Linux is a UNIX derivative that is available for free. However, commercial versions of Linux can also be purchased that contain proprietary additional features.

A variety of Web server software products are available for UNIX operating systems. The one that is probably most widely used is Apache, which is developed by the Apache Software Foundation.

At the time of writing, Apache is the most widely used web server software on the Internet – see **http//www.netcraft.net.survey/**.

3.1.3.3 UNIX v Windows NT – filenaming considerations

It is not the role of these guidelines to suggest which operating system would be best for an organisation's web hosting requirements, but certain elements of each operating system's filesystems are quite different.

Case sensitivity
The Windows NT filesystem is for practical purposes case-insensitive but UNIX filesystems are case-sensitive.

A file called HomePage.htm on a Windows NT system will be accessed whether the reference to it is homepage.htm, HOMEPAGE.HTM or HOMepaGE.hTM. All three references in the example would be to the same file.

The same example would work quite differently on a UNIX system. If HomePage.htm is required then HomePage.htm is the reference that must be used. Homepage.htm, HOMEPAGE.HTM and HOMepaGE.hTM would all be different files in UNIX filesystems.

It is for this reason it is recommended that in general *lower case* should be used for an organisation's website filenames regardless of which system they are stored on. All hypertext links and references to images and downloadable files within HTML files should all also be in lower-case. Following this recommendation will help ensure that website content can easily be moved between Windows and UNIX operating systems. This will, for example, facilitate the use of Windows PCs for the development of website content that will be served to the Internet from UNIX systems.

There are add-on components available for popular UNIX web server software that can eliminate the problems for users that can arise from having a case-sensitive web server filesystem that propagates through to case-sensitive file paths in URLs. For example, the Apache web server 'mod_spelling' module and others can be used to effectively produce case-insensitive URL paths in websites served from UNIX systems. When this kind of technology is deployed, the general recommendation in the preceding paragraph may not be appropriate. The important point is to devise a live service, development and test environment combination that results in a website that is easy for visitors to use, straightforward for web managers to develop and test and is resilient to future changes in the underlying system technology. It is recommended that the server administrators should be involved from the earliest stages in the design of a website's operational and management regime.

File name length
Both Windows NT and UNIX allow file names of up to 256 characters so these names can be as descriptive as is required. Filenames should be kept as short as possible but remaining consistent with the recommendation that they should be descriptive.

Spaces
Although both operating systems will allow spaces within the file names, URL file paths containing them are unwieldy in many web browsers. For this reason use the

hyphen or underscore character, eg consultation-2001.htm, to break up file names. No other character should be used for this purpose.

File extensions
In principle, HTML pages can be saved and served with any filename extension. However, the web server must have been configured to serve files whose extensions indicate to it that they contain HTML with an 'internal label' that indicates to the browser that it is receiving an HMTL file and should render it as such. [Technically, the server has to be configured to serve files that have specific filename extensions as MIME type 'text/html'.]

In practice HTML pages are conventionally saved using either the .htm or the .html extension. However, server-side scripting and programming systems often bring their own conventions for filename extensions, for example .php for PHP scripted pages and .asp for Active Server Pages. For web content authors and editors it is important to establish a standard and adhere to it. The use of multiple extensions for a specific type of file will only cause confusion when building hyperlinks within your site.

See **Annex H** for information on access standards and common file extensions.

3.2 Document structure

The web is a very different medium than the printed page. Data on the web is not structured like a printed book, as links enable users to go from one source of data to another in a completely transparent way.

Readers must be able to orientate themselves immediately, know that the data can be trusted and find it easy to understand. Most importantly it must be demonstrable that the document is up-to-date.

For this reason it is important to ensure that the document has been constructed correctly with the user in mind.

Use each checklist to ensure that your web pages comply with these guidelines

3.2.1 Checklist and Summary	Core guidance
Checklist	❑ The document should include the HTML title element
	❑ All HTML pages within the site should contain the department's standard-text navigation bar, which should be consistent throughout the site
	❑ The document must have a meaningful heading at the very top
	❑ A long document which requires scrolling by the user should contain an informative summary of 40/50 words, placed directly beneath the heading
	❑ If the document requires it there should be a hyperlinked downloadable alternative versions (eg, PDF or text) listed beneath the summary description
	❑ If the document to be published is broken into smaller sections for the web, there must be clear navigation to enable users to go forward or backwards within the document
	❑ If the web page is part of a larger document there should be clear identification of this, for example, Page 5 of 12
	❑ Each document should contain 'published' or 'last updated' date clearly shown at the top or bottom of the document
Summary	Because web users can surf using other pages or search facilities as a first step, it cannot be guaranteed that they have come to your document through the front door.
	Therefore each page in your website must have a self-contained identity and be capable of being seen as the first page. It should contain context orientating data for the user, such as:
	• meaningful document headings;
	• informative summaries;
	• page numbering;
	• document dating;
	• consistent navigation to the rest of your site.

3.2.2   Structuring documents for the Web

By using file downloads, plug-ins, graphics and hyperlinks, there is no real limitation on what can be accomplished.

A site looked at as a whole may make complete sense and have a form of logical construction, but this picture can look somewhat different when a single page of that site is looked at out of context. This is the situation that many web users have to contend with on a daily basis.

There are many different ways of getting to a particular piece of information, and going through a website's homepage to get to it is perhaps one of the less likely. Another site may have linked to this information, a newspaper may have given a particular page's URL or a user may have located the information using a search facility.

Any one of these situations may mean that a user is introduced to your site without seeing your introduction. They will be unfamiliar with your navigation system and may not necessarily know who the owner of the information actually is.

The design of each page within a website must therefore be consistent, usable, and immediately identifiable with the information's owner. Ultimately this means that each separate page of information should be seen as an island, existing on its own but identifiably part of a whole.

Each of these ingredients will affect the experience the user has while in your care.

There are examples of each of the following in the **section 8.3.4**.

> *IMPORTANT*
>
> *Do not use splash screens with automatic client-side redirection as an introduction to your site or to a section of your site. Some browsers still do not support this HTML feature and will therefore not automatically redirect. This just adds another click to a user's journey through your site.*

3.2.3 File naming

The file name component of a URL will be displayed in the address bar in the user's web browser and will be exposed in the status bar at the bottom of the browser window when the user moves their pointing device onto a link in the document. For this reason it is better to make file names indicative of the document's name or purpose. This will also help with the general housekeeping of the website file structure, as file names should be fairly obvious. For example, section three of the corporate business plan for 2001 is far more meaningful if called 'businessplan01-03.htm' rather than '350165.htm'.

Where file names include dates these should conform to the ISO and W3C standard, that is they should be in yyyy-mm-dd format. This ensures that file names have meaning in the long term and lists of such files will sort in a sensible order.

A number of conventions should be considered when naming your web files, most of which may well be determined by your hosting service:

- An '8.3' file-naming configuration may be required (eight digits for the file name, a full point and then the required extension).
- File names should be in lower case, lessening the likelihood of broken links or images as pages are moved from one system to another because, for example, Linux file systems are case sensitive but Windows NT's is not.
- There should be no spaces in file names.
- Where the file name is split, use the hyphen (-) character, and avoid use of the underscore (_). It is easier to read corp-plan.htm than corp_plan.htm.
- Other forms of punctuation and special characters should be avoided.
- File names should be kept short but should also be descriptive.

- The HTML file-type extension (.htm .html, .asp or whatever) should be used consistently throughout the site. Note that the allowable extensions depend upon the web server's file system and the MIME type mappings in the server software. Decisions such as this need to be made in consultation with the server administrator.

3.2.4 File sizes

Large files are time-consuming and expensive to load, particularly for clients with slow modems. Large homepages have the added disadvantage that the user cannot choose a more economical means of accessing the site.

Different types of web page require different file size restrictions, thus:

- Homepage total file sizes should not exceed 40kB.
- Standard, informational page total file sizes should not exceed 120kB.
- Special pages (such as reports, statistical data, etc, where it is advantageous for the user to be able to download the file in one transaction) total file sizes should not exceed 300kB.

In all cases, if the file size exceeds our recommended maximum, the user should be warned. Good internal navigation within a larger publication is also required (this is covered in **section 4.1.4**).

File size can be an issue because of the differing levels of formatting data contained within them. Depending upon the text-to-graphic ratio of a document, either a PDF or RTF file may be considerably smaller or larger than the originating document. Plain-text will always save with the smallest file size as it contains the bare minimum of document structure and no images at all.

Whenever these options are offered they should be listed at the top of the HTML document, directly under the document summary. The file size for each should be shown next to each file to inform the user of potential download time.

If a proprietary format such as PDF or Microsoft Word is used, a link to the reader software download site, using a standard form of words, should be included next to the document.

Subsequent sections of a long document should have a link to these downloadable formats at the very top, as many users may not have been introduced to the document from its homepage.

3.2.5 Sequential structure

A long document, for example an organisation's business plan, may be 80 pages long in its printed format. This document would not transfer satisfactorily to the web as one file - so it is better to break it up into manageable sections, which may well translate into a number of separate HTML files reflecting natural breaks in the content.

As stated earlier in this section, a user visiting your website may not have been introduced to a document from its home page. A link from another site, such as a search engine or another department's website, may have brought them to page 5 of a 10-page document. It must therefore be made obvious from the very start, where they are and how they can access other information within the document.

This can be accomplished by adding section numbering to the top of the page, to illustrate each element of the document in a linear sequence.

- Each section of a publication will be accessible from any other section.
- The contents page of the document can always be accessed.
- A user can choose simply to go to the previous or the next section.

Consider providing a single file downloadable version of large documents, suitable for reading off-line.

3.2.6 Document identification

Any document or section of a document prepared for print will invariably be larger than what can be physically displayed within a web browser's window at any one time. Most users will have monitors with a screen size of 800 pixels by 600 pixels, although many will have smaller screens.

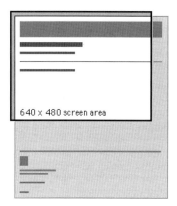

640 x 480 screen area

Documents written in English are read left to right, top to bottom. A document displayed on a browser will always have the information contained in the top left-hand corner on screen when the page is first delivered to the user. It is very important to make best use of this space.

A browser has a scrolling function that enables the user to move up and down a page. At worst, the need to scroll through a document may discourage its use by users with a motor disability who find it difficult to use a mouse.

Each page should include a selection of internal links to different parts of the document that has been loaded. This will enable users to access important information as soon as they receive the page.

Each of the sections contained within the document should include a **Back to top** button and internal hyperlink so that a user can quickly return to the top of the displayed page.

3.2.7 Information to be included in every document

A user should always be informed that each publication contained within the organisation's website is relevant and up-to-date.

This could be made obvious by the use of a document footer within each of the files, whether they be in HTML, PDF, RTF, XLS, CSV or text format.

Your approach could include the following information:

- the organisation's name, so that the user can identify the originators of the

  information;
- the document's date of publishing/date updated or a version number;
- the expiry date of the publication's relevance;
- an email address of the document's owner so that any discrepancies or comments regarding the publication can be directed to the correct area.

3.2.8   Version control of web documents

Making information available on your website is a publishing process and organisations have established procedures for content approval prior to posting. Because of the nature of web publishing some information, for example, press notices, can be produced in a very short time and changes or updates to existing web pages can sometimes be undertaken in a matter of minutes. It is therefore important that users are aware how current the information is that you are publishing.

Every web page should clearly display the date it was first published on your website. And this date should subsequently be updated if you amend the information.

With information that is frequently updated web managers should consider maintaining a version control record.

The simplest record would be to track the published version as an HTML comment note – the HTML mark up which is ignored by browsers but which can be seen by viewing the source code. For example:

```
<!-- version control record of page /annex01.htm -->
<!-- first published 01/02/2001 -->
<!-- updated 21/02/2001, 06/03/2001, 09/08/2001 -->
```

The latest date recorded here should correspond with that displayed via the browser

4.1 HTML markup, other formats and scripting

The development of Web content markup standards continues at a very fast pace. It is for web managers to decide which version of the key markup standards, eg, HTML and CSS, should be employed in the construction of their websites.

Markup standards for government websites

At the time of writing this document, the W3C recommendations are XHTML 1.0 and CSS2. Given the current state of browser developments and that of the software tools typically used to generate and maintain websites, it may be appropriate to adopt XHTML 1.0 with CSS1 or HTML 4.01 with CSS1. It may also be appropriate to adopt the *'transitional'* rather than *'strict'* sub-versions of XHTML 1.0 or HTML 4.01 in order to accommodate browsers that have incomplete or faulty CSS1 implementations.

e-Government Interoperability Framework for information on latest standards
http://www.e-envoy.gov.uk/publications/frameworks_index.htm

The Open Source (previously W3C) 'Tidy' program can be used to convert HTML to XHTML. Tidy and a number of other available applications can also perform a number of useful jobs, such as, cleaning up the 'bulked out' HTML that is produced by a number of proprietary word processing and HTML editing packages.

Currently, HTML tables are frequently used to effect screen layout designs. Where HTML tables are used for this purpose, care should be taken that the resulting pages work properly with assistive technologies, eg, screen readers that are used to make the Web available to impaired users.

When server-side scripting and related 'dynamic publishing' techniques are employed, consideration should be given to developing an implementation capable of serving markup customised for the browser or other client technology with which a user is accessing the site.

When planning websites that are intended to be long-lived, it should be borne in mind that the appropriate versions of the markup languages and the range of versions of client technology used to access the site will almost inevitably change during the site's lifetime. A strategy for dealing with these evolutionary processes should form a part of the website project plan.

Regardless of which versions of the markup languages are adopted, the critical issues are for web managers to keep abreast of developments and to ensure that their website remains accessible to the full range of client technology with which users visit it. Web managers should ensure that their sites 'transform gracefully' when viewed with older client technology and that their site does not become 'broken' when viewed in newly released browsers.

See **section 4.5** and **section 4.6** for specific considerations when using plug-ins, client-side scripting or other client-side active components, also see **section 6.3** HTML tables.

The analysis of webserver logfiles can give a useful insight into the range of browsers that visitors use to access the site. Of course, the absence of a browser from the logs may just indicate that the website is inaccessible to that browser.

See **section 2.4** Building in universal accessibility
See **Annex C** HTML editor applications
See **Annex E** Plug-ins

World Wide Consortium (W3C)
http://www.w3.org

HTML Tidy Library Project
http://tidy.sourceforge.net

Overview of Tidy
http://www.w3c.org/People/Raggett/tidy/

4.2 HTML pages

Creating a website is not just a matter of taking all of an organisation's previously printed publications, turning them into HTML and throwing them online.

Careful thought must be put into the online web publishing medium, which has its own advantages and idiosyncrasies. Only once these basic considerations have been understood will a department be in a position to start implementing a website.

Use each checklist to ensure that your web pages comply with these guidelines

4.2.1 Checklist and summary   *Core Guidance*

Checklist	<ul><li>The site's HTML homepage should be no larger than 40kB in total</li><li>Subsequent HTML pages *should* be no larger than 120kB in total</li><li>The site must use colours for text only from the basic 216 colour *web-safe* palette</li><li>The site should not use background graphics within HTML pages that are confusing or could contribute to page illegibility</li><li>No area of the site should contain messages such as *'under construction'*</li><li>Every hypertext link within the site must work and take the user to the expected document</li><li>It must be clearly indicated if a hypertext link takes the user out of the site's control</li><li>Text must not flash and should be static at all times</li><li>The marquee and blink elements must be avoided</li><li>Each page should use clear, precise language</li><li>There should be no spelling or grammatical errors within any document</li><li>All web pages should be printer friendly</li></ul>
Summary	An overly complex document on paper will not transfer gracefully to a website. There are a number of publishing conditions that are specific to the web. Legibility, clear and concise language, small file sizes, relevant hyperlinking and good use of colours will always add to a document on the web and never detracts.

4.2.2 Browser specification

Web browser applications have been available for a number of years. In that time each of the suppliers such as Microsoft, Netscape and Opera, have made a succession of modifications resulting in a variety of differing version numbers. There are often a number of different systems on which each version can run.

Each of these renders HTML in different ways. A particular browser release may only recognise specific revisions of the HTML and CSS markup languages or they only have partial implementations of the markup standards. Either way, this has resulted in pages rendering and working very differently in different browsers and on different operating system platforms.

This range of available viewing systems and devices has required Web managers and authors to cater for common denominators rather than individual applications or versions of them. This can mean that the latest fashion or gimmick in the web publishing world cannot be used because it can, for example, only be viewed using the latest version of a particular browser. Although some may see this as limiting it is essential to avoid building web pages that will only work with specific browsers, or releases of them.

Departments must always ensure that all of their web presence is accessible by the widest possible audience. No part of an Internet site should be designed specifically for a particular browser. This would disenfranchise users who happen to use other, equally popular applications.

4.2.3 HTML (Hypertext Markup Language)

HTML files are plain-text files containing special codes that give information to the browser about the structure of the file. HTML is rather similar to the typesetting codes used by modern typesetters, in which blocks of text are surrounded with codes that indicate how the text should appear. An HTML file can point to graphics (see below for formats) and can contain pointers to other files (and thus create a hypertext link). HTML files are intended to be viewed with a World Wide Web client program (known as a browser), such as Netscape Navigator or Microsoft Internet Explorer.

The HTML4 and later recommendations have provisions to assist accessibility of documents, such as:

- Better distinction between document presentation and structure.
- Better forms, including the addition of accesskeys.
- Requirement that alternative text accompany images included with the <img> element and image maps included with the area element.
- Support for the abbr and acronym elements.
- Support for the title and lang attributes on all elements.
- A wider range of target media, such as, large type and Braille, for use with style sheets.

A major benefit of HTML is the consistently small file sizes in comparison to other formats such as PDF and word processor files.

4.2.3.1 HTML title element

This should be included in the HTML head element on each page. It is important because it will identify the page if the user decides to bookmark the page.

The title element:

- must be included in each page;
- should be no longer than 60 characters in length; and
- should have a meaningful syntax, describing your organisation and the content of the page, for example, organisation – section – page: `<title>`Department of XXX – frequently asked questions`</title>`.

4.2.3.3 Text navigation

The homepage of an organisation's website should set the *shape and feel* for the design and user functionality. This should in turn be adhered to by all other parts of the site. The most important part of this template's function is to establish a consistent and intuitive navigation policy.

To optimise usability and functionality, the first aspect of a page to appear on a user's browser, after the title, should be a text navigation bar. This will help establish a content for the website and will also be an important guide for those users who find using a standard web browser difficult.

4.2.3.4 Core navigational elements

Each page within an organisation's website should aim not to contain more than **ten** navigational elements in a string. Consider for example:

Skip navigation
This should be the first option available in the text navigation area and should be internally linked to the document's main heading. This enables users with a screen reader to jump past repetitive navigational elements that they may not wish to use on the page.

Homepage
Each individual element of a website should have a direct link back to the website's homepage.

Description of organisation
A user may have entered the organisation's website from a number of different routes, linking from another site or via a search facility. A user should always have the ability to link directly to an introduction explaining the organisation's responsibilities and duties.

Site map
This is an extremely useful option to enable users to orient themselves in an organisation's website structure. A sitemap should not be offered only in a graphic format, a text option should always be provided as well.

What's new?
A user should always be able to link directly to an organisation's 'What's new' listing if the website has one.

Feedback or Comments
This should either link to a structured form asking particular questions or offer a free-

format email submission.

If a free-format text email option is chosen it is best to avoid using 'bucket' email addresses, ie one email address for all enquiries because over time this could become very difficult and time consuming to administer.

Whatever system is implemented, a number of points should be considered:

- Is the comment system regulated and standardised throughout the website?
- Are all requests and comments directed to the appropriate areas within the organisation?
- Do all submissions receive a reply?
- If replies are automated, do users receive a personal follow-up reply at a later date?
- Are all replies to users' communications clearly formatted to the organisation's standards?
- Is there any value to this consultative input from users?
- Are all comment and feedback links clearly labelled as such?

Help
A direct link to an organisation's help section will inform users of any proprietary formats used on the website and how to access any required plug-in software.

Search facility
This should be a site-specific search facility for the organisation's website. This is extremely useful for larger organisations that have large, diverse sites. Small organisations may feel there is no requirement for this facility, although it is always desirable.

Access keys
A user should always be able to link directly to an organisation's 'access key information' and use the UK Government Access Key System. See **section 2.4.4** UK Government accesskeys standard.

Press notices/speeches
This service may already be available for organisations through the Central Office of Information (COI). If not, this facility can be a valuable information resource for users.

4.2.3.5 Graphic navigation

A text navigation area at the very top of the page will not replace graphic navigation; rather it will complement it. The same rules must be adhered to whatever tool is used to help the user navigate round the website.

Whenever graphics are employed as navigational aids it is important that each button or icon carrying a link has a meaningful 'alt' attribute and value (this is covered in **section 2.4.6 .2** Alt attribute for accessibility).

Navigational aids must be consistent and intuitive in their appearance and function. A basic number of major areas within the website should be linked to. These can then be expanded as the user goes deeper into the site.

4.2.4 Internal links

Any document or section of a document will invariably be larger than what can be physically displayed within a web browser's window at any one time. Most users will have monitors with a screen size of 800 pixels by 600 pixels, although many will have smaller screens.

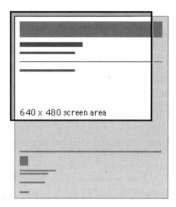

640 x 480 screen area

Documents written in English are read left to right, top to bottom. A document displayed on a browser will always have the information contained in the top left-hand corner on screen when the page is first delivered to the user. It is very important to make best use of this space.

A browser has a scrolling function that enables the user to move up and down a page. At worst, this may discourage use of the document by users with a motor disability who find it difficult to use a mouse.

Each page should include a selection of internal links to different parts of the document that has been loaded. This will enable users to access important information as soon as they receive the page.

Each of the sections contained within the document should include a **Back to top** button that is an internal hyperlink so that a user can quickly return to the top of the displayed page.

Place an identifier at the top of the page, such as

```
<a name="top"></a>
```

Then place this message at the end of each section of the document's report. The hash signifies to the browser that the hyperlink is internal, within the document displayed on the user's browsers.

```
<a href="#top">Top of page</a>
```

Each of these elements reduces the need for a user to scroll unnecessarily.

4.2.4.1 Headings

For documents to be clearly understandable they need to be broken up into manageable, coherent sections. The correct use of the various headings available in HTML can be a very effective tool.

Header tags should be used in order to give a document clear, and concise, structure, ie, <h1> for main heading, <h2> for sub headings, <h3> etc. These can then be given the required styling in the CSS.

Headings should always be in lower case, except for the initial capital of the first word. This will aid readability.

4.2.4.2 Summary information

A document of any length can cover a wide range of information that may not be immediately obvious to the user.

To ensure that the appropriate audience reads a document it is good practice to include an informative summary of the document at the very top, directly under the document heading. The summary should:

- consist of no more than 40 to 50 words;
- cover the important information contained within the document;
- contain as many keywords as practical.

This will help the user identify whether the document is appropriate to them and will also be used by the free text search engines that do not utilise metadata (see **section 1.7** Getting users to your site). These search facilities will take the document title, document heading and possibly the summary as their information resource to be delivered to users.

4.2.5 Uses for metatags

As well as containing data for search engines and electronically cataloguing pages, metatags can be used for a number of other actions, for example, refreshing pages and re-directs.

It should be remembered that W3C advises against these practices because some browsers do not support them and therefore they cannot to be relied upon to work.

The implementation of metadata is covered in **section 1.7.2**.

4.2.5.1 PICS labelling

This style of metatag enables the author of a document to categorise and rate the page to established standards on the Internet. The ratings can be assigned to any content, ie a page, a collection of pages or an entire website.

This area is covered in greater detail in **section 1.8** Platform for Internet Content Selection.

4.2.6 Validation and testing

Validation is important in ensuring platform independence, but alone is not sufficient. Developers should ensure that web pages are not dependent on a certain resolution, colour depth or font size. They should test and evaluate an early working version (a beta test) of a site with representative users.

Well-authored HTML is a highly structured and usable markup language that is backward compatible ensuring that many web browsers can display information contained within a web page and equally providing accessibility at little or no cost. Although the web is often seen as a visual environment, accessible web pages should adjust and remain accessible in any browsing medium and adapt to allow audio and Braille presentations.

Once the page is completed it can be checked for conformity to a specific version of HTML by running it against the World Wide Web Consortium (W3C) automated validator. Cascading Style Sheets should be validated using the W3C automated validator. These validators are available online from the following URLs:

| **HTML validator service** |
| *http://validator.w3.org* |

| **CSS validation service** |
| *http://jigsaw.w3.org/css-validator/* |

Also refer to **section 2.4.7** Validation and testing.

4.3 Non-HTML file formats

Most documents published within on websites are produced in HTML (see section 4.2). This is the primary format used on the web. It is easy to produce and is understood by all web browsers.

There will, however, be many occasions when a document published in HTML is not enough, or is not suitable to the task. Organisations produce publications that are not only large but also complex in structure, using multiple-column text, formulae and many graphics and detailed tabular information. It may be decided that these documents will also need to be published in their print-ready format.

There are a number of other formats that can be used by the web audience – PDF, RTF, plain text, Microsoft Word and CSV.

4.3.1 PDF (Portable Document Format)

PDF files are created using a proprietary application from Adobe. To read these files the user will require the Adobe Acrobat Reader program that is available free of charge on the web.

Adobe Acrobat Readers
http://www.adobe.co.uk/

A file saved in PDF will display text and graphics, in black and white or full colour. While file sizes are sometimes larger than those using HTML and combined graphics files, there are additional benefits when using PDF. These include:

- There is a single file to maintain.
- Files are easy to produce from the majority of word-processing and desktop publishing packages (using the proprietary PDF-creating applications).
- Pages retain almost the exact rendering of printed pages, (which is not possible in HTML).

While PDF offers many conveniences, the format has historically suffered from severe limitations in terms of ease of access by people with disabilities, since it has been difficult to reconstruct the text into another format. Adobe has always had a commitment to working towards overcoming accessibility problems with the format.

Since 1995 Adobe have issued accessibility add-ons for Acrobat, some with more success than others have. This has greatly improved with version 5.

Adobe online accessibility resource
http:// access.adobe.com

A free online PDF to HTML or text conversion service is also available at
http://access.adobe.com/access_info.html

While the Access plug-in is felt to represent an improvement, it is clear that disabled access to PDF documents still falls short of the ideal. Because of these current accessibility limitations, it is recommended that PDF is not used indiscriminately without alternative versions being offered and is not regarded as the 'natural' file format for the web.

See **Section 4.4** Portable Document Format (PDF)

4.3.2 RTF (Rich Text Format)

RTF (Rich Text Format) is a file format that lets you exchange text files between different word processors in different operating systems. For example, you can create a file using Microsoft Word 97 on Windows 95, save it as an RTF file (it will have an '. rtf' three-letter file extension), and send it to someone who uses WordPerfect 6.0 on Windows 3.1 and they will be able to open the file and read it. There are many different revisions of Microsoft's proprietary Rich Text Format and portability of files will depend on what version of RTF is being used.

In some cases, the RTF capability may be built into the word processor. In others, a separate reader or writer may be required.

When saving a file in RTF, the file is processed by an RTF writer that converts the word processor's internal file format to the RTF language. When being read, the control words and symbols are processed by an RTF reader that converts the RTF language into formatting for the work processor that will display the document.

4.3.3 Plain text (.TXT files)

Plain text is the simplest format for storing text files in computers and on the Internet. In a plain-text file, each alphabetic, numeric or special character is represented by a 7-binary digit binary number (a string of seven 0s or 1s). 128 characters are defined (upper and lower case letters, numbers, and a few punctuation and other characters).

A document saved as a text file will be legible but will lose all the formatting apart from line- and paragraph breaks.

4.3.4 Microsoft Word (.DOC)

Microsoft Word (DOC)
Documents can also be saved in Microsoft Word format. A range of free Word readers is available from Microsoft. This is the least desirable format as it is proprietary and it cannot be guaranteed that a reader exists for a particular user's computer.

A number of different versions of Microsoft Word are commonly used. It should therefore be clearly shown on the web page which version has been used to create the document.

> **Microsoft Word reader software**
> *http://www.microsoft.com/Office/000/viewers.htm*

Web Guidelines v2 in Word format
http://www.e-envoy.gov.uk/webguidelines/download/guidelines2001-1.doc

---

4.3.5 Spreadsheet formats

Microsoft Excel (.XLS)/Lotus 1-2-3(.wk1)
Spreadsheet documents can be saved in Microsoft Excel format or as Lotus 1-2-3.
Both are proprietary but are widely importable into spreadsheet and word processors.

Microsoft Excel reader software
http://www.microsoft.com/Office/000/viewers.htm

Comma-Separated Values (.CSV)
This is the simplest way in which tabular information can be saved for importing into
table-orientated applications such as Microsoft Excel or database applications such
as Microsoft Access. A CSV or 'flat file' is a common standard among computers
and is understood by a wide range of software. In CSV a comma separates each
column of data and each row is shown on a separate line.

No special reader is required for this format.

4.3.6 Compressed file formats

.ZIP
ZIP software stores single documents or collections of files and their directory
structure in a lossless compressed format. Zip archive files have the extension - .zip.

The commercial WinZip application can be downloaded for free trial but must be
purchased after a fixed period. When ZIP files are prepared on MacOS systems,
care should be taken to exclude the MacOS resource fork from the Zipped file. After
you download a Zip file, you usually need to use a Zip-capable decompression
program to 'unzip' it.

WinZip software
http://www.winzip.com

4.3.7 File download sizes

File size can be an issue because of the differing levels of formatting data contained
within the various file formats. Depending upon the text-to-graphic ratio of a
document, PDF or RTF files may be considerably smaller or larger than the original
documents. Plain-text will always save with the smallest file size as it contains the
minimum of document structure and no images at all.

Whenever these options are employed they should be listed at the top of the HTML
document, directly under the document summary. The file size for each should be
shown next to each file to give the user an idea of the potential download time.

If a proprietary format such as PDF or Microsoft Word is used, a link to the reader software download site should be included next to the document using a standard form of words.

Subsequent sections of a long document should have a link to these downloadable formats at the very top, as many users may not have been introduced to the document from its homepage.

---

e-Government Interoperability Framework (e-GIF)
http://www.govtalk.gov.uk

How long does it take to download a file?

When linking to a video or audio file, you should indicate to users the format and size. The latter is particularly important as large file sizes and associated long download times can make the delivery of multimedia a difficult feature. Consider listing indicative download times for standard file sizes against different modem connection speeds. However, such guidance should incorporate a caveat because it is difficult to determine the exact amount of time it takes to download any file. There are many factors that can affect download time, such as, modem speeds and network traffic.

File size	Modem speed: 28.8	56	ISDN (128)	Cable/DSL (512)
500 kB	4 mins	2 mins	1 min	0.20 secs
1 MB	7 mins	4 mins	1 min	0.40 secs

4.3.8 Audio files

To be suitable for publishing on your website, recorded sound has to be prepared to professional standards. DAT (Digital AudioTape) and audio CD-ROMs are satisfactory for Web broadcasting. Audio captured via professional quality sound cards from professional standard recordings on analogue compact cassettes will also be satisfactory for Web broadcasting. Amateur quality recordings are unacceptable.

4.3.8.1 TV and cinema commercials

Web managers asked to stream TV or cinema commercials should check that they do not have a BACC viewing 'watershed restriction' or a similar restriction. The web page carrying the direct link to such a commercial should carry a warning, for example:

This television advertisement carries images
that some viewers may find disturbing.

4.4 Portable Document Format (PDF)
(Adobe Acrobat files)

Adobe's Portable Document Format (PDF) is an example of a proprietary format which over time has become an industry standard.

Documents previously held in a variety of different formats can be saved in PostScript form by using one of the appropriate Adobe Acrobat applications. These can then be read by anyone using the free reader software available from Adobe.

Use each checklist to ensure that your web pages comply with these guidelines

4.4.1 Checklist and summary	Core guidance
Checklist	❑ Each PDF file included for download should show the size of the file on the page from which it is downloaded ❑ A general notification that the file is in PDF format should always be shown by the file download ❑ The means to download the free reader should always be shown on the page containing the PDF file ❑ Backwards version compatibility testing should be carried out on all PDF files ❑ Metadata should be completed when saving any PDF file ❑ Security features should be incorporated in each file.
Summary	There is virtually no limit to the types of file that can be converted into Adobe Acrobat files. They have proved popular with authors and users alike. However, information in PDF is generally considered inaccessible to web users whose disabilities make it difficult to interact with computer technologies PDF files retain all of their formatting, type styles and illustrative images. The PDF files use compression, so large documents can be saved using significantly less space than the original files. Nonetheless there can be performance issues with PDFs and those containing graphics should be tested to check their rendering times.

4.4.2 How PDFs work

Documents or any other form of information for a user of the organisation's website should always be produced in HTML as the standard default, but any other formats can be employed to support this.

The Adobe Acrobat software is proprietary but has also become the standard tool for saving complicated and graphically rich documents in a compressed, platform-neutral format.

Producing PDF files is now a simple process. The software to make PDFs can be installed in a matter of minutes and works with most office productivity software. Once installed, it will even offer new menu options within other applications, such as Microsoft Word.

A PDF file is created in a broadly similar way to sending a document to an office PostScript printer. The PC creates a Postscript file, but instead of sending it directly to the printer, the Acrobat application intercepts it and saves it as a PDF document.

This file retains all the formatting, images and colour whilst also compressing the embedded images usually making the PDF smaller than the original file. The Adobe Distiller application allows the user to specify the degree of compression that is applied to images.

It is recommended that a PDF document be saved at no more than 300 dpi. Specifying higher resolutions, for example, 600 dpi produces large file sizes and does not improve on-screen resolution or indeed most printouts.

The Acrobat Reader software is available for the most popular operating systems and is free. The Reader software works as a plug-in to modern browsers or as a stand-alone application.

IMPORTANT

Viewers with visual difficulties may find it useful to investigate components that improve the accessibility of Acrobat documents at:

http://access.adobe.com

One example of a government organisation that has used PDF to good effect, is the Office for Standards in Education (OFSTED). Each of the school reports for state schools is available free of charge on the Web. With a planned workflow process and a dedicated IT system reports can be made available with minimum fuss. A piece of information that could possibly have taken weeks to get hold of before can now be accessed in a matter of minutes.

OFSTED website
http://www.ofsted.gov.uk

These guidelines are also available online in PDF format. They can be downloaded from the following URL.

Guidelines for UK Government Websites in PDF
http://www.e-envoy.gov.uk/webguidelines.htm

When PDF files are created care should be taken to ensure that the document is always legible. It is not enough for printers to take a paper publication and save it in PDF format. The following should all be noted:

- Care must be taken to crop pages correctly to the appropriate paper size.

- Subject to font licensing considerations any custom fonts should be embedded in the PDF file, as failure to do so will affect the way the document is presented to the user.
- Avoid the use of dark coloured backgrounds to text.
- Where possible, save the PDF in a format that is compatible with Acrobat Reader 3.
- Text and images within the document should be compressed as much as possible. The smaller it is the easier it will be for the user to load.
- A PDF document can be searched and indexed and it can be linked in a manner similar to an HTML document.
- Web hyperlinks can be placed within PDF pages.

4.4.3 Versions of Adobe Acrobat

PDF has been used on the web for many years, and this longevity has established it as an industry standard. Unfortunately, this has also resulted in some usability issues, as there are now a number of different versions of Acrobat creation and reading tools in use.

Adobe's file format specification (PDF1.4) incorporated in Acrobat version 5 is the newest release and is a major improvement on previous versions. It supports Scalable Vector Graphics (SVG), has a word search facility and has accessibility features. See **section 4.4.7** Accessibility and PDFs. As with much purchased software, many production houses upgraded as soon as possible.

The real problem on the Web is that many users have not upgraded their reader software and continue to use an older version. Being a free product it is generally downloaded once and then forgotten about. Unless users have only recently gone online, or they have taken the trouble to upgrade their reader, it should be assumed that the majority of the readership would still be using version 3 or version 4.

Documents created with Acrobat version 4 can be compatible with older versions of the Reader if saved correctly. The version 3 reader may not have all the functionality but the document will be legible. The Acrobat 5 Reader is able to read document formats all the way back to PDF version 1

These problems must either be completely overcome by the department or clear warnings should be added to the downloadable files to inform users that the files are only compatible with the latest version and that they may have to update their reader software to use them.

4.4.4   Metadata and PDFs

When creating a PDF document the author should always include as much detail within the metadata section as possible. This is completed in the following way.

Once an author selects to save a file as a PDF the Acrobat software will want to know what the file is to be called and where it should be saved.

When this information has been filled in, the next screen presented to the author is the metadata-input screen, as illustrated below. Here information can be inserted in the Subject and Keywords areas.

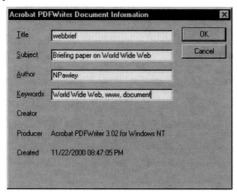

4.4.5 Security with PDFs

When creating a PDF document in Acrobat versions 4 and 5 the author has the ability to give a document security settings by assigning passwords. This can be used to restrict certain features, such as, copying and pasting, editing and printing. In Acrobat version 5, for example, copying and pasting can disallowed but Content Accessibility remains enabled. The Acrobat security feature can also be used to include a requirement to enter a password before an individual document can be opened and read.

4.4.6 Forms and PDFs

Conventionally, the PDF format has been used as a distribution medium for forms; a PDF form would be downloaded, printed out, completed manually and returned by traditional mail. Adobe's PDF1.3 specification incorporated in Acrobat 4.0 included support for on-line forms. Acrobat 5 has enhanced support for on-line forms.

PDF forms can include familiar elements, such as, radio buttons, check boxes, drop down boxes and text boxes can be built to be completed on-screen. On-line forms can then be submitted for sever-side management using, for example, CGI scripts, XML or via open database connectivity (ODBC) connections into databases.

Accessible Adobe PDF forms can be created using a tagged Adobe PDF file or by converting a pre-existing PDF file using Acrobat 5's Make Accessible plug-in. Acrobat 5.0 also has a digital signature feature and offers a PKI plug-in.

4.4.7 Accessibility and PDFs

Adobe PDFs have become the portable document format standard for government on the World Wide Web. Hitherto PDF documents could not have been considered as accessible. However, Adobe have taken considerable steps to improve the accessibility of both their Acrobat software and the information contained in their PDF files. Their latest specification (PDF1.4) is incorporated in Acrobat 5.0 and features some of the following usability enhancements:

- support for assistive technology such as screen readers and/or refreshable Braille output devices through the Microsoft Active Accessibility (MSAA) application programming interface for the Windows operating system;
- the level of contrast between text and background can make a big difference in the legibility of a page and Acrobat allows users to increase contract by creating custom colour schemes that override the colours specified in a document;
- the ability to zoom in and reflow text on the screen;
- keyboard shortcuts to enable navigation without the use of a mouse.

It is important to understand that your legacy PDF documents (those not originally created using the PDF1.4 specification) will remain inaccessible. To give them a level of accessibility you have either to:

- redistill them from their source material into tagged Adobe PDF files using the PDF1.4 specification in Acrobat version 5, or
- view your documents using the Acrobat Reader 5 with the Make Accessible plug-in.

4.4.7.1 Make Accessible plug-in

The Acrobat 5.0 Make Accessible plug-in automatically analyses the logical structure of a document and creates a new version of that file that will read more logically with assistive technology. The plug-in allows the users of Acrobat 5.0 for Windows to convert untagged legacy PDF files into tagged Adobe PDF files. A tagged Adobe PDF file is designed to ensure:

- the information is in the correct reading order on the page;
- it includes paragraph attributes needed to reflow text correctly;
- the reliable translation of all text into Unicode so that all characters, for example, hyphens and ligatures, can be read correctly by a screen reader.

4.4.7.2 Accessibility checker

The Adobe Accessibility Checker is a tool intended to identify common accessibility problems in Adobe PDF documents. This tool will, for example, check a document for missing 'alt' tags on images, and for unrecognisable character encodings. When found they are logged and reported so that you can decide whether or not to fix the identified problem.

4.4.7.3 Validation and testing

Tagged Adobe PDF files should be tested using a screen reader. This will demonstrate how your information will actually be presented to a user and how the reading order and navigational links will work.

Adobe online accessibility resource *http:// access.adobe.com*

PDF Techniques for Web Content Accessibility Guidelines *http:// www.w3.org/AAI/GL/2000/12/pdf.html*

4.4.8 Example notification and prompt to obtain the Acrobat Reader

Web managers should consider placing this prompt on all pages that link to PDF documents:

This document is available in portable document format for downloading. The Adobe Acrobat Reader can be freely downloaded from *http://www.adobe.co.uk*

Viewers with visual difficulties may find it useful to investigate services provided to improve the accessibility of Acrobat documents *http://access.adobe.com*

4.5 Plug-ins

Although a standard web page allows the author to do many things, some effects can only be achieved by using particular add-on applications.

A web author must bear in mind that each of these files will add to the document weight and download times for the user, and will complicate the accessibility of the page for many.

As well as the author requiring proprietary software to construct these added extras, the end user will also require proprietary software to make use of them.

Such software is usually available to a user free of charge but can take some time to download and install.

Use each checklist to ensure that your web pages comply with these guidelines

4.5.1 Checklist and summary	*Core guidance*
Checklist	❑ Any information contained in a proprietary format must also be available in HTML ❑ Clear notification should be given to the user of the file sizes of any plug-in content that have to be downloaded ❑ Users should be notified of the plug-ins required to access information ❑ Site-wide standard text and links should be included, making it easier for a user to download and install relevant plug-in software ❑ No plug-ins should be used on the organisation's website homepage
Summary	Many plug-in technologies are available to a web author, each offering possibilities for presentation and content that cannot be achieved in standard HTML pages. Plug-ins require the content author to have the skills and relevant software to construct the files, and the end-user to have the (usually) free reader software for the plug-in application on their browser. Training, development and implementation costs will have to be considered by an organisation, as well as the end usability of the website. Wherever plug-ins are used accessible alternatives must also be provided.

4.5.2 What plug-ins are

Web browsers interpret and display the HTML and CSS content contained in web pages. Most web browsers are also capable of rendering text and image content generated from the JavaScript scripting language and the Java programming language.

In addition, most recent web browsers have the ability to extend the repertoire of file formats they can process by means of software plug-in components.

The following are short descriptions of some of the most popular plug-ins used on websites today.

4.5.2.1 Portable Document Format (PDF)   *Adobe Corporation*

This is probably the most common plug-in and helper software on the web today. A document saved as a PDF file retains its entire document layout, including images and font formatting. Any user can now download this file using the free Adobe Acrobat Reader software. Once downloaded, PDF files can be read on screen, saved to local disk or printed.

Adobe Acrobat Reader (free)
http://www.adobe.co.uk

4.5.2.2 Flash   *Macromedia*

This plug-in is popular for websites that are required to convey interactive graphical information, such as animated menu disclosures. The image files are stored in vector format, which allows users to zoom in on images without them degrading. The files' size could be a major limitation to the popularity of the format, but this is overcome by streaming. Streaming allows the start of a file to play while the rest of it is downloading, thereby giving users rapid access to the content no matter what the speed of their modem.

Flash player (free)
http://www.macromedia.com/software/flash/

4.5.2.3 Shockwave   *Macromedia*

Websites that include this plug-in are referred to as 'Shocked' sites. A popular plug-in, it is used for more sophisticated interactive animations, such as, demonstrations, presentations and games that require the full power of a sprite-based animated system. Shockwave filesizes can be large.

Shockwave player (free)
http://www.macromedia.com/shockwave/

4.5.2.4 Quicktime   *Apple Corporation*

This plug-in is a very versatile application for the playing of digital video and audio on the web. Although this plug-in was developed by Apple Computer, it can be used by any operating system. It will play many-streamed video and audio formats.

Quicktime player (free)
http://www.apple.com/quicktime/download/

4.5.2.5 RealPlayer   *RealNetworks Inc*

One of the main uses of this plug-in is to allow real-time television and radio transfers across the web. The viewer is very user friendly although there are significant privacy concerns over the information that is elicited from users as part of the installation and registration process.

RealPlayer Basic player (free)
http://www.real.com/player/index.html?src=001121realhome_2

4.5.3 Usability considerations

All the above examples require proprietary software to construct and to view the files. Each can be useful and informative to a user if used in an appropriate manner.

It must be remembered that each different example that is used will require the user to have the plug-in already installed. If a user does not have a required browser plug-in installed, they will have to download it, which can be a lengthy and confusing process to users not used to downloading and installing software. These sites often based in the USA and download times can be anything from 2 to 20 minutes.

If information that is formatted and contained within a plug-in is essential to the user, the data must also be formatted in other ways.

A 'Flash' presentation is quite acceptable in a website as long as it is not on the organisation's homepage and an HTML version is delivered first from the same location.

> **IMPORTANT**
>
> *It is not just users with disabilities that will have difficulties with certain plug-ins. Many users choose not to use them because HTML versions are quicker to download, or their version of the required plug-in is not compatible with the one being used on the website.*

Plug-ins should never be needed for files on a department's homepage or other major locations.

Any file requiring a plug-in must also carry an explanation of the data in the file. There must also be a clearly defined link to a replica of the data in static HTML.

All video and audio formats will cause difficulty for certain sectors of the web-using community. Whenever these are used, text versions should be available, either within the plug-in (using closed captions or speech) or as a separate HTML file containing the transcript.

THE CORPORATE USER

Web managers must be aware that many corporate users are prohibited by security measures from downloading plug-ins or adding additional software to their workstations.

4.6 Scripting and programming

Web managers should be aware that scripting and programming could be used to add interactivity and style to their web pages. Three major forms of scripting and programming are now used within web browsers. JavaScript from Netscape/ECMA, Java from Sun Microsystems and ActiveX components from Microsoft.

Use each checklist to ensure your web pages comply with these guidelines

4.6.1 Checklist and summary	*Core guidance*
Checklist	❏ Do not rely on client-side scripting or programming to convey meaning or data: use standard HTML ❏ Ensure that your website is still usable in browsers that have scripting turned off ❏ Does the website benefit from the scripting? If not, don't use it ❏ Thoroughly test scripting on a range of browsers and operating systems
Summary	A variety of different scripting languages and programming can be incorporated into HTML pages. All are very powerful and can be put to good use. It is important to ensure that your website remains usable in browsers that have scripting and/or Java/ActiveX turned off.

4.6.2 Introduction to scripts

A substitute for any information or action generated with client-side scripting or component or Java programming must be made available in standard HTML format for users with browsers that do not use these technologies.

Particular attention should be paid to the version number of the script being used. For example, browsers that only understand JavaScript 1 will not be able to interpret JavaScript 1.2. There are a number of ways around this problem. Historically, JavaScript routines typically first established the version of the user's browser and then branched accordingly. Some parts of a script would, for example, be executed in Microsoft Internet Explorer and others in Netscape Navigator

The rapid development of the browser document object models (DOMs) and of JavaScript language variants has the result that the traditional 'browser sniffing' approach is no longer considered adequate because it does not offer a fine enough degree of granularity. The recommended approach is to test for the existence of each specific DOM and scripting language object, property and method before attempting to use it.

The only way to fully test the compatibility of any script is to test the pages using a range of browsers (see **section 2.5**).

4.6.3 Problems with scripts

On the Internet, there are many occasions when scripts do not work as intended either because the scripting is incompatible with the user's browser or as a consequence of the user's inability through physical or motor impairment to use the functions presented by the script.

Any scripts used on the website must be thoroughly tested on a range of different browsers and operating systems to ensure full compatibility. Even then, there is a number of Web browsers that cannot render any script functions so no essential information should also be presented in standard HTML format.

In the process of testing the script, the author should always ensure that the page is not adversely affected if the scripting abilities of the browser are disabled.

Finally, the hosting service for the departments Website may possibly have policies regarding the use of scripting languages. It is advisable to check with your server administrator before implementing.

4.6.4 Scripting and programming technologies

4.6.4.1 Java

The Java programming language was introduced by Sun Microsystems in 1995 and instantly created a new sense of the interactive possibilities of the web. Both of the major web browsers include a Java virtual machine than can run Java 'applets'.

Java is a programming language that uses an object-oriented programming model. Java can be used to create complete applications that may run on a single computer or be distributed among servers and clients in a network. It can also be used to build a small application module or 'applet' for use as part of a web page. Applets make it possible for a web page user to interact with the page.

The major characteristics of Java are:

- The programs created are portable in a network. A source program is compiled and can be run on any server or client that has a Java virtual machine. The Java virtual machine translates the compiled code into a recognised run-time code for a particular computer. This means that individual computer platform differences such as instruction lengths can be recognised and accommodated locally just as the program is being executed. Platform-specific versions of your program are no longer needed.

- The code is robust, meaning that the Java objects can contain no references to data external to themselves or other known objects. This ensures that an instruction cannot contain the address of data storage in another application or in the operating system itself, either of which would cause the program and perhaps the operating system itself to terminate or 'crash.' The Java virtual machine makes a number of checks on each object to ensure integrity.

- In addition to being executed at the client rather than the server, a Java applet has other characteristics designed to make it run fast.

4.6.4.2 JavaScript (ECMAScript)

JavaScript is a scripting language developed originally by Netscape specifically for the web. In general, script languages are easier and faster to code in than precompiled languages such as Java. In the past script languages have generally take longer to process than compiled languages, but the just-in-time compilation techniques used in recent browsers mean this is no longer necessarily the case.

JavaScript is used in web pages to do such things as:

- automatically change a formatted date on a web page;
- cause a linked-to page to appear in a popup window;
- cause text or a graphic image to change during a mouse rollover.

JavaScript uses some of the same ideas found in Java. JavaScript code can be embedded in HTML pages and is executed by the web browser. JavaScript can also be run at the server, as in Microsoft's Active Server Pages (ASP), before the page is sent to the requestor. ASP uses JScript that is a proprietary version of JavaScript.

Both Microsoft and Netscape browsers support JavaScript. The JavaScript language interacts with, but is distinct from the Document Object Model (DOM) in each browser. (See **section 4.6.7**.)

The widely encountered problem of web pages containing JavaScript that goes wrong arises from the large number of generations and dialects of the language that browser manufacturers have implemented many of which contain subtle and not-so-subtle incompatibilities. Such is the complexity of this issue that the commonly-used technique of testing the browser make and version number and making assumptions on that basis about the capabilities of the JavaScript language and Document Object Model now barely constitutes an adequate defensive programming approach. Instead, it is recommended that JavaScipt programmers should write code that tests for the presence of individual objects, properties and methods before attempting to use them.

The European Computer and Manufacturer's Association (ECMA) has attempted to standardise JavaScript under the name ECMAScript. The third edition of the ECMAScript language specification was produced in December 1999.

| **ECMAScript** |
| *http://www.ecma.ch/ecma1/STAND/ECMA-262.htm* |

4.6.4.3 ActiveX

ActiveX is the name Microsoft gave to a set of 'strategic' object-oriented programming technologies and tools. Recent versions have changed the name to COM and most recently to DCOM.

The main thing that is created when writing a program to run in the ActiveX environment is a component, a self-sufficient program that can be run anywhere in your ActiveX network (currently a network consisting of Windows systems). This component is known as an ActiveX control. There is no full implementation of the ActiveX component run-time environment in the MacOS version of Internet Explorer.

ActiveX is Microsoft's answer to the Java technology from Sun Microsystems. An ActiveX component can be considered to be very roughly equivalent to a Java applet.

One of the main advantages of a component is that it can be reused by many applications (referred to as component containers). A COM component object (ActiveX control) can be created using one of several languages or development tools, including C++ and Visual Basic.

4.6.5   Use of NOSCRIPT element

All browsers do not support scripts. Some firewalls do not permit their passage to the desktop and browsers behind such firewalls work with the script's disabled. When, for example, JavaScript is used, it should not be relied on. You should,

- Provide an alternative with equivalent text using the NOSCRIPT element. This element should enclose the content that you wish to be displayed by the non-script supporting browsers.
- The NOSCRIPT element can also contain a hyperlink to an alternative accessible web page with the same content. Examples:

```
<noscript><a href="summary.htm">This is a summary of
alternative information.</a></noscript>
```

4.6.6   CGI (Common Gateway Interface) scripts

CGI (common gateway interface) scripts were the first to add interactivity to web pages. CGI is not a programming language but a specification for writing programs that enable transactions between a web server and other programs on that server. CGI applications are usually developed in the Perl scripting languages, but compiled programming languages such as, C, C++, Java, and Visual Basic are often also used.

Typical applications of CGI scripts include:

- online forms – when the user clicks on the 'Submit' button, the CGI script on the web server processes the user's form data that is passed to it;
- searchable indexes of documents held in a database.

CGI scripts run as programs on the servers and therefore must be considered as potential security risks. Because of this some ISPs and commercial websites limit the use of CGI applications.

4.6.7 Document Object Model

The Document Object Model (DOM) is a browser scripting and programming interface that represents the contents of HTML documents as objects that can be manipulated by scripts and programs. Each structural element in a document (heading, paragraphs, lists etc) is available to be manipulated. Using the DOM, a programmer can write a script or program that modifies, creates, and deletes document objects dynamically from within the browser. A virtually endless array of multimedia effects can be created, and page content can be dynamically modified in response to user input. The DOM can also be used in conjunction with CSS to change the display characteristics of a page dynamically.

The DOM is in principle programming language independent. Document objects can be manipulated with JavaScript, Java, VBScript, Perl etc. In practice, JavaScript is almost always used because a language interpreter for it is installed as part of both the Internet Explorer and Netscape browsers.

4.7 Cookies

The basic function of a cookie is to allow Web servers to store and retrieve information on the user's machine. Although there are no major security considerations in using these cookies there are privacy and usability issues which affect their deployment.

Use each checklist to ensure that your web pages comply with these guidelines

4.7.1 Checklist and summary

Checklist	<ul><li>The content and purpose of any cookie that is delivered by your website should always be communicated to the user.</li><li>Users should have the ability to refuse a cookie without it affecting the basic usability of your website.</li><li>Your website should notify your users if technical features of your site will be degraded as a result of their declining to accept cookies from it.</li></ul>
Summary	Cookies provide a way to track individual users' usage of your website. The ability to identify a specific user opens the possibility of having your website deliver content customised to individual users' interests and needs. Using cookies to track individual users' usage of your website raises concerns about their privacy. The user privacy implications of any proposed cookie regime should be investigated and understood before deployment.

4.7.2 Explanation

When a web server receives a request from a browser for an HTML page or other document, it may include a cookie along with the returned content.

A cookie is a *token* that the web browser stores on disk in the form of a small text file. Depending on the user's browser preferences settings, a browser may automatically store cookies without notifying the user that they have arrived, may ask users whether to accept each individual cookie that arrives, or automatically reject all cookies.

Cookies are stored in a text file whose name and location depends upon the user's operating system and browser. These can be viewed and deleted by the user. For example:

- Microsoft's Internet Explorer stores each cookie as a separate file under a Windows sub-directory,
- Netscape stores all cookies in a single cookies.txt file, and

- Opera stores them in a single cookies.data file.

A cookie contains three parts:

- The web server DNS domain name(s) to which the cookie should be sent. The cookie will be included as a part of any future requests for HTML pages or other documents from web server(s) with the specified DNS domain name(s).
- An expiry date, after which the cookie will be discarded by the web browser, and will no longer be included in requests to web servers.
- Arbitrary text set by the web server when the cookie was first sent to the browser.

Note that the expiry date can be set to *end of session* in which case the cookie will be discarded when the browser application program is ended.

By setting the arbitrary text portion of a cookie to something different in every cookie it issues, and setting the domain name section to refer to itself, a web server is then able to recognise individual users' sessions (sequences of requests from the same user). By setting an expiry date that is in the distant future, a web server is additionally able to recognise users that return to the site on subsequent days, weeks or whatever (repeat visitors). Cookies set to expire beyond the end of the current browser session are usually referred to as *persistent*.

Cookies do not contain executable code and therefore do not provide a potential point of entry into users' computers for viruses, Trojan horses or other malicious software.

Establishing user sessions at the server in this way also enable the development of new classes of web-based applications ranging from multi-page forms to websites that can record user preferences and customise the content they deliver according to users expressed preferences.

A practical example is Amazon.com, the online bookseller. They use cookies for site personalisation, to aid established customers by informing them of offers and discounts in areas they have previously used. For example the personalised message when your log in:

```
'Hello John Doe, we have recommendations for you in books
and video'
```

Hyperlinks then take you to a personalised page that highlight products based on your personal profile.

4.7.2.1 User privacy implications

Any proposal to implement a website cookie regime inevitably and properly raises concerns about user privacy. To clarify and assess user privacy implications it is useful to categorise cookies into several basic types as follows:

Anonymous session tracker – a cookie used to track user sessions. It contains no personal information about the user, nor does the website elicit or store any information from the users. Appropriately used this is a valuable tool in user analysis and it also enables the provision of features such as multi-page forms. This cookie may be made persistent in order to detect repeat visitors and returning users respectively.

Session tracker – this is a cookie that the web server uses to relate page and other content requests to user preferences stored on the server. The cookie is used to establish the session and the web server ties the session to the user profile that it has stored. The use of the cookie does not in itself add any additional privacy considerations to those that arise as a consequence of eliciting and storing data that may be considered to be private. Note, however, that it is not acceptable for a browser's presentation of a cookie to be interpreted by the web server as adequate authentication for access to private data held on a web server or back-end database. Additional authentication and data encryption techniques must be used for application involving the transfer of private information over the Internet. This category of cookie may or may not be persistent. For example, you may belong to an online group that issues a session cookie each time you log into it. If you select the *login automatically* option it will then send you a persistent. See **section 1.11** Backgrounder on securing websites, and **section 5.5** Online transactions.

Cookies containing private data – cookie regimes that involve storing private or potentially private data, such as names, addresses, credit card numbers, within the cookie itself are sometimes mooted. This approach should be avoided in Government websites.

It is important that the user is always made aware if your website uses cookies, what data they contain and what they are used for. This information should be communicated on every entry page to a service that uses cookies. Most browsers let the user specify whether to allow cookies – always, never or case-by-case, but you could consider using a more direct approach for consent: For example:

- 'opt-in arrangement' whereby express consent is communicated to the user, eg, 'If you are happy for us to use cookies and provide you with a personalised service use the OK button'.
- 'opt-out arrangement' – a less customer friendly approach which may say, eg, 'If you proceed, then we assume that you are happy with how this service works'.

A website that uses cookies should also work if users decline to accept them. Your site should perform with and without the use of cookies. If your site offers a degraded service to users who do not accept cookies then they should be informed that they would have to put up with a less sophisticated service.

4.7.3 Third-party cookies

Web managers should be aware of the use of cookies by third parties, for example, advertisers or others making use of part of a web page. It is possible that they may employ a cookie (sometimes called a web bug) that seeks to track a user across the Web by using globally unique identity and a DNS domain name that is not related to the DNS server of your department/agency. Such third-party cookies may impinge upon your published privacy policy.

See **section 1.3** for advertising and sponsorship
See **section 1.10.2** for Data Protection Act

5.1 Dynamic publishing

Many government organisations use static, HTML files to deliver their information on the web. However, for appropriate applications, dynamic publishing methods offer great advantages over websites constructed from static HTML pages.

Instead of a website comprising a collection of manually constructed HTML pages, server-side scripting and database access techniques are used to piece together web pages directly in response to requests from users' browsers.

The development and implementation costs of dynamically generated websites are can be substantially higher than the alternative. However, for appropriate applications, there will be savings in running costs including efficiency gains in the management of content updates and changes to the site structure.

The use of dynamic publishing techniques offers the opportunity to deliver web content that is highly customised to the needs of individual users.

Before embarking on a dynamic publishing project, web managers should ensure they have the necessary information systems project management, development and implementation resources available to ensure the project's success.

In order to simplify procurement procedures and avoid 're-inventing the wheel' the Office of the e-Envoy is developing a centralised offering that will include database and content management functionality.

Use each checklist to ensure that your web pages comply with these guidelines

5.1.1 Checklist and summary

Checklist	❏ Does the method of dynamic publishing create HTML pages that are accessible to everyone? ❏ Can all web browsers read the dynamic pages? ❏ Is the system simple to administer and manage? ❏ Does the system respond to user requests sufficiently quickly ❏ URLs of key documents should be stable and be able to be bookmarked
Summary	The decision on which dynamic web publishing system will be used is likely to take into account the systems technologies and products already supported within the organisation.

5.1.2 Introduction

Most dynamic page publishing solutions involve a 'scripting language'. Normal web pages are created, with extra instructions embedded in them. These instructions access databases, other websites, or system services, and format the results returned.

The raw page, containing a mixture of HTML and scripting language, is served through a special type of program ('interpreter') which executes the scripting instructions and renders their results into HTML. The resulting 'page' is then served through a web server.

5.1.3 Personalised content delivery

Dynamic publishing enables the construction of websites capable of delivering content that is highly tailored to the needs of individual users. Site content, navigation and appearance can be customised in response to preferences and queries expressed by users via HTML forms. It can also be customised to work optimally with individual user's browser and Internet connection technology.

The distinction between a dynamically published website and a transactional website (that passes information into, and retrieves information from, back-end business systems) is a fine one. Many of the underlying technologies involved are the same.

5.1.4 Content management

It is common for dynamic publishing website developments to employ databases to store some or all of the sites' content, structure and appearance data. Such implementations typically also include a 'content management' application of some degree of sophistication that allows the stored data to be updated and otherwise manipulated.

Content management systems, which may themselves be web-based applications, are usually designed to allow website managers to update and manipulate the content of their sites without having to be concerned with the intricacies of HTML, CSS and so on. They typically also automate a lot of the routine website management work.

5.1.5 Web server performance and resource considerations

Since each dynamically published Web page is created on- the-fly, the web server must work harder to produce results. This will typically have a performance overhead that may be substantial.

Most dynamic publishing implementation systems try to deal with this problem in different ways. Often a reverse-proxy server such as Squid can address performance problems. Other solutions involve the periodic bulk generation of static HTML pages from the dynamic publishing system that can then be served to the Internet as if the site were a traditional static one. However, the latter approach will reduce the extent to which the website can deliver personalised responses to user requests. It is entirely possible to employ different server resource conservation techniques on different sections of a single website.

These issues should be considered when developing the specification for a dynamic publishing website project.

5.1.6 Technologies and tools

It is beyond the scope of this handbook to go into the detail of the technologies and tools available for the development and deployment of dynamic websites. This section lists a number of widely used products and technologies to illustrative the huge range and variation in scope that is available.

It is recommended that the advice of your organisation's information technology professionals should always be sought from the outset when contemplating the development of a dynamic publishing website.

5.1.6.1 Active Server Pages (ASP)

ASP is a scripting platform and is a part of Microsoft's Internet Information Server. In particular, it provides interfaces to other Microsoft products and technologies such as SQL Server, COM and .NET. For the scripting language, ASP uses VBScript (which is similar to Microsoft Visual Basic) or JScript (which is Microsoft's server-side version of JavaScript).

A third-party implementation, Sun's ChiliSoft ASP, will run ASP on a range of non-Microsoft platforms and servers.

5.1.6.2 CGI

CGI (Common Gateway Interface) is a basic standard for web servers to interact with programmed content. All web servers support CGI.

CGI programs can be written in any programming language. The most common being Perl. CGIs are usually less flexible than scripted web pages, but are easier to install and run.

5.1.6.3 ColdFusion

Cold Fusion is a complete authoring system made by Macromedia (formerly Allaire). Scripting instructions are usually embedded in pages using CFML, with the help of the Cold Fusion Studio programming environment.

It has a wide range of third party libraries available and runs on a variety of operating systems.

5.1.6.4 Java Server Pages (JSP) / J2EE

Java Server Pages are written using Sun's cross-platform programming language, Java. However, they work on a very similar basis to other scripting languages, and can be served by any one of a number of 'Servlet containers', the most popular of which is the free Open Source Tomcat server (now part of the Apache Foundation).

J2EE is a more ambitious specification for building entire "web applications." It is used in very large enterprise-scale projects. JBoss, is an open source J2EE server.

5.1.6.5 Lotus Notes and Domino

Lotus uses the Domino name to refer to a set of Notes server applications specifically designed for web usage. Notes itself refers to the overall product.

A Domino server can effectively be configured to serve an Intranet-style GroupWare solution implemented in Notes, on the Internet.

It is a solution for projects where integration with an existing Notes network is required.

5.1.6.6 Mediasurface

MediaSurface is another example of a product that enables the development of complete dynamically published websites and the collateral content management systems. It also uses the Oracle RDBMS as the repository for the website data. It has its own built-in web server.

5.1.6.7 Perl

Perl is one of the first all-purpose scripting languages. It excels at fast text processing, and is widely used. An important feature is the enormous range of third party libraries available.

It can be used to create dynamic pages both using CGI scripts, or special server modules like mod_perl for Apache.

5.1.6.8 PHP Hypertext Pre-processor

PHP is also a scripting system. It runs on most web servers and operating system platforms. It is Open Source software, and therefore free.

Its main features are speed at runtime and fast development speed. It has a large library of third party components, and can interface with COM, CORBA, MySQL, etc.

5.1.6.9 Vignette Storyserver

Vignette Story server is an example of a product that enables the development of complete dynamically published websites and the collateral content management systems. It uses a version of the TCL scripting language and the Oracle RDBMS as the repository for the website data.

5.1.6.10 Zope

Zope serves pages written using the cross-platform scripting language, Python. It can use its internal database or external databases for storing content. It also comes with a number of basic content management needs provided for 'out of the box'.

Refer to **section 2.4** Building in universal accessibility

5.2 Your website on television

Although the number of computers in households is still growing they are still complex and expensive pieces of equipment that can be difficult for the average user to get to grips with.

Virtually all families in the UK own a television and it is the main source of information and entertainment in the household. Interactive Digital Television (DiTV) is undoubtedly going to become a popular way of viewing information not least because of analogue switch off later this decade.

In principle it is easy for broadcasting companies to tie in information presented on screen to further, more detailed data within a DiTV site. Pressing a button on the remote control could access this data. Television, including digital TV, is regulated by the ITC, making these guidelines an additional source of guidance for the developers of websites.

Access to interactive pages via a television is achieved using either an in-built modem or a 'set-top box' (STB) attached to the PSTN (public service telephone network), an ISDN (integrated services digital network) line or a Broadband connection. These relay any requests for pages through their system and out onto security systems via the Internet.

At present there are no definitive national standards for producing and formatting information for this medium. Navigation through a service on the TV is done through either a television remote control or a keyboard. Be aware that a website designed for accessing via a PC may not work on a television set or be available on a particular platform.

5.2.1 General

As many as two in three television viewer's users may not have surfed the web previously using a computer. Therefore keep everything simple and clear. Don't think of them as web pages; think instead of the way TV graphics look and feel. This is what users expect. Phrases like 'click here to…' are not appropriate in a mouse-less environment. Where possible, refer to a 'service' rather than a 'site'. Although the contents are built using Internet technologies and may be re-purposed from a website, viewers who have not experienced the Internet may be confused by the use of Internet terminology.

The example below of a screenshot from the UK online Interactive service illustrates the power of simplicity.

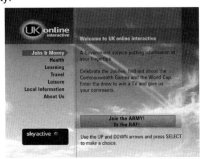

5.2.2 Three main TV-friendly principles

Three main principles are the key to making TV-friendly websites.

Readability
The size of the fonts used by set-top boxes to render text on the TV needs to be larger than those rendered by web browsers, simply because people are watching TV from a lot further away than they are when viewing their computer monitors.

The user can enlarge the size of the text displayed by some set-top boxes (to improve readability on small TV sets), but the user cannot of course change the size of the window used for the general display (PC browser windows can be resized manually).

Simplicity
Human-factors research has shown that for most computing tasks the threshold of frustration is around 10 seconds. Web page designs employing complex layouts and 'pretty' graphics just will not work. Whilst some DiTV services use high-speed access to the Internet, phone line connections represent the only option for many users. Therefore, it is recommended that HTML pages should not exceed 50kB in size. They cannot include dozens of links where this can be avoided. Navigation similar to UKonline Interactive is recommended, being more intuitive than computer menus.

Television users do not have a mouse so imagine what it is like navigating around the page using only arrow keys. Frames and complex tables are not possible.

Avoid writing long pages: remember that the normal user will saturate their cognitive capacity if they have more than seven things to look at. Viewers are not used to scrolling, so it is entirely possible that items below the viewable area will be completely missed. If you cannot say it in 40 words – then you need to re-work the page.

Entertaining content
Televisions are far less business-like than computers. Users expect to be entertained as well as educated or informed. Boredom thresholds can be quite high, and this is typified by the viewing culture of channel hopping at the press of a single button. This is likely to be the fate of dry content that does not capture the imagination or encourage the viewer to read on. Content must be compelling and of value to the user – not just what you want to say! Keep detail to a minimum -- remembering to provide back buttons to return the viewer to the page they have just left.

5.2.3 Design

Design guidelines can be summarised in ten rules that can be applied to any of the three TV-friendly principles:

- Your site should look good on small screens.
- Beware of certain colour combinations – use TV safe colours
- Use large sans serif fonts – TV safe fonts, eg, Tiresias, which was developed in conjunction with the Royal National Institute for the Blind.
- Scrolling is not possible on some platforms.
- Simple navigation

- Facilitate navigation with a remote control keypad.
- Limit data entry as most viewers have to use SMS
- Limit text to 40 words per page (screen)
- Be short, be simple, and be entertaining!
- Make use of video where the bandwidth permits
- It is inappropriate to try to just link a website to a DiTV platform.

5.2.4 Screen sizes

Scrolling is not simple or even possible for TV viewers. Most TV browsers will not support horizontal scrolling so pages that exceed the display window width may need to be reformatted to fit in. This can have unexpected effects on page layouts and may even result in parts of the page not being displayed at all.

Vertical scrolling is supported on most TV browsers, but viewers may miss items below the viewable area if they are not expecting them to be there. Examples of actual screen sizes are as follows:

- **Telewest Active Digital** The width of a page is 640 pixels while the length is 400 pixels, excluding the title bar. If the page size exceeds this then the transcoder may either reduce the scale or add scroll bars.

- **KIT (Kingston Interactive TV)** The actual screen size is 720 x 576 pixels. Not all of this is visible because of Overscan. This requires a 'safe area' which will appear on all TV sets. Important screen elements and all HTML have to be 600 x 480 to fit.

5.2.5 Colours

Colours for TV need to be PAL (Phase Alternating Line) safe. This means developers should avoid using RGB values including 0-16 and 236-256. This can be done in, for example, Adobe Photoshop using the Levels function. Using 90 per cent of the true colour will reduce colour bleed and distortion.

Colours displayed on TV look a lot brighter and more saturated than they do on a computer monitor, and certain colours when placed in close proximity to each other can cause effects on neighbouring elements such as jittering or shimmering (visible movement), chroma crawl (colour smearing) and interference. Try and use web safe colours for Liberate platforms.

Always check the colours on a TV before committing to a whole series of pages. Keep small items such as icons greyscale or mono as colour tends to bleed and distort on the TV. Some transcoders attempt to adjust colours on the fly to ensure that they are broadcast safe, but some combinations may still cause problems and different platforms may behave differently.

Overly bright colours may be limited by transmitter technology, resulting in grey, patchy colours.

5.2.6 Text

It is harder to read text on a TV screen. It takes a lot more concentration and can take up to 25% longer to read. The optimum common text font is a sans serif font of size 12pt. Where the platform has a transcoder (Liberate and Netgem) this will be automatically increased by 50 per cent to 18pt. Fonts are limited to those few available in the set top box (STB) so keep text clear and concise.

- Avoid the use of too many fonts.
- Lower case is easier to read for body text on screen.
- Italics can also be hard to read.
- There is only one embedded typeface for Liberate. This is Tiresias, which was developed in conjunction with the Royal National Institute for the Blind to ensure legibility for the partially sighted and also to remain legible when stretched to 16:9 wide-screen formats.

Above all, keep it simple, avoid too many on-screen elements and try to focus attention on one area of the screen at any one time. Work to a maximum of 40 words on a page.

5.2.7 Graphics

Authors should always present all images in either GIF or JPEG format.

All images are converted by the Liberate transcoder to a 15-bit palette, and dithered accordingly, but to optimize the quality to transfer delay ratio, images should be stored with a 256-colour palette (8-bit format).

Although TV browsers generally support imagemaps, they make the cursor very small and are almost impossible to navigate without a mouse.

5.2.8 Plug-ins

- RealVideo and RealAudio plug-ins are **not** supported.

- Flash and Shockwave plug-ins are **not** supported.

- AVI and MOV video formats are not generally supported. Those that are supported have limitations on the size of the clip owing to the lack of a hard drive and the relatively small amount of available RAM.

- MPEG 1 or 2 is the only video format commonly supported across set-top boxes. MPEG video has to conform to defined sizes and bit-rates and must also be stored on a special video server at the head end, so video clips cannot be played over the Internet or from external video servers.

5.2.9 Audio

- Some boxes play WAV and MIDI files.
- Liberate does not support sound.

- The best rate is generally 22kbps 16-bit mono. Size is also an issue: limit file sizes to between 500kB and 1MB. They can be clicked on to play or they can play automatically in the background of a page. Both the standard `embed` and `bgsound` HTML elements function as normal.

5.2.10   Animation

Animated GIFs work well. They should have a plain background or one that matches the background of the HTML page. Keep the file size down, as large animations slow down the loading of the page.

5.2.11   Frames

Frames should be avoided. However, they can be used to avoid having to load one section of a screen more than once, for example a menu. Too many frames can make on-screen navigation awkward so stick to standard templates and make sure that there are only links in the same frame throughout the website.

5.2.12   Forms and data entry

Not all iDTV customers will have keyboards, and entering text from a television remote control keypad is a similar operation to sending text messages from a mobile phone. HTML 3.2 form elements are supported by the Liberate and Netgem platforms. The design and use of forms should follow these guidelines:

- Simplify the form as much as possible and remove unnecessary fields.

- Use drop-down lists and radio buttons instead of text entry fields. For instance, provide a drop-down list for titles – 'Mr', 'Mrs', 'Ms' etc – rather than requiring a user to type them out.

- 'Submit' and 'Clear' buttons should be in line with other hyperlinks so that they will be included within the cursor navigation sequence.

- Avoid scrolling screens with forms. Break up forms into multiple screens, and indicate how many steps are required to complete the form.

- It should be made very clear to the user if and when any action on their part may incur costs, eg, telephone cost may be incurred when entering competitions, voting, etc.

See **Section 1.10.2** Data Protection Act

5.2.13   WebTV

WebTV was formed in 1995 and was acquired by Microsoft in 1997. It is popular in the USA and Japan. Although there are some special considerations in publishing data on this system, it basically works and renders in the same way as standard web browsers on a computer and can handle CSS, JavaScript and common audio and video formats.

Screen

One of the biggest controlling issues is the displayable screen size. This is only 420 x 560 pixels, smaller than the old standard 640 x 480 VGA resolution. When this is coupled with the requirement for larger font and graphic sizes, it becomes clear that web managers must carefully control and limit document contents.

The browser window is quite different from that usually seen on a PC screen. It is quite restricted and can render pages in a suprising way, for example, will crush a page to make it fit

Navigation

Internal hyperlinking navigation now becomes essential in order to reduce the amount of scrolling that any user must undertake.

Text

Only 12 characters of a page's title will be stored in the 'recent' panel, but 25 characters will be stored in the bookmark section. All titling must therefore be very specific and meaningful.

Colours

The colour palette available on a television is not as large as that on a full-colour PC so images must be designed carefully. This is especially important when text is used within the graphic. The system does support all standard graphic formats such as GIF, JPEG and PNG.

Frames

A website that is organised around a frames environment will not render well on a WebTV system. All frames are automatically converted into tables, which can result in very unfriendly sites.

Version of HTML

WebTV supports the use of HTML 4.

Downloadable files

The user cannot download files when using this system. Because there is no hard disk, there is nowhere to store files such as images or PDFs.

There is a WebTV browser emulator available for computers. Using this allows a web manager to see what pages will look like when they are displayed on WebTV. The emulator can be downloaded from the WebTV website.

WebTV website
http://www.webtv.com

5.2.14 Example

The Bush Internet TV allows Internet access via a modem that connects to a telephone line and normal television viewing via a standard coaxial aerial connection. The user interface is via a remote control that contains a mouse controller and a QWERTY keyboard.

Screen resolution is quite good and the automatic text resizing carried out by the internal ANT Fresco browser assists legibility. Cascading Style Sheets are disabled but graphic rendering is standard.

Service provision is via Virgin.net and cannot be changed. Users may bookmark and go back to previously accessed pages in a very similar fashion to standard computer browser applications.

UK online interactive

In April 2002, the Office of the e-Envoy (OeE) launched the pilot service on the Sky (and ITV Digital) platforms with the intention to be on NTL and Telewest when agreements are in place. The service includes a database of UK online centres, a questionnaire, an email feedback functionality and topic-based content. OeE is now looking into the introduction of personalisation, regionalisation, transactions and forms to the service.

The OeE have negotiated commercial arrangements with platform providers, where there are considerable benefits to using the UK online interactive as an access point to your DiTV service. Using UK online interactive provides benefits of a Partnership with UK online:

- *Shared knowledge providing best practice, best price and best partnering advice.*

- *Create continuity of navigation and design to increase the user experience.*

- *Single entry point to Government information – on the Sky service they have secured a position on page 1 of the main interactive menu.*

- *UK online holds the Government's Independent Television Commission (ITC) broadcasting license, which is essential if you wish to be on the Sky platform.*

- *You get to use an effective advertising medium at a percentage of the normal cost for interactive advertising campaigns.*

*For further information email **DiTV@e-envoy.gsi.gov.uk***

Telewest website
http://www.telewest.co.uk

ntl: interactive TV developer's website
http://www.digitalcabletv.co.uk

Independent Television Commission
http://www.itc.org.uk/

Broadcasting Standards Commission
http://www.bsc.org.uk//

Digital Television Group
http://www.dtg.org.uk//

Office of Communications
http://www.ofcom.gov.uk

Bush Internet TV
http://www.bush-Internet.com

5.3 Other digital communication media

In the past few years a number of other methods have been made available to users to view information on websites. Different devices, both mobile and static in nature, are beginning to transform the Internet.

Information can be accessed from home via a computer or games console. The same data can be retrieved on the move using mobile phones and personal digital assistants (PDAs).

In an ideal world, one website could be multi-purposed to allow all of these channels to see the same thing, but unfortunately, this may not always be possible.

This section is aimed at familiarising the web manager with the available media and how best to deal with them. See section 5.2 Your website on television.

Use each checklist to ensure that your web pages comply with these guidelines

5.3.1 Checklist and summary

Checklist	❑ Test all pages on as many platforms as possible ❑ Make content displayable within 544 horizontal pixels ❑ Avoid the use of small text ❑ Only use supported code and file formats ❑ Keep page titles short and descriptive ❑ Write concise text ❑ Avoid complex tables and frames ❑ Only use simple forms ❑ Do not use server-side or irregular imagemaps ❑ All pages should be smaller than 250kb
Summary	Web managers should be aware that many of these new browsing modes would cause severe disruption to the end-view of their websites. Games consoles and browsers on PDAs allow only a small viewable area at any one time and users can find it difficult to scroll up and down. WAP is a completely different protocol and will not interact with a standard HTML website. If all these browser modes were to be supported, it would not be unrealistic to suggest that a number of versions of a website will have to be maintained. Content Management Systems and multisource DTDs, XSL-T and XML may well be the saving grace in this field, but much of the technology is quite new and untested by public sector organisations.

5.3.2   Range of browsing devices

The world is now a very different place to that of seven years ago. Then, the web was new and all browsing of websites was based on a relatively small monitor, connected to a relatively large computer.

Now users can access an organisation's website on a wide range of browsing devices ranging from televisions to mobile phones. These all have very different ways of interpreting and rendering data within very different screen sizes.

Three basic questions that a content provider is faced with today are:

- What will the client use to access our information?
- How will we deal with this request?
- How will we manage the data?

The following sections cover some of the more common ways in which data will be accessed and also what Web managers can do to ensure that their information is displayed correctly on them.

5.3.3   Mobile access

5.3.3.1 Personal digital assistants (PDAs)

This is really a generic name given to small computing devices that offer more facilities than a mobile phone. Many different varieties are available on the market.

Some run very simple operating systems which are designed to allow the user to store memos, read and write emails, keep phone details and have calculator functions. The Palm Pilot and current Psion ranges are good examples of this type of product. The new versions of the Psion range now contain the Opera web browser application.

The other more versatile, and therefore more expensive, option is the miniature PC which runs the Microsoft CE operating system. These machines have very few differences to the average desktop PC. They have lower levels of RAM and smaller hard disks but run many of the common software programs used by Microsoft operating systems. They have versions of Microsoft Word, Outlook and Internet Explorer as well as many others and can therefore handle CSS, cookies, etc.

When hooked up to a modem these pocket PCs can browse the web as well as any other PC. They have a smaller viewable area and limited capabilities to run plug-ins, but other than that they are very good at what they do.

There are no special considerations for these machines as they either have no online capabilities, they use a CE version of the Microsoft Internet Explore, which deals with data in the same way as any other browser, or they use the WAP communication protocol. This is covered in the next section.

> **Information on best practice issues with PDAs**
> *http://ami.avantgo.com/support/developer/channels*

5.3.3.2 Wireless Application Protocol (WAP)

Newspapers and television are now starting to carry adverts for the new WAP-enabled mobile phones. The companies' promises are a little exaggerated, and the ability to surf the web effectively on the phone is still some way off.

The WAP application strategy involves taking existing services that are at present supplied through a fixed-line environment and tailoring them to be user friendly and useful in a mobile wireless environment.

The WAP specifications define a set of protocols for applications, transactions, security and transport. They also define a Wireless Application Environment (WAE), which enables operators and manufacturers to develop applications such as microbrowsers, email and web-to-mobile messaging facilities.

If a device is said to be WAP capable it means that it has a microbrowser loaded into it which allows it to communicate, understand and handle all entities specified in the WML 1.1 DTD.

Many of the protocols are based around existing Internet standards such as HTTP but have been optimised for the unique constraints of the wireless environment, such as low bandwidth and connection instability.

Although this is a collection of new standards, these are all based on the use of XML. Every document and all output are in XML. In fact, there is very little within WAP that is new. The diagram below illustrates how a mobile device requests and receives data using this service.

A 'GET' request from a user is transmitted as a URL from the mobile phone to a WAP gateway, from where it is sent via standard HTTP to the Internet content provider. The request is handled by the server, which then transmits the requested data back across the same network.

Standard XHTML data could not be sent to mobile phones because of the size and complexity of content in the pages, the requirement to continually link to other pages within the server and the small screen size of the device. So another mark up language was needed to serve this environment.

WAP documents are written in Wireless Mark up Language (WML), which is a subset of XML. A WML document is known as a deck, and a single interaction by a user agent (ie the microbrowser) is called a card. A deck may consist of several cards. This simple architecture means that WAP sessions can cope with intermittent

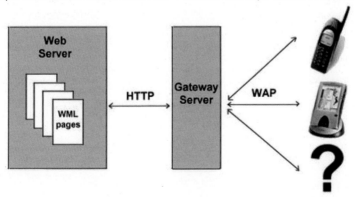

coverage and loss of server connection by downloading multiple screens to the client in one transaction.

The reduced processing power of the mobile devices concerned has the result that decks cannot contain too much information. This limitation means that multiple cards will have to be split into multiple decks to complete a complicated transaction.

Below is a very simple example of a WML deck as defined by everything contained within the <wml> tag being turned on and off. It actually looks very similar to an HTML page, using similar tags, but it is actually an XML document. As stated in the earlier section, there is an XML statement at the top of the document, and there is a DTD statement. This deck containing three cards allows the user to select different options and then return to the front page.

```
<?xml version="1.0"?>
<!DOCTYPE wml PUBLIC "-//WAPFORUM//DTD WML 1.1//EN"
"http://www.wapforum.org/DTD/wml_1.1.xml">

<wml>

    <card id="card1" title="Neil Pawley">
        <p>
        <a href="#card2">My email
address</a> CARD 1
        <a href="#card3">My phone
number</a>
        </p>
    </card>

    <card id="card2" title="Neils email address">
        <p>
        npawley@ccta.gov.uk<br/>
        CARD 2
        <a href="#card1"><small>Back
</small></a>
        </p>
    </card>

    <card id="card3" title="Neils phone no">
        <p>
        01603 704852<br/>
        CARD 3
        <a href="#card1"><small>Back
</small></a>
        </p>
    </card>

</wml>
```

This example will display on a WAP phone or WAP emulator as follows:

Neil Pawley	Neils email	Neils phone no
My email address My phone number	npawley@ccta.gov.uk Back	01603 704852 Back
Screen 1	Screen 2	Screen 3

The user can navigate from the front page (card 1), by either selecting the email address or phone number option. The secondary screens (defined by card 2 and card 3) give simple information and a link back to the first screen (card 1 again).

This example has only a limited amount of client interaction as there are only three cards in the deck and the only navigation is backwards and forwards.

As well as this basic display there are many features which allow client transactions to be completed. Variables within WML provide a mechanism for carrying selected data from one card to another. WMLScript, a slimmed-down version JavaScript, can deal with more complex elements.

It is obvious from this section that a standard HTML website will not deliver data across this medium. Further information on the structuring of documents, server architecture and delivery protocols can be seen at the following website.

WAP Forum + specification
http://www.wapforum.org

5.3.4 Games consoles

Of the games consoles available at the time of writing, Sega Dreamcast, Sony PlayStation 2 and Microsoft's Xbox offer web browsing facilities to the user at home. For example, with the Sega Dreamcast the browser it uses is called DreamKey, which is based on a quite early version of the Netscape browser. Because of the browser's limitations there are some very specific requirements in presenting information on this system.

It should be remembered that this is a games console and is not primarily designed for browsing the web. This limitation is very obvious when trying to use the scrolling and selecting mechanisms. There is no mouse for the unit: the user can either use the joystick control or the extra keyboard. Neither is particularly good and takes some time to master.

As the system is based on an early version of Netscape it does not have the ability to use Cascading Style Sheets. All fonts and colours are subsequently rendered in a flat format. This does not inhibit the use of most pages, but they do lose a degree of presentational style.

Images rendered by the browser are relatively good, but any images that contain small text can be very difficult to read. This can be overcome by using the zoom facility.

Below is a screenshot of a template site accessed through this games system compared to the same website on a standard web browser. Although the rendering quality of the Dreamcast is quite obviously lower, the website is still usable.

SEGA Dreamcast browser   Microsoft IE browser

Screen rendering
30 pixels of the screen are given over to a Dreamcast status bar at the bottom of each page. Three screen resolutions are offered to users:

- Small   607 x 453 (default setting)
- Medium   640 x 480
- Large   768 x 576 (equates to a standard SVGA monitor resolution)

This limited screen rendering capability usually results in a user having to scroll left and right as well as up and down to get the full information from the screen.

Text
The Dreamcast also suffers from the same limitations that the digital television systems do. All text should be large to ensure that it is rendered correctly on the lower-specification viewing screen. Text size is controlled by the system and can be set to one of two levels, small or large.

Colours
The colour palette available on a television is not as rich as that on a full-colour PC so images should be designed carefully. This is especially important when text is used within the graphic. The system does support all standard graphic formats such as GIF, JPEG and PNG.

Client-side imagemaps
Imagemaps are supported and work well. As mentioned earlier, the usability of these maps depends on the text size within the given image.

Frames
Frames are supported but may not render as well as expected particularly if groups of nested frames are used.

Version of HTML
Dreamcast will only support the use of HTML 3.2. This is not a problem for any website using the HTML 4 standard, as the browser will simply ignore what it does not understand. HTML 3.2 does not support many of the WAI recommendations.

Presentational tools

JavaScript 1.1 and 1.2, cookies and Flash 3 are supported.

Downloadable files

The user cannot download files when using this system. A system CD should be running within the game console to load the browser, so there is no storage capability.

Dreamcast website
http://www.dreamcast.com

5.4 eXtensible Markup Language (XML) and eXtensible Stylesheet Language (XSL)

XML provides a universal, standardised and well-supported mechanism for marking up data, for use on the web and in other applications. Unlike HTML, which is a language based around displaying data in a web browser, XML puts no constraints on the purpose for which the data will be used, but merely describes the structure of the data. XML can therefore be used (and is used) for applications that involve the transfer of data across the Internet either for display or computational purposes.

It is important to understand that XML does not, on its own, constitute a presentation markup language – it is a markup metalanguage. That is, a syntax within which we can define other languages. The Wireless Markup Language used by WAP phones and XHTML, which provides HTML functionality in XML syntax and is intended to supersede HTML, are two aimed at displaying information. The Extensible Business Reporting Language (XBRL) is an example of a language developed for transferring data for processing by computer. A major strength of XML is that the same data can be used directly by a computer and displayed for human users.

XML has many supporting standards. The Extensible Stylesheet Language (XSL) is used to display XML directly in a web browser or other client software. XML Schema is used to define XML languages for specific uses. XLink and XPointer provide powerful linking facilities between and within XML documents and the Document Object Model (DOM) provides a standard programming interface.

XML was developed and is maintained by the World Wide Web Consortium (W3C), which also maintains the HTML standards. It is widely supported by industry and has good commercial tool support.

Within the UK Government, the e-GIF mandates the use of XML for both display and data transfer applications. Use of XML is supported by the UK GovTalk™ initiative and the web site at *www.govtalk.gov.uk.*

5.4.1 Summary	
Summary	XML has three major uses within the UK public sector. 1. XML languages are being used for transferring information between citizens and government, between businesses and government and across government. Examples are the submission of personal and business tax returns. 2. XML is increasingly being used in web site development. For example, where information is drawn from a database, using XML as an intermediate format between the database and the display code speeds development and eases maintenance. 3. XML can be used for archiving data. Rather than storing archive data in proprietary database formats that could make reading old archives hard in the future, careful design of an XML language allows data to be self-describing. Coupling this with the text-based nature of XML ensures that data can be retrieved and understood easily in the future. Web sites can use XML both to provide and consume services. For example, both public and private sector web sites can provide a change of residence service that submits an XML message to multiple public sector organisations that store the information in their databases. While holding a dialogue with the citizen, this service might itself send XML messages to the National Land and Property Gazetteer to ensure that the addresses provided are both unambiguous and valid.

5.4.2 What is XML?

The concept of XML is very different to that of HTML. HTML is an application of Standard Generalised Mark up Language (SGML), that is to say the various revisions of the HTML mark-up language are each defined using SGML as a SGML 'document type' - XML is a simplified, and more powerful version of SGML itself.

The following quote is from the W3C XML WG (Working Group):

"XML is primarily intended to meet the requirements of large-scale web content providers for industry-specific mark up, vendor-neutral data exchange, media-independent publishing, one-on-one marketing, workflow management in collaborative authoring environments, and the processing of web documents by intelligent clients. It is also expected to find use in certain metadata applications. XML is fully internationalised for both European and Asian languages, with all conforming processors required to support the Unicode character set in both its UTF-8 and UTF-16 encodings. The language is designed for the quickest possible client-side processing consistent with its primary purpose as an electronic publishing and data interchange format.

The key to how it works is descriptive mark-up. This allows you to tag data not by its structure in the document or how it will be displayed, but by what kind of data it is. For example, this means it can break an address down into individual descriptive elements such as street, street number, town, and postcode. This is very useful if the address has to be used by different databases each of which records addresses in different ways."

In order for different databases or systems to use this markup, a XML schema has to be developed to establish what the descriptive mark-up will be for different purposes.

For example, as part of developing a cross-departmental schema that included a representation of people's names, the participating Departments would need to agree the names and meaning of the XML elements to be used. In the case of this example, it might be agreed that the XML element to represent a person's first name would be `<first-name>`, as opposed to anything else, such as, `<fst-nme>`, `<christian-name>` or whatever.

5.4.3 What is XSL?

XML does not provide any way to describe how XML-structured data should be laid-out or formatted when it is rendered on any physical medium, such as, PC monitors, paper, or whatever. eXensible Stylesheet Language (XSL) is a system for specifying the relationship between XML data and how it should be rendered on arbitrary media.

Suppose, for example, as an application developer, you wanted to be able to display the content of email boxes on a number of devices ranging from PC monitors to the very small screens on mobile devices. If the mail were stored in XML, defining the way the messages would be laid-out and formatted on the different display devices would, in principle, be a matter of developing an XSL stylesheet for each device.

5.4.2 Developing XML and XSL for the UK Government

The use of XML is mandated for the UK Government in the e-Government Interoperability Framework. There is an ongoing program of development of schemas for use across the public sector and these are available on UK GovTalk™, see *http://www.govtalk.gov.uk/interoperability/xmlschema.asp*

The adoption of XML and XSL form the cornerstone of the government data interoperability and integration strategy. To make implementation easier, best practice guidance, training and toolkits is being developed and provided at *www.govtalk.uk.gov/interoperability/egif.asp*

A non-government source of information about XML can be found at: *www.xml.org/*

5.4.3 XML and accessibility

See **Section 2.4** Building in universal accessibility.

5.4.4 Scalable Vector Graphics (SVG)

Scalable Vector Graphics is an open standard language based on XML for describing two-dimensional images. SVG allows for three types of graphic objects:

- vector graphic shapes, eg, paths consisting of straight lines and curves;
- bitmap graphics, and
- text.

The format allows objects to be interactive and dynamic. There are also animation facilities. Users can adjust some parameters of the image – zoom or pan around the image without it becoming blurry. The image can be scaled up or down to fit proportionally to any size computer screen or mobile device screen. Generally it will have smaller file sizes than regular bitmap graphics, such as, GIF and JPEG files.

SVG documents (often saved with the file extension .svg) always start with <svg>. Currently SVG images cannot be seen through a web browser. You must download an SVG viewer.

XML specification
http://www.w3.org/XML/

---

e-Government Interoperability Framework V3
http://www.e-envoy.gov.uk/publications/frameworks/egif3/egif3.htm

---

SVG 1.0 specification
http://www.w3.org/TR/SVG/

Accessibility features of SVG (Scalable Vector Graphics)
http://www.w3.org/TR/SVG-access/

5.5 On-line transactions

The functionality of websites is increasing as the Internet and technology mature. Previously, websites were seen solely as communicators of information, but this view is changing as more sites are built that are capable of transacting with users.

Encryption of user's personal data and authentication of their identity are key issues in the e-Economy. These have security implications are a likely to be dealt with by a Departmental Security Officer and an IT Security Officer.

The acceptance of orders and payments and their fulfillment electronically will require a change to your business practices and systems.

Use each checklist to ensure that your web pages comply with these guidelines

5.5.1 Introduction

The concept of electronic business was around before the Internet became popular. An example of this is Electronic Data Interchange (EDI). However, e-business would not be possible on such a large scale without the Internet. This provides the environment for suppliers to conduct dealings with their customers through computer and communications networks. The development of networks and electronic transference of funds have contributed to the growth of operational websites. These sites allow users to conduct transactions electronically on a large scale, making the business process more accessible and more efficient.

There are many issues with electronic business, most prominently information security. Additionally government business transactions need to have record capturing mechanisms appropriate to their nature. This is to record what has taken place robustly for the benefit of both parties. In addition public business needs to be accountable. A variety of approaches to this are outlined in guidance from the Public Record Office at *http://www.pro.gov.uk/recordsmanagement/default.htm*

5.5.2 Information security

5.5.2.1 Confidentiality and trust

Confidentiality and trust are implemented through the use of cryptography. Encryption makes sure that if information is intercepted or sent to the wrong person, it cannot be read. Only the recipient has the knowledge to decrypt it. This knowledge is called the key. Traditional encryption involved both sender and user sharing the same key. In order to make encryption more generally available, e-commerce usually relies on two completely separate keys, one to encrypt and another to decrypt. The **public key** is openly available to anyone wanting to encrypt data. The **private key** needed to decrypt the data is held only by authorised recipients. Those sending the information can trust that only those with the private key can read the information.

Data protection and privacy is a sensitive issue for Internet users and modern web browsers now support encryption. Many Internet services also offer **Public Key Infrastructure** (PKI) which combines encryption with authentication.

See **Section 1.10.2** Legal issues – Data Protection Act.

5.5.2.2 Authentication

Authentication is a means of checking a user's identity. This is usually done through a user ID and a password. Websites requiring authentication will not allow a user entry into the site unless the authorised ID and password details have been entered.

Traditionally, a person's signature is recognised as authentication of an individual. However, it is impossible to sign in pen and ink when undertaking an online transaction. An alternative was needed and a security mechanism known as a **digital signature** was initiated. Documents can be digitally signed which then allows verification of who signed it and whether or not the document was changed during transmission.

5.5.2.3 Legal issues

For a contract to be made, under English law, a number of factors have to be in place. An 'offer' has to be made and accepted, a 'consideration' has to be given by each side, eg, usually in the form of goods or services exchanged for cash, and the parties have to have the intention of making a contract. When setting up an e-Commerce website it is recommended that it be structured so that the user (customer) makes the offer to you – which you either accept or decline – and not the other way round. If you get this the wrong way round it can lead to contracts being concluded by the user (customer) accepting an offer on the website – which you may not be able to fulfil.

Digital signatures are the basis for a legally binding agreement, just as a hand written signature would be on a paper-based contract. Their legal status is confirmed in the *Electronic Communications Act 2000*.

5.5.3 Explanation of e-commerce terms

Authentication
Electronic means of identifying and verifying legitimate application users and devices.

Digital signature
A security mechanism that includes a user's private and public keys, which the browser uses to validate from the user.

Encryption
The conversion or transformation of readable data into an unreadable steam of data using a reversible coding processes.

SHTTP (Secure HTTP)
A protocol that provides server authentication, digital signatures and encrypted sessions for web traffic.

SSL (Secure Sockets Layer)

A technology from Netscape for encrypting data sent between client and server.

5.5.4 e-Trust Charter

It is essential that customers of electronic public services have confidence in how their personal data are handled. In line with recommendations from the Performance and Innovation Unit, the Office of the e-Envoy has developed a draft **Trust Charter for Electronic Service Delivery** (e-Trust Charter) with the aim that departments will adopt it as individual electronic services come online. This has been issued for consultation and seeks to provide such necessary reassurance. It has a two-tier structure of e-Trust Charter and context-specific privacy statements that will apply to particular electronic services. The need for Codes of Practice, Information Sharing Protocols and Management Guidance should also be considered.

e-Trust Charter
http://www.e-envoy.gov.uk/publications/guidelines_index.htm

UK GovTalk™ with XML Schemas
http://www.ukgovtalk.gov.uk

Authentication Framework
http://www.e-envoy.gov.uk/publications/frameworks/authentication/authentication.htm

Framework for Information Age Government Security
http://www.e-envoy.gov.uk/publications/frameworks/security/security.htm

6 Technical detail and tutorials

The technical detail in section 6 does not provide a full tutorial on how to write HTML. It assumes that you have a basic understanding of HTML and is intended to provide clear instructions and sample markup on how to successfully achieve much of what is contained in the previous section of these guidelines.

Section contents

6.1   Hypertext Markup Language (HTML 4.01)

6.2   Cascading Style Sheets (CSS)

6.3   HTML tables

6.4   HTML frames

6.5   HTML forms

6.6   Web page navigation

6.1 Hypertext Mark up Language (HTML4.01)

Web pages are formatted using Hypertext Mark up Language (HTML). Systems of document formatting have been around, in one form or another, since the 1960s. The popularity of HTML stems from the fact that it is fairly easy to learn. However, in common with most systems of instructing computers, it has to be done with precision in order to produce the intended result.

Use each checklist to ensure that your web pages comply with these guidelines

6.1.1 Checklist and Summary	*Core guidance*
Checklist	❏ The page should contain the appropriate DTD ❏ The page should contain syntactically correct HTML that validates against the DTD ❏ Each element which requires it must be closed correctly ❏ To meet evolving markup standards attribute values must be contained within speech marks (" ") ❏ The completed HTML document must validate cleanly using the W3C validation service
Summary	To ensure that any browser can read a published web page it must first be marked-up correctly, to the open standard of HTML 4.01. HTML version 3.2 should be considered the standard for non-PC device channels.

6.1.2 Implementation

The primary consideration for any public sector body in the UK is to ensure that data presented on the web is available to all.

The public's ability to access the data should not be conditional on their having the latest version of a browser, the fastest modem or the most powerful processor or having the physical attributes to be able to see the page on screen or to use a mouse.

Because of the wide variety of web browsers available today and the legacy issues that exist because of older browsers that are still in use, it is fundamentally important that a recognised international standard is set that is understood by all.

Any standard that is used must be implemented correctly on each and every page. It is only when this is done is it that a content provider can reasonably expect its information to be interpreted and rendered correctly by all browsers.

An automated service is available to ensure that pages do comply with the recommendations. This is provided by the World Wide Web Consortium (W3C) that exists to promote the development and use of standards in Web technology.

W3C HTML validation service *http://www.w3.org/*

6.1.3 Simple introduction to HTML

HTML is a markup language for expressing the structure of documents published on the World Wide Web. The display arrangements were originally under the control of the browsers' implicit built-in style sheet. Subsequent versions of HTML started incorporating display instructions into the markup languages but these have now been taken back out of HTML and more appropriately put into Cascading Style Sheets (CSS). What started off as a very simple, efficient markup language has now become a rich, multimedia publishing language.

However, the fundamentals of HTML are still very simple and can be understood by anyone after an hour or two. It is also this simplicity which has led to the incorrectly marked-up HTML documents that are found on many websites.

Below is a simple HTML page. The document structure shows a collection of markup tags each contained within angle brackets (< >). Anything inside these brackets is an instruction to the browser that reads and interprets them, but does not display them on screen.

HTML markup tags are usually combined in pairs, for example <title> and </title> that indicate the start and end of an HTML element, the document title element in the case of this example. Note, however, that some elements do not enclose text and do not have a closing counterpart tag.

An HTML page should always contain correctly nested html, head, title and body elements. The start and end of each element is indicated in the markup by the opening and closing tags. The example below shows the structure that should be used in all pages.

The opening html tag is the first to appear and is consequently the last to be closed. Everything included within this element is recognised as HTML.

In this example, the head element serves only to contain the title element. The content of the title element will be displayed in the Web browser's window title bar.

The opening <body> tag is next. Whatever is contained within the body element will appear in the user's web browser window. If any of these fundamental elements are placed in the wrong order, or not used at all, an author cannot guarantee that the page will render correctly.

In this example, the word 'hello' has been emboldened by using the strong markup element. This is another example of an element that has opening and closing tags. The element is closed by repeating the opening tag name prefaced with a forward slash, ie **Hello**.

```
<html>
      <head>
            <title>My document</title>
      </head>
      <body>
            <strong>Hello</strong> world
      </body>
</html>
```

The diagram below shows how our simple example page looks when it is rendered by a browser.

Adding attributes and values can extend tags. A simple example would be an author assigning the colour yellow to the background of an HTML page by adding the following attribute and value to the opening <body> tag.

Two features not mentioned yet have really given the web life and helped ensure its enduring popularity. These are:

- the ability to link to graphics and display them within a page; and
- the ability to link to other pages on the web, wherever they might be.

HTML also contains many other content structuring elements which control the way the browser renders text (see **section 6.1**), tables (see **section 6.3**), frames (see **section 6.4**) and forms (see **section 6.5**).

Detailed information on the correct implementation of the latest version of HTML 4.01 can be gained from the World Wide Web Consortiums (W3C) website.

HTML4.01 specification from W3C
http://www.w3.org/TR/html4/

6.1.4 Using the appropriate Document Type Definition (DTD)

The Document Type Definition (DTD) must be included at the very top of each HTML page. This line informs the validation services which revision of the HTML standard you have used to construct the page. It should be entered into the page in the following manner:

```
<!DOCTYPE HTML PUBLIC "-//W3C//DTD HTML 4.0//EN"
"http://www.w3.org/TR/REC-html40/strict.dtd">

<html>
...The head, body, etc. goes here...
</html>
```

Three specific DTDs are available within the HTML 4.01 standard, one of which must be quoted on each HTML page to ensure the correct validation and subsequent guaranteed usability. They are as follows:

HTML 4.01 Strict DTD
This includes all elements and attributes that have not been deprecated or do not appear in frameset documents. For documents that use this DTD, use this document type declaration:

```
<!DOCTYPE HTML PUBLIC "-//W3C//DTD HTML 4.01//EN"
"http://www.w3.org/TR/REC-html40/strict.dtd">
```

HTML 4.01 Transitional DTD
This includes everything in the strict DTD plus deprecated elements and attributes (most of which concern visual presentation). For documents that use this DTD, use this DOCTYPE:

```
<!DOCTYPE HTML PUBLIC "-//W3C//DTD HTML 4.01 Transitional//EN"
"http://www.w3.org/TR/REC-html40/loose.dtd">
```

HTML 4.01 Frameset DTD
This includes everything in the transitional DTD plus frames as well. For documents that use this DTD, use this DOCTYPE:

```
<!DOCTYPE HTML PUBLIC "-//W3C//DTD HTML 4.01 Frameset//EN"
"http://www.w3.org/TR/REC-html40/frameset.dtd">
```

6.1.5 HTML 4.01

Once an appropriate Document Type Definition (DTD) has been decided upon the corresponding standard must be adhered to. The set of DTDs available with HTML 4.01 is listed in the previous section.

It is important to use the correct HTML elements and the tags that represent them when marking-up a document. The rendered document must be as legible and understandable to a user with a visual impairment as to anyone else. To accomplish this there are certain elements that render in the same way on a visual browser but which actually have subtle differences when read by a disability browser.

`<i>` … text … `</i>`
This tag will make all text contained within it italic.

`<em>` … text … `</em>`
This tag will make all text contained within it italic but will change the inflection of a speech browser, placing emphasis on the text within the containers.

`<b>` … text … `</b>`
This tag will make all text contained within it bold.

`<strong>` … text … `</strong>`
This tag will make all text contained within it bold but will change the inflection of a speech browser, placing emphasis on the text within the containers.

Other elements should **only** be used for structuring the document rather than styling it.

`<body></body>`
This tag should not be used as a styling device, and no font styling, margin control or link colouring should be contained within this element. Many of the commonly used attributes and values are proprietary extensions and will not work for all browsers. The only styling element that may be included is the specification of a background colour for the page. Any other styling information that is used to control the entire page should be included in the website's Cascading Style Sheet.

`<h1>` … text … `</h1>`
There are six levels of heading within HTML, h1 is the most prominent, and h6 is the least prominent. These should only be used when headings are required for separating individual groups of data within a publication. <h1> through to <h6> should be used hierarchically.

`<hr>`
A horizontal rule should be used to separate information. It should never be used as a styling device.

`<blockquote>` … text … `</blockquote>`
This tag should be used when formatting a speech quotation within a document. It should never be used for indenting information in a web publication as it could be misleading to browsers with access technology.

Many HTML elements can have extra attributes and values added to them. The basic HTML element will, for example allow an author to add a paragraph break (<p>) or a horizontal rule (<hr>) but on many occasions this is not enough to obtain the full effect that is required.

The extra attributes provide further controls over the way elements are rendered by a web browser. Entire paragraphs can be justified or aligned to the left, and the width, height and the thickness of horizontal rules can be adjusted. Each attribute will have a value, which must always be preceded by an equals sign and contained within quotation marks.

An example of an HTML tag being extended with attributes and values is as follows:

```
<hr width="90%" size="5">
```

The resulting horizontal rule will stretch across 90 per cent of the viewable web browser screen, and will be five pixels in height.

Always remember that:

- any attribute value must be contained within quotation marks (" ");
- not all browsers will recognise a particular attribute;
- most of these attributes can and should alternatively be added using Cascading Style Sheets;
- care should be taken that chosen colours do not cause difficulty for users.

All formatting of textual and tabular information should be added by using Cascading Style Sheets. This is explained within **section 6.2**.

HTML 4.01 – ISO/IEC 15445:2000 specification from W3C
http://www.cs.tcd.ie/15445/15445.html

6.1.6 Validation

The W3C automatic online validation service is free of charge and enables Web managers to test and correct their HTML document.

The URL to be tested is entered; enabling the W3C website validation service to validate the HTML page against the DTD specified at the top of the file. A results page will then be sent to the user with either a congratulatory message or a full list of errors.

The error page is well constructed, reporting exact problems, showing the line that the mistake occurred on and stating where in the HTML standard the correct formatting can be found.

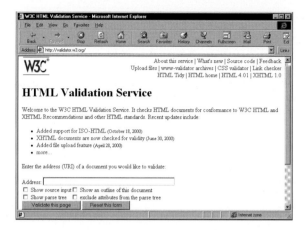

Only once a page has been completely cleared by the validation service will the Web manager see the congratulatory message. This message page also gives the graphic that can be displayed on the organisation's website homepage:

Also listed is a sample URL that enables the Web manager to keep a continual link to this successful validation message, which might be for example:

```
http://validator.w3.org/check?uri=http%3A%2F%2Fwww.ukonline.go
v.uk
```

> **IMPORTANT**
> *It is easy to learn HTML, but it takes a long time to learn how to use it correctly.*

It should be remembered that every page within the website should validate correctly. It is simply not enough to have a well-written homepage that validates correctly and other pages within the website that do not.

If the production of HTML pages within the organisation is automated it is still worthwhile validating the output, as it is not uncommon for these pages to be badly constructed. Mistakes can always be corrected as the templates that the automated process uses are usually straightforward to change.

Many of the features of WAI rely on the Web manager knowing how to format a page correctly in HTML, and only validation and display of the logo and link will prove that this is the case.

HTML pages should never be published on the web in what is in effect a half-finished format. If an open standard is going to be used it should be used correctly – this is the only way in which it can be checked properly.

W3C HTML validation service

http://validator.w3.org/

6.1.7 eXtensible Hypertext Mark up Language (XHTML1.0)

The W3C's December 2000 recommendation for the latest revision of the HTML markup language is XHTML 1.0 (eXtensible Hypertext Mark up Language). There are two main questions that need to be answered before any Web manager seriously considers this move:

- What is the difference between HTML 4.01 and XHTML 1.0?
- What does XHTML1.0 look like?

6.1.7.1 What is the difference?

XHTML1.0 is the first major change to HTML since HTML 4.0 was released in 1997. It brings the rigour of XML to web pages and is the keystone in W3C's work to create standards that provide richer web pages on an ever increasing range of browser platforms including cellular phones, televisions, in-cars devices, wallet-sized wireless communicators, kiosks and desktops.

XHTML1.0 is modular in construction, making it easy to combine with markup tags for technologies like vector graphics, multimedia, mathematics, electronic commerce and more. Content providers will find it easier to produce content for a wide range of platforms, with greater assurance as to how the content is rendered.

The modular design reflects the realisation that a one-size-fits-all approach will no longer work in a world where browsers vary enormously in their capabilities. A browser in a mobile phone can't offer the same experience as a top-of-the-range multimedia desktop machine. The mobile phone doesn't even have the memory to load one page designed for the desktop browser.

XHTML1.0 is the first step. XHTML reformulates HTML as an XML application. This makes it easier to process and easier to maintain. XHTML borrows the tags from W3C's earlier work on HTML 4, and can be interpreted by existing browsers, by following a few simple guidelines.

All old HTML documents can be changed into XHTML1.0 using W3C's open source HTML Tidy utility. This tool also cleans up markup errors, removes clutter and structures the markup, making it easier to maintain.

6.1.7.2 What does XHTML1.0 look like?

Instead of the normal HTML Document Type Definition at the top of each page, the following needs to be used:

```
<!DOCTYPE html PUBLIC "-//W3C//DTD XHTML 1.0 Strict//EN"
"DTD/xhtml1-strict.dtd">
```

This informs the browser that the document is marked up using XHTML. The elements that are used are basically the same as the ones used in all other HTML documents, but there are some subtle differences that need to be understood to ensure that the document validates correctly.

Well-formed

This concept introduced with XML, means that every markup element must be closed correctly. This is not an issue with many elements in HTML as most are closed by replicating the tag name but preceding it with a /, as in this example:

```
<html>
        <head>
                <title>Document</title>
        </head>

        <body>
                <h1>Document Title</h1>
                <p>This is a short paragraph</p>
                <table>
                        <tr><td>cell 1</td><td>cell2</td></tr>
                        <tr><td>cell 3</td><td>cell4</td></tr>
                </table>
        </body>
</html>
```

In this simple example, every markup tag is turned on and off, with the contents of that element being affected by the specified formatting.

However, a number of HTML elements do not have a closing tag. In this case a special notation is needed:

```
<meta name="DC.Identifier" scheme="URI"
content="http://www.open.gov.uk" />

<link rel="stylesheet" href="css/open.css"
type="text/css" />
        <body>
                This is a short line of text<br />
                Followed by another line of text<br />
                <hr />
                <img src="test.gif" />
        </body>
```

In this example a number of common elements are shown that are normally left open – that is, they actually terminate themselves once their formatting instruction has been read. In XHTML each of these needs to be closed to be considered well formed so a space and / needs to be incorporated at the end of each tag. This is effect on the following these simple examples.

Line Break	` `	` `
Horizontal Rule	`<hr>`	`<hr />`
Image	`<img>`	`<img />`
Metatag Enabler	`<meta>`	`<meta />`
Link Reference	`<link>`	`<link />`

Nested elements

As with HTML it is important that elements are written in the correct order and are always closed in reverse sequence. The first tag turned on must be the last tag turned off.

An example of nested elements:

`<p>`here is an emphasised `<em>`paragraph`</em>`.`</p>`

An example of overlapping elements:

`<p>`here is an emphasised `<em>`paragraph.`</p></em>`

Both will probably work in most browsers but only the first example with correctly nested elements will work in all and will also validate correctly to the XHTML standard.

Case sensitivity
Unlike HTML, the elements used in XHTML1.0 must all be in lower case. This is because XML is case sensitive and the element written as `<p>` can be different to the one written as `<P>`.

Values
All attribute values must be given in quotation marks, as in the following example:

`<table border="0" width="100%">`

not this:

`<table border=0 width=100%>`

Although the latter does not constitute correct HTML either because an attribute value that includes the percentage symbol should also be enclosed in quotation marks in all versions of HTML>

6.1.7.3 Validation

If XHTML1.0 has been employed on the organisation's website it should be validated using the online W3C validator in the same way that HTML is. When pages pass, the following logo can be displayed on the website:

The specification for XHTML1.0 can be accessed at the W3C website.

W3C The Extensible HyperText Markup Language
http://www.w3.org/TR/xhtml1/

XHTML
http://www.xhtml.org

6.2 Cascading Style Sheets (CSS)

Cascading Style Sheets (CSS) give the author of an HTML page the ability to separate the styling elements from the content of a document. They are of fundamental importance to the usability of a page for everyone.

They are simple to implement and extremely powerful. Their use should be controlled centrally by the organisation's Web manager and should set the formatting standards for the entire organisation.

Use each checklist to ensure that your web pages comply with these guidelines

6.2.1 Checklist and summary   *Core Guidance*

Checklist	❑ All documents using CSS for formatting must be usable when CSS is disabled ❑ Management of CSS formatting should be centralised using an external CSS file ❑ Care should be taken when using CSS absolute and relative positioning to ensure that content remains presented in the correct order in browsers that do not implement CSS positioning ❑ All Cascading Style Sheets should be validated by W3C
Summary	Although Cascading Style Sheets use a slightly different language to that of HTML they are quite easy to master. When appropriate, web managers should ensure that the organisation's website is consistently formatted using this technique.

6.2.2 Introduction

Until a few years ago all HTML documents were a mixture of content plus structural and styling markup elements. When viewed the source code looked complicated and cluttered. This clutter could make it difficult to actually see the data amongst all of the mark up information. These elements not only got in the way when the information was viewed and edited but could also cause many usability issues for non-graphical browsers and screen readers.

With the advent of Cascading Style Sheets the Web manager now has the ability to separate styling instructions from the entire page content and structure.

Any element within an HTML page can be referred to as an object – a word, an image or a style of formatting. Using CSS the Web manager can name these objects and assign a particular style to them. These styling elements can be for the formatting of a page or the font style of all text, but they can also be used to format an individual line or word.

There are three main ways in which CSS can be implemented in an HTML document:

- in-line styles;
- a style sheet at the top of each document; or
- an external style file.

Each of these works in exactly the same way and all use the same syntax.

6.2.3 Cascading Style Sheet language

The descriptive syntax used in CSS has its own language and construction rules, which are different from those of HTML.

In the past, if a Web manager wished to format a line of text in red, make it larger, specify a particular font, embolden and italicise it, the following HTML commands would have to be used on each occasion:

```
<p><b><i><font face="arial, helvetica, sans-serif" size="+1"
color="#ff0000"> A line of text </font></i></b></p>
```

This is very inefficient, particularly if many instances of this formatting are required throughout the document or the website.

Using CSS an author can now specify the above example as:

```
<p class="redtext"> A line of red text</p>
```

In this example the author has reused a required HTML element and applied a class attribute and value to it. This class refers to a line in the CSS section. The browser recognises that the line needs to be styled a particular way and displays the results. In this way all objects can be styled.

If this element of the CSS file is examined it will become obvious how this instruction is formatted correctly:

```
.redtext    { color: #ff0000;
              font-family: arial, helvetica, sans-serif;
              font-size: 1.5em;
              font-weight: bold;
              font-style: italic }
```

Firstly the class is listed, which in this case is 'redtext'. A full point must precede this listing, as this is the class identifier.

Each class has a series of CSS formatting rules, which are contained within braces (curly brackets) { }.

Each rule has an attribute and a value. The separation of these is slightly different to that used in HTML. An author would normally use the equals symbol and quotation marks to separate the attribute and value in HTML. In CSS specifications, a colon is all that is used. Each set of attribute(s) and value(s) is separated by a semicolon.

In the example above, the 'font-family' attribute has a multiple value: it states not only two values for the font family name (Arial and Helvetica) but also the generic typeface name (sans-serif). This is to ensure that if a user's browser does not contain the required fonts it will still display the information in a style that is acceptable.

The font-size can be specified in a number of different ways. Pixel height, point value and percentage size can all be used. Pixel and point are particularly inflexible and cannot be changed by a user (known as *hard coded*). It is recommend that text formatting is stated either by 'ems' or by using the x-small, small, medium, large or larger technique.

An author should always make the size of text as legible as possible. It is not sufficient to rely on users to change their font size as some will not bother. Start with a font size equivalent to 10 or 12 pixels, which will render acceptably on most web browsers.

Many browsers are still being used that have no understanding of CSS. Although information on an HTML page should always be formatted using this method it is important to ensure that you website is still legible if this facility is disabled.

> **IMPORTANT**
>
> *An easy way to test that a page is usable on non -CSS-capable browsers is to disable the CSS line in the document, ie:*
>
> *<! - - <link rel="stylesheet" href="css/deptx.css" type="text/css"> - ->*
>
> *Once this line has been commented out and viewed on any browser, the page will be displayed without the desired formatting.*
>
> *Can it still be read? Can you still navigate around the page?*
>
> *If not, you will have to make corrections.*

This difference can be illustrated very easily. The following diagram shows exactly the same page – on the left it is accessed by a browser that can understand CSS and uses the formatting rules that have been specified, while on the right is rendered by a browser that does not understand CSS and therefore displays the page with the basic HTML formatting.

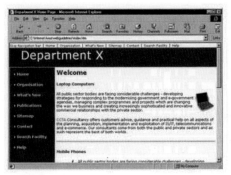 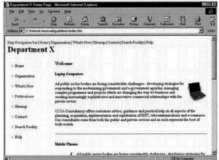

Because this page has been formatted correctly, it is also readily accessible by all varieties of browsers. The next illustration is the same page viewed through the Lynx browser. This really is the most basic of web browsers: it works within the MS DOS screen of a PC and therefore does not support graphics or font manipulation at all.

Lynx

Even though it has been rendered basically, the page is still structured and easy to use. The navigational elements are listed at the top and the real content of the page is shown underneath.

Although CSS are one of the latest advances in web publishing, a Web manager must always ensure that it is implemented correctly and that it does not interfere with the basic construction and usability of the website. Ensure that your CSS is validated by W3C.

These screen shots are from the template website that supports these guidelines use CSS to format all of the major elements on the page.

More detailed explanations of the correct use of CSS can be obtained from the W3C website.

See **section 2.6.6.2** Fonts

CSS specification from W3C *http://www.w3.org/TR/1999/REC-CSS1-19990111*

CSS validation from W3C *http:// jigsaw.w3.org/css-validator/*

6.2.4 Examples

The following very simple example can be styled using any one of the three methods mentioned above.

In a standard HTML document a heading would be formatted as follows:

`<h1>`This is a heading`</h1>`

This text would be displayed as a heading 1, in bold and black text, aligned to the left-hand margin and displayed in the base document font.

A Web manager may wish to display a particular heading within a document in red, indented from the top and left of the document's margins, italicised and in a particular font face.

This can be accomplished in several ways as outlined in the following sections.

6.2.4.1 In-line styles

To format the `<h1>` in the required style, each of the CSS elements is added to the opening `<h1>` tag.

```
<h1 style="margin-left: 2em; margin-top: 2em; color: #ff0000;
font-family: arial; font-style: italic">This is a heading</h1>
```

The margin-left and margin-top attributes each have a value of two ems. An em is useful as it scales to the size of the font employed and is safer to use than pixels or points, which can cause problems for users who require large font sizes.

This method is fine but becomes unmanageable if all `<h1>` tags in the document need to be formatted in the same way because all the CSS specification would have to be repeated on every opening `<h1>` tag. This can be overcome by using a style sheet at the very top of the document.

6.2.4.2 Style Sheet inclusion

Including a style element at the top of a page within the `head` element of an HTML file is another way to achieve the same results as the previous example. In this way all `h1` elements within the document will be styled in the same way. The following shows how this is accomplished:

```
<html>
<head>
<title>Cascading Style Sheets</title>

<style type="text/css">
h1      { margin-left: 2em;
          margin-top: 2em;
          color: #ff0000;
          font-family: arial;
          font-style: italic; }
</style>
</head>

<body>

<h1>This is a heading</h1>

</body>
</html>
```

This has the benefit of simplifying the HTML markup and locating all styling elements at the top of the page. Now all that is left within the body of the document are the structural elements.

This method is fine for a single document but would become unmanageable if all `h1` elements in the organisation's website needed to be formatted in the same way. This problem can be overcome by using a separate style sheet file to which all other files refer for their styling.

6.2.4.3 Style sheet file (CSS)

The final example will give exactly the same results but will add even more flexibility to the formatting of publications within a website.

All documents can refer to the styling elements contained in a centrally located CSS file. In this way one change to the external file will effect the change on every page within the website. This is far more efficient for a Web manager and helps co-ordinate the organisation's publishing style.

For this to work each document within the website must link to the external style sheet. The following is an example of how to do this:

```
<html>
<head>
<title>Cascading Style Sheets</title>

<link rel="stylesheet" href="style.css" type="text/css">

</head>
<body>

<h1>This is a heading</h1>

</body>
</html>
```

The link element shown after the opening `<title>` tag tells the browser where the style sheet is located. The browser will access this file and format the specified tags in the appropriate manner. The contents of the 'style.css' file are as follows;

```
h1      { margin-left: 2em;
          margin-top: 2em;
          color: #ff0000;
          font-family: arial;
          font-style: italic; }
```

This method is the preferred authoring style when managing complex websites. It is flexible and easily controlled. All authors and editors of web pages within the website only need to know the location of the CSS file and how to link to it. All other styling is then completed automatically for them.

6.2.5 Implementation of CSS

The example given in the previous section was very simple. As Cascading Style Sheets can be used to format virtually all elements of an HTML page, the CSS file can get very long and complicated, very quickly. It is the Web manager's role to ensure that it is maintained correctly.

As well as ensuring that all styles are correct the Web manager must also make sure that access to the CSS file is limited to staff who have responsibility for styling and no-one else, as any change to this file will have an immediate effect on the entire website.

> **IMPORTANT**
>
> Care should be taken when using CSS absolute and relative positioning to ensure that content remains presented in the correct order in browsers that do not implement CSS positioning
>
> **Relative values** – *allow the author to specify that the next object on a page should be placed 40 pixels down and 40 pixels to the right of the last object.*
>
> **Absolute values** – *allow an author to specify page x, y and z co-ordinates for an object.*
>
> *Although this is potentially very useful, it is likely to cause layout problems in browsers that do not implement it.*

CSS specification from W3C
http://www.w3.org/TR/1999/REC-CSS1-19990111

6.3 HTML tables

Table formatting is used in the layout of websites for a variety of reasons. Displaying data in tabular format is only one use, and designers often use it to physically structure the layout of a page.

To ensure that pages remain usable for all, it is important to use tables correctly and with restraint.

Use each checklist to ensure that your web pages comply with these guidelines

6.3.1 Checklist and summary	*Core guidance*
Checklist	❑ All table markup elements must have closing tags ❑ All tables should contain summary information ❑ Background colours within the table must not detract from the legibility of the contents ❑ Tables should be used sparingly ❑ Tabular information must always be clearly labelled and easy to follow ❑ All tabular information should be displayed in a standard way throughout the website ❑ Consider expressing table and cell widths in percentage terms
Summary	Tables are easy to construct in HTML, but they are also very easy to get wrong. A single mistake in the construction of a table can cause the entire page to fail to render in some web browsers although it may still render as intended in others. Another aspect to consider is that what may look great in a graphical web browser may be completely unintelligible to a screen reader used by a section of the community.

6.3.2 Implementation

Although tables were initially added to the HTML standard to allow the formatting of regular tabular information, HTML authors quickly found that they could also be used to control the layout of HTML pages.

This ability to use tables to place images and textual information in specific parts of a page is widely employed on the majority of websites and has certainly made web presentation more aesthetically pleasing.

Any HTML mark up that is allowed in the body element can also be contained within in a table cell. This means that tables can be built within tables that are built within tables and so on. These 'nested tables' can add flexibility to a website design – for example, they can be used to build a single graphic from multiple images.

The downside of all this is that many users with visual disabilities and special purpose web browsers can have difficulty in separating the information from the layout.

Some special purpose browsers will only read web pages from left to right. The best way to illustrate this is to take a ruler, hold it to the screen displaying the page and draw it down the page one line at a time. If the page displays information in a number of columns it can be very confusing when read aloud.

An HTML author needs to answer two questions when using tables:

- Is a table required to format this information?
- Will the consequence of the table be that certain users cannot easily access the information?

> **IMPORTANT**
> WYSIWYG ('What you see is what you get') HTML editors are not as useful at creating tables as those that show the HTML markup. Good background knowledge of HTML is essential to avoid common markup mistakes.

Many elements go into the construction of HTML tables. The following sections cover the basic elements and attributes that should always be included to construct a table.

6.3.2.1 Table element

This is the element that establishes the table within an HTML document. As soon as a browser reads this markup it knows that everything included after it that is contained within cells is to be constructed in a tabular format.

```
<table>
<tr><td>cell 1</td><td>cell 2</td></tr>
<tr><td>cell 3</td><td>cell 4</td></tr>
</table>
```

6.3.2.2 Table widths in percentages

If you wish to ensure that an entire table displays on the screen regardless of screen size, use percentages for specifying the table and cell widths rather than fixed widths. The former allows the browser to size the table cells in proportion to the dimensions of the user's screen. A fixed value that is larger than the displayable area will cause a page to scroll from left to right, which can be difficult to negotiate.

The following example set up a table whose width is 80% of the width of the browser window. Within the table there are two columns, each of whose width is 50% of the width of the table.

```
<table width="80%">
<tr><td width="50%">cell 1</td><td width="50%">cell 2</td></tr>
<tr><td width="50%">cell 3</td><td width="50%">cell 4</td></tr>
</table>
```

If the user re-sizes the width of their window, the browser will re-render the table to take account of the changed window width.

Care should be taken with this technique when tables contain body text. Text set in wide measures (column widths) can be very inconvenient to read.

6.3.2.3 Border attribute

Any value added to this attribute will affect the dimensions of the border surrounding the tabular information. This value can be any pixel value from zero upwards. A value of zero will mean that the table border will not be displayed. The following example has a one-pixel border and illustrates various alignments of text within the table cells.

```
<table border="1">
<tr>
<td width="200">This is cell one</td>
<td width="200" align="right">This is cell two</td></tr>
<tr>
<td valign="bottom" align="center" height="100">Cell 3</td>
<td align="center">And this<br>is cell 4</td></tr>
</table>
```

This is cell one	This is cell two
	And this is cell 4
Cell 3	

6.3.2.4 Cellpadding attribute

The value given to this attribute will control the space around data within cells the table. A larger value will increase the space between the data and the table grid lines.

```
<table border="1" cellpadding="5">
<tr><td>cell 1</td><td>cell 2</td></tr>
<tr><td>cell 3</td><td>cell 4</td></tr>
</table>
```

cell 1	cell 2
cell 3	cell 4

cellpadding of 5 pixels

6.3.2.5 Cellspacing attribute

The value given to this attribute will control the space between cells in the table. A
larger value will increase the thickness of the table grid lines.

```
<table border="0" cellpadding="0" cellspacing="5">
<tr><td>cell 1</td><td>cell 2</td></tr>
<tr><td>cell 3</td><td>cell 4</td></tr>
</table>
```

cellspacing of 5 pixels

6.3.2.6 Alignment attributes

Alignment attributes can be specified for a number of table-related elements. The
entire table can be left, center (note the American spelling of centre, which is used in
HTML markup) or right aligned on an HTML page with the 'align' attribute. This same
attribute can be used to position data within individual cells. The 'valign' attribute (for
vertical alignment) can be specified for td elements and takes a value of top, middle
or bottom. The align and valign attributes may also be specified on a table row
element to set a default alignment for all the cells in the row.

```
<table border="0" width="90%" align="center">
<tr><td>cell 1</td><td>cell 2</td></tr>
<tr><td>cell 3</td><td>cell 4</td></tr>
</table>
```

6.3.2.7 Summary attribute

This attribute allows the author to give a descriptive value to a table. The summary
attribute gives a user with a visual impairment an indication of the content of the
table, which will either be spoken or presented by a Braille device.

```
<table border="0" width="90%" summary="this is an example
table">
<tr><td>cell 1</td><td>cell 2</td></tr>
<tr><td>cell 3</td><td>cell 4</td></tr>
</table>
```

6.3.2.8 Caption attribute

This attribute and value will be shown on screen. It allows an author to attach a
descriptive title to a table. This should not replicate the summary information already
included, but should complement it.

```
<table border="0" bgcolor="#ff0000">
<caption><em>A test table</em></caption>
<tr><td>cell 1</td><td>cell 2</td></tr>
```

```
<tr><td>cell 3</td><td>cell 4</td></tr>
</table>
```

6.3.2.9 Table headers for accessibility

The following example shows how to use the table header element to enable screen-reader software to convey the structure of tables. The headers attribute of the table data item elements is used to indicate beneath which header each data item falls.

```
<table border="0"
summary="This table charts the number of cups of coffee
consumed by each e-Communicator, the type of coffee
(decaffeinated or regular), and whether taken with sugar.">
<caption>Cups of coffee consumed by each
e-Communicator</caption>
<tr>
<th id="header1">Name</th>
<th id="header2">Cups</th>
<th id="header3" abbr="Type">Type of Coffee</th>
<th id="header4">Sugar?</th>
</tr>
<tr>
<td headers="header1">G. Ryman</td>
<td headers="header2">10</td>
<td headers="header3">Espresso</td>
<td headers="header4">No</td>
</tr>
<tr>
<td headers="header1">T. Levy</td>
<td headers="header2">5</td>
<td headers="header3">Decaf</td>
<td headers="header4">Yes</td>
</tr>
</table>
```

A screen reader would typically render this table as follows:

```
Caption: Cups of coffee consumed by each e-Communicator
Summary: This table charts the number of cups of coffee
         consumed by each e-Communicator, the type of coffee
         decaf or regular), and whether taken with sugar.
Name: G. Ryman, Cups: 10, Type: Espresso, Sugar: No
Name: T. Levy, Cups: 5, Type: Decaf, Sugar: Yes
```

- Complex tables can have an alternative page that presents the data in a linear fashion or as a <longdesc> file. Although adopted by the W3C WAI, the <longdesc> is not widely supported by current browsers. A solution may to use a [D] (description) link. The D-link is a letter 'D' added to the document next to the table and links to a detailed description.

- To understand how a screen reader will read a table, run a straight edge down the page and read your table line-by-line.

6.3.2.10 Bgcolor attribute

This attribute can be added to a table or a cell to apply a background colour. Wherever it is placed, an author must always ensure that there is sufficient contrast between the contents of the cells and the background colours used in order to avoid user difficulty in reading the data. The example below would colour the entire table background red.

```
<table border="0" bgcolor="#ff0000">
<tr><td>cell 1</td><td>cell 2</td></tr>
<tr><td>cell 3</td><td>cell 4</td></tr>
</table>
```

6.3.2.11 Colspan attribute

This attribute can be added to a cell. Its value will control how many columns individual cell's contents will span across horizontally.

```
<table border="0">
<tr><td colspan="2">This data spans two table cells</td></tr>
<tr><td>cell 1</td><td>cell 2</td></tr>
<tr><td>cell 3</td><td>cell 4</td></tr>
</table>
```

6.3.2.12 Rowspan attribute

This attribute can be added to a cell. Its value will decide how many rows the individual cell's contents will span across vertically.

```
<table border="0">
<tr><td rowspan="2">This data spans two table rows</td>
<td> cell 2</td></tr>
<tr><td>cell 4</td></tr>
</table>
```

> **IMPORTANT**
> *Netscape Navigator tends to be far less forgiving in its rendering of HTML. If HTML markup for a table contains syntax errors, there is a good chance the table will not display correctly. The same table viewed in Microsoft Internet Explorer 4 will often render apparently without a problem.*

6.3.3   Examples of tables

The following example illustrates the range of HTML elements and attributes that may be used in the construction of tables.

```
<table border="1" width="40%" cellpadding="1" cellspacing="1"
align="center" summary="An example of tables using all basic
elements">
<caption><em>A test table</em></caption>
```

```
<tr><th rowspan="2"></th><th colspan="2"
align="center">Average</th>
<th rowspan="2">Red<br> eyes</th></tr>
<tr><th>height</th><th>weight</th></tr>
<tr><th>Males</th><td>1.9</td><td>0.003</td><td>40%</td></tr>
<tr><th>Females</th><td>1.7</td><td>0.002</td><td>43%</td>
</tr>
</table>
```

Every tag that has been opened has been closed correctly. It should also be noted that the text within the caption has been formatted with the `<em>` tag rather than the `<i>`. This ensures that correct emphasis is given to the caption when read by a voice browser.

This table will render as shown:

A test table

	Average		Red
	height	weight	eyes
Males	1.9	0.003	40%
Females	1.7	0.002	43%

Further, more detailed instructions on using and implementing HTML tables within a website can be found in the W3C HTML4.01 specification.

HTML4 .01 specification from W3C
http://www.w3.org/TR/1998/REC-html40-19980424/

HTML Techniques for Web Content Accessibility Guidelines 1.0
http://www.w3.org/TR/WCAG10-HTML-TECHS/

6.4 HTML frames

HTML frames allow the web author to split the browsing window into a number of different sub-windows, each of which can be used to display the content of a separate HTML file.

HTML frames need to be used carefully if they are to enhance, rather than detract from, users' experience of a website.

Use each checklist to ensure that your web pages comply with these guidelines

6.4.1 Checklist and summary	*Recommended*
Checklist	❑ Any website constructed using frames must include a `noframes` alternative ❑ Any website constructed using frames must be usable on a browser that cannot render frames ❑ Each frame must be named ❑ Frames should not be multiply nested within frames ❑ Do not rely on the frames environment for website navigation ❑ Navigational elements should be included on each individual web document ❑ All links outside the website should be loaded into the top-level window: avoid displaying other websites framed by yours.
Summary	The use of frames in a website is a source of some contention. Some Web managers have been under the impression that they should not be used at all. Others have employed them without proper consideration for their implication for their whole user community. Frames are part of the HTML4.01 specification and the WAI, which means that they can be used by most browsers and users. If frames are implemented correctly they can be a useful technique for designing the user interface. If used incorrectly, they can make a website incomprehensible and very difficult to navigate around.

6.4.2 Background information

Netscape introduced frames to the web in 1995 and they have since become part of the HTML standard maintained by W3C.

They give the author the ability to break up a single browser window into multiple sections, referred to as 'frames', each displaying a different HTML page. Each of these pages can be manipulated separately by the user, and hyperlinks in each separate frame can target another frame.

The development of frames made it easier for Web managers to incorporate a corporate look and feel into websites. On a standard webpage an organisation's logos and navigational areas will usually be displayed at the very top. This is fine until a user has to scroll down a page to retrieve some information. When the page scrolls down, the logo and navigational area will disappear from the browser screen.

The following screen-shots show how this is rendered within a web browser:

Top of the document   Scrolled down

Using frames, the designer can ensure that both of these elements remain visible, when the user scrolls down the page displayed in the main content frame.

The main content pages within the website need only contain the substantive data because all the organisation and navigation information is contained within the non-scrolling frame(s). The following illustration shows how a departmental name and logo will always be displayed within a browser, even when the page has been scrolled downwards:

Top of the document   Scrolled down

Using frames to build websites in this way has been popular. It has eliminated the need to repeat section within pages and helped browsers avoid repetitive rendering of graphics. However, there are potential problems with this approach:

- The frames would only be set up if the user came through the homepage. Users entering through search facilities or links from other websites would not get the frames set up and therefore may not be able to navigate further through the website
- The time taken for a browser to display the initial set-up of a website using frames would be longer because there would be multiple HTML files to fetch from the server and render rather than just one.

- Bookmarking pages of interest is more difficult for users as only the page establishing the frames would normally be recorded.
- Printing documents is more complex, as the browser would not necessarily know which frame or frames are to be printed.
- Individual page titles are lost as because only the title element of the page that sets up the frameset is displayed.
- Badly managed links can result in frames being rendered within parent frames.
- Differing user monitor sizes can result in large proportions of the screen being used by the frames containing logos, navigation and whatever, leaving very little screen space for the substantive data.

Many of these issues, such as bookmarking and printing, have become easier with the development of more advanced browsers. Use of the right-hand mouse button allows particular pages to be specified for both functions.

Scripting techniques can also be used to improve the usability of websites that use frames. For example, it is possible to have a script in each page that detects whether it is being displayed outside of the intended frames set-up and, if so, re-establishes the required frameset. This technique can be used to resolve the problem of user's bookmarking or following links to individual HTML pages that would otherwise be displayed out of the frames context.

> **IMPORTANT**
> *It is often said that a user, in any given website, is only three clicks away from an unpleasant external website. Given this it is extremely important that any website that uses frames should ensure that all links to websites outside its control should be launched outside the frame environment.*

Unfortunately, many problems with the implementation of frames remain and careful management of the website is needed in order to avoid the potential snags.

> **IMPORTANT**
> *In a website that uses frame it is essential that all documents within the website contain all of the navigational elements. Users with browsers that cannot render frames will still use these elements to get around the website. However, these same documents can be used in the frames website but users will benefit from the extra navigational aids that can be implemented as a result of the use of frames.*

There are a number of pros and cons in the use of frames. Each must be considered before using them in an organisation's website.

6.4.3   Implementation

Not all browsers can display frames, some because they were released before were invented and others, such as screen readers and digital TV, because they just do not work with them. For this reason, a noframes version of the website must always be provided for users.

The first document of the website, (the one usually called index.htm or default.htm) establishes the frames environment. This page is not actually displayed to the user:

it just sets the frame structure used by the rest of the website. It is this page that places the website's title in the browser's window title bar and divides the screen up into the frames with in which subsequent HTML pages are displayed.

The following is a basic introduction to the HTML attributes that should always be used in a frames environment.

6.4.3.1 Frameset

This HTML tag establishes a frames environment. It specifies the dimensions of each of the frames to be set-up with either percentage or fixed pixel values. A frameset element may specify that the users' display window is to be divided up either row-wise or column-wise. Frameset elements may be nested in order to divide the display window both row- and column-wise.

The attributes used with this element are all marked up in the standard HTML way (ie, `attribute="value"`, with each attribute and value pair separated by one or more spaces).

`rows="30%,20%,*"`	In this example three frame windows are established in percentages of the viewable screen area. The first window is given 30 per cent, the second 20 per cent and the third set to the asterisk character which means it is to fill whatever is left of the display window after the specified frame sizes have been set up.
`cols="200,100,*"`	In this example three frame windows are established in columns of fixed pixel values. The first window is given 200 pixels, the second 100. The size of the third column is set to the asterisk character, which specifies that it is to fill whatever is left of the display window after the specified frame sizes have been set up.

6.4.3.2 Frame

This element is used to specify which page should be loaded from the website and displayed within each of the frames established by a frameset element. Each frame should be given an individual identifier or name. The name of a frame is quite separate from the frame's title attribute and from any setting of the HTML title element inside an HTML file that is displayed with the frame.

`src="top.htm"`	Each frame must have a URL attribute. The browser will load the resource at the URL into the frame. The URL can be either relative or absolute.
`name="top"`	Each frame should be given an individual identifier. This is used to target hyperlinks between pages and frames.
`title="This is the navigational frame"`	This title attribute and value will help accessibility browsers identify different frames to their users. Using these correctly will enable users of accessibility technologies to orientate themselves to your website's design and functionality.

`scrolling="no"`	This attribute instructs the browser to turn off the scrolling bars within that specific frame. Other available values are "yes", which displays the scrolling bar, and "auto", which only shows the scroll bar if the information contained in the frame is larger than the displayable area.
`noresize`	This attribute prevents the user from being able to resize the frame by grabbing the visible frame divider and dragging it across the screen.

`marginheight="2 0"`
 	
`marginwidth="15 "`
	These two attributes control the size of the margin depth around a given frame. In this example the frame data would only be displayed after a vertical gap of 20 pixels and a horizontal gap of 15 pixels.

`frameborder="0"`	This attribute controls the border size of each of the frames. In this example, the value of zero means the frame will not display a frame border.

6.4.3.3 Noframes

It is essential that this element be used when a frames environment is chosen for an organisation's website. Many browsers do not understand frames, so if this tag is not included on the frame set-up page the browser will display nothing at all.

Web browsers are programmed to display only the contents of HTML elements that they recognise and to ignore any elements that they do not. The `noframes` element has a `body` element nested immediately within it so a browser that does not understand frames will recognise the content of the `noframes` element as what it will consider to be the `body` element of a legitimate HTML page. On the other hand, a frame-capable browser will read and display all of the frames data and will ignore everything contained within the `noframes` element.

6.4.3.4 Target

The target attribute may be added to any hypertext link (href element) to instruct browsers to load the object of the hyperlink into the frame whose name is specified as the value of the target attribute.

Specifying a name of a frame (the name given to it on its frame element) will make the object of the hyperlink load into that frame. Specifying a value that does not match the name of any frame element will cause the object to load into a new browser window, which will be created with the specified names.

There are a number of other special values for the target attribute:

- Specifying "_top" will ensure that the object of the hyperlinks will be loaded into the same browser window but will replace all of the currently set up frames.
- Specifying "_parent" will load the new document into the parent window or frameset containing the frame that contains the hyperlink anchor.

- Specifying "_blank" will open a new unnamed window.
- Specifying "_self" has the same result as is obtained by omitting the target attribute altogether: the object of the hyperlink is loaded into the same frame as the hyperlink anchor.

6.4.4 Example

The examples below will illustrate how frames should be implemented.

For illustrative purposes each of the individual frames have its own background colour so that is immediately obvious which page has been placed in which frame. All hotkey attributes and styling by Cascading Style Sheets have been deleted from the example to simplify the illustration of the frame commands.

6.4.4.1 side.htm

This page contains all the navigation elements within the website. It will have a light red background colour and will be displayed along the left-hand side of the browser. Each of the hyperlinks uses the `target="display"` attribute and value to ensure that each linked document appears in the correct frame.

Only frames-capable browsers will ever use this page.

```
<!DOCTYPE HTML PUBLIC "-//W3C//DTD HTML 4.0//EN"
"http://www.w3.org/TR/REC-html40/strict.dtd">

<html>
<head>
<title>Side</title>
</head>

<body bgcolor="#ffccff">

<h3>Nav Bar</h3>
<p><a href="home.htm" target="display">Homepage</a></p>
<p><a href="info.htm" target="display">Organisation
Information</a></p>
<p><a href="whatsnew.htm" target="display">What's New</a></p>
<p><a href="sitemap.htm" target="display">Sitemap</a></p>
<p><a href="contact.htm" target="display">Contact</a></p>
<p><a href="search.htm" target="display">Search</a></p>
<p><a href="help.htm" target="display">Help</a></p>

</body>
</html>
```

6.4.4.2 top.htm

This document will be displayed across the top of the browser and will have a light yellow background. Its only content will be the organisation's title.

Only frames-capable browsers will ever use this page.

```
<!DOCTYPE HTML PUBLIC "-//W3C//DTD HTML 4.0//EN"
"http://www.w3.org/TR/REC-html40/strict.dtd">

<html>
<head>
<title>Top</title>
</head>

<body bgcolor="#ffffcc">

<h1>Department X</h1>

</body>
</html>
```

6.4.4.3 home.htm

This document will take up the majority of the browser screen, will have a lime
background colour and will display the substantive content of the website. This and
all subsequent pages that are displayed in this frame should also contain the basic
navigational elements. This will ensures that users of browsers that do not display
frames will be able to navigate the website.

Only frames-capable browsers will ever use this initial page. This information is
replicated in the <noframes> area of the index.htm file.

```
<!DOCTYPE HTML PUBLIC "-//W3C//DTD HTML 4.0//EN"
"http://www.w3.org/TR/REC-html40/strict.dtd">

<html>
<head>
<title>Home</title>
</head>

<body bgcolor="#66ff66">

<p>
<a href="home.htm">Homepage</a> | <a
href="info.htm">Organisation Information</a> | <a
href="whatsnew.htm">What's New</a> | <a
href="sitemap.htm">Sitemap</a> | <a
href="contact.htm">Contact</a> | <a
href="search.htm">Search</a> | <a href="help.htm">Help</a>
</p>

<h2>Display Area</h2>
<p>This is the main area that all documents and links to
documents will be displayed</p>

</body>
</html>
```

6.4.4.4 index.htm – frame setup page

If a website did not use frames, this page would normally be the website's homepage. In a website that uses frames, it contains the frameset, frame and noframes elements.

This example shows the frames structure established by the `frameset` element.

The index.htm page instructs the browser to display three pages, side.htm, top.htm and home.htm. A number of attributes are used to specify margin width, border width, size of frame, etc.

The information contained within the noframes element will only be displayed if a user's browser does cannot use frames.

```
<!DOCTYPE HTML PUBLIC "-//W3C//DTD HTML 4.0//EN"
"http://www.w3.org/TR/REC-html40/strict.dtd">

<html>
<head>
<title>Example of Frames</title>
</head>

<frameset  cols="23%,*">
<frame name="sidebar" src="side.htm" marginwidth="5"
marginheight="0" scrolling="no" frameborder="1" noresize
title="Navigational Area">
<frameset  rows="18%,*">
<frame name="logo" src="top.htm" marginwidth="10"
marginheight="10" scrolling="no" frameborder="0" noresize
title="Department X logo">
<frame name="display" src="home.htm" marginwidth="5"
marginheight="5" scrolling="auto" frameborder="0" noresize
title="Main Display Area">
</frameset>
</frameset>

<noframes>
<body bgcolor="#ffffff">

<p>This information will only be displayed if your browser
cannot read frames.</p>

<p>
<a href="home.htm">Homepage</a> | <a
href="info.htm">Organisation Information</a> | <a
href="whatsnew.htm">What's New</a> | <a
href="sitemap.htm">Sitemap</a> | <a
href="contact.htm">Contact</a> | <a
href="search.htm">Search</a> | <a href="help.htm">Help</a>
</p>
```

```
<h1>Department X</h1>

<h2>Display Area</h2>
<p>This is the main area that all documents and links to
documents will be displayed</p>
</body>
</noframes>

</html>
```

6.4.4.5 Basic concept of page construction

The combination of HTML pages are held together by the frame setup page
(index.htm). The illustration below shows how the four separate HTML frame
documents given in this section relate to each other, combining to complete the
window displayed by the web browser.

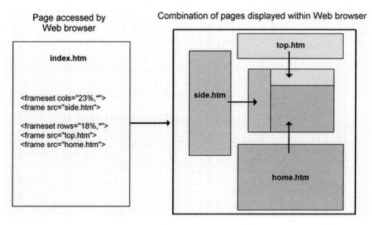

6.4.4.6 View on a frames-capable browser

The example frame setup will be rendered as follows on a frames-capable browser.

For illustrative purposes Microsoft's Internet Explorer 4 has been used. Each of the
frames can be seen.

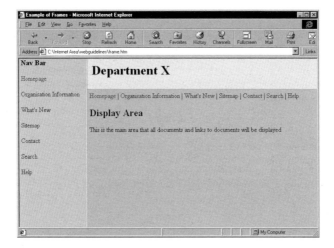

6.4.4.7 View on a non-frames-capable browser

The same HTML page (index.htm) when viewed on a non-frames-capable browser looks very different. The browser ignores all of the elements it does not understand and only the data contained within the `noframes` element is displayed.

Further, more detailed instructions on using and implementing frames within a website can be found in the W3C HTML4.1 specification.

HTML4.01 specification from W3C
http://www.w3.org/TR/html4/

6.5 HTML forms

HTML forms provide way in which an organisation can collect structured feedback from the users of its website. They can range from simple suggestion or problem reporting forms to complex user feedback surveys.

However they are used, there are a number of elements that must be implemented correctly to ensure accessibility to as wide a range of users as possible.

Use each checklist to ensure that your web pages comply with these guidelines

6.5.1 Checklist and summary	*Core guidance*
Checklist	❑ Forms are contained within the HTML `form` element. ❑ Tables can be used to help format an HTML form but should not get in the way of its usability or accessibility ❑ All styling of the form can be accomplished using Cascading Style Sheets. ❑ If webserver CGI software is used to process the data submitted from forms, the web manager will need to check with the organisation's hosting service about the location of the cgi-bin directory. ❑ All elements that are required to be closed, must be closed and elements must be properly nested. ❑ Where possible, HTML forms should bear a resemblance to the design of the paper-based form. ❑ Form design should be consistent throughout the organisation's website.
Summary	If constructed correctly forms can add value to a website and be of value to the organisation itself. For this reason it is important to ensure that the correct elements are used and that forms are designed with the user in mind.

6.5.2 Implementation

A form is constructed in HTML 4.01. It allows a user to set the values of the form elements on the page by clicking on pre-selected options or inputting text into designated fields. The contents of the form elements can then be submitted to a URL, specified in the form element markup, for processing.

This completed information can either be sent directly to a Web manager's email address or, more usually, to the organisation's hosting server where it is typically stored until it is outputted according to some pre-arranged timetable. The collected information can then be analysed using applications such as spreadsheets or databases.

If form submissions are to be collected by the organisation's web hosting service, it is important to liaise with your server administrator to ensure that they are willing to take form submissions, and for a suitable server-side CGI script or ASP to be put in place.

Many HTML elements go into the construction of an HTML form. The following are the basic elements that are commonly used.

6.5.2.1 Form

The `form` element is the container for an HTML form.

A form can be sent directly to a webserver for processing by adding the URL of the resource that is to perform the processing.

```
<form action="http://www.domainname.gov.uk/cgi-bin/postit.pl"
method="post">
. . . form contents . . .
</form>
```

The action attribute can also be used to trigger a client-side email user agent to send the submitted form contents directly to an email address.

```
<form action="mailto:webmaster@department.gov.uk"
method="post">
. . . form contents . . .
</form>
```

There are a number of cautions concerning the latter approach. First, some early browsers do not support mailto in form actions. Second, the approach contains the inherent assumption that the user has a properly configured email client installed on the computer from which they are submitting the HTML form.

6.5.2.2 Input elements

There are a number of methods by which forms can allow users to input data. Each is specified using a variation of the input element markup, and each has a number of additional attributes and values that can be added.

Text
Creates a single-line text input box.

```
<input type="text" name="firstname">
```

Checkbox
Creates an on/off button box that can be toggled (ticked and unticked) by the user. Only the value of boxes that have been selected will be included with the submitted form data.

```
<input type="checkbox" name="internet" value="car">
```

Radio

Works in a similar way as 'checkbox' except that when several buttons share the same control name (eg `name="sex"`) they are mutually exclusive. When one is switched on, all others with the same name are switched off.

```
<input type="radio" name="sex" value="Male">
<input type="radio" name="sex" value="Female">
```

Both 'checkbox' and 'radio' can be selected by default by including the 'checked' attribute (which does not take a value).

Submit

When activated, a 'submit' button sends the contents of the form to the URL specified on the form element. Any value added to the 'value' attribute will be rendered as a text label on the button.

```
<input type="submit" value="Send form">
```

Although it is possible, authors should not use graphic buttons for the submission of forms.

Reset

A 'reset' button resets all controls in the form, clearing the user input and returning controls to their initial values.

```
<input type="reset"> value="Reset form">
```

6.5.2.3 Select control element

This control offers the user a pull-down menu option from which to choose one option.

```
<select name="age">
      <option>18-40</option>
      <option>41-65</option>
      <option>65 upwards</option>
</select>
```

When used with the size attribute, the select control renders as a multi-select scrolling list that displays the number of entries that is specified as the value of the size attribute.

6.5.2.4 Textarea

This element creates a multi-line input control, allowing users to type in and view larger amounts of data. The author specifies the geometry of the area by including the 'rows' and 'cols' attributes.

```
<textarea name="furtherdetails" rows="6" cols="50">
</textarea>
```

6.5.2.5 Tabindex

This attribute and value can be added to any form element. It controls the order of input for users who do not wish to or who cannot use pointing devices such as a mouse. In the example given in **section 6.5.3** each tag has been given a 'tabindex' value, help to ensure that fields are completed in the correct order. This has no controlling effect on anyone using a mouse to complete the form.

See **section 2.4.4** UK government accesskeys standard.

6.5.3 Example

The following example illustrates a very basic feedback form that uses some of the elements discussed in the previous section.

```
<form action="http://www.domainname.gov.uk/cgi-bin/postit.pl"
method="post">
<p>First name : <input tabindex="1" type="text"
name="firstname"><br>
Last name : <input tabindex="2" type="text"
name="lastname"><br>
email : <input tabindex="3" type="text" name="email"><br></p>
<p>Which of the following do you own:<br>
<input tabindex="6" type="checkbox" name="possession"
value="car">Car
<input tabindex="7" type="checkbox" name="possession"
value="house">House
<input tabindex="8" type="checkbox" name="possession"
value="boat">Boat</p>
<p>What sex are you?:<br>
<input tabindex="4" type="radio" name="sex" value="Male">
Male<br>
<input tabindex="5" type="radio" name="sex" value="Female">
Female</p>
<p>Age : <select tabindex="9" name="age">
<option>1-10</option>
<option>11-20</option>
<option>21-30</option>
<option>31-40</option>
<option>41-50</option>
<option>51-60</option>
</select></p>
<p>
<textarea tabindex="10" name="furtherdetails" rows="6"
cols="50">
Add further details within this box:
</textarea></p>
<p>
<input tabindex="11" type="submit" value="Send">
<input tabindex="12" type="reset"
value= "Reset form and start again">
</p>
</form>
```

There is no validation of the form content on this example form. The form could be submitted without any of the fields being completed.

An author may wish to add client-side scripting to validate the form contents before it is submitted. For example, scripting could be used to ensure that a minimum of fields has been completed before submission, or that only numerical values are added to a telephone number input field. Technically this can be accomplished by including the JavaScript in the page, and having it triggered by an onClick event on the form submit button.

A web browser like this would render this form:

First name :
Last name :
email :

Which of the following do you own:
☐ Car ☐ House ☐ Boat

What sex are you?:
○ Male
○ Female

Age : 1-10 ▼

Add further details within this box:

Send   Reset

Further, more detailed instructions on constructing and implementing forms can be found in the W3C HTML 4 .01specification.

HTML 4.01 specification from W3C
http://www.w3.org/TR/1998/REC-html40-19980424/

IMPORTANT
If you collect personal data via forms the Data Protection Act applies.
See section 1.10.2.

6.6 Web page navigation

Navigation around a web page can be achieved in a number of ways. Text, graphic buttons, imagemaps and keyboard shortcuts can all be used in any number of combinations.

Each of these tools may be implemented within a website as long as measures are put in place to ensure that every user can gain access to every page.

Use each checklist to ensure that your web pages comply with these guidelines

6.6.1 Text navigation bar	*Core Guidance*
Checklist	❑ An HTML text navigation bar is best placed at the top of every page ❑ The `accesskey` attribute should be used for each link ❑ Text should be formatted by Cascading Style Sheets ❑ Text must be legible without the use of Cascading Style Sheets ❑ Text must be easily distinguishable against a clear background colour ❑ A 'skip navigation' option should be the first element in the list ❑ There must be no dead-end links
Summary	Not all users choose to view websites using graphics, and many are unable, because of impaired vision, to use images at all. These users may be using small-screen browsers that only display text, or may be visually impaired users using access technology. It is for this reason that text is the simplest and most powerful tool available to construct a navigational aid for users.

6.6.1.1 Implementation

To ensure that the most important element of the page is loaded first and is accessible to all, it is imperative that all UK public sector websites offer text navigation, containing each of the important links, at the very top of each page.

The text elements within this top navigation bar should be separated by spare + vertical bar (|) character + space which is not part of the link. This avoids the problem with the access technology reading all the links as one.

This text navigation should also use the hotkey capabilities referred to in the WAI guidelines (see **section 2.4**). This allows authors to assign keyboard actions to hyperlinks. As well as being a useful tool for getting around a website, its primary role is to aid users with motor disabilities who find controlling a pointing device difficult.

This keyboard access is part of the HTML 4 recommendation for all browsers, although this facility can only be used by the Microsoft Internet Explorer browser at present.

> **IMPORTANT**
>
> *It is essential that once the order of the text navigation be decided on, it is adhered to throughout each page on the website. This allows users to quickly become accustomed to your website structure.*

The text elements of the top navigation bar are best formatted using a CSS, ensuring that the text is legible against the background colour and easily displayed by browsers that are unable to interpret CSS.

A sighted person will scan a page and ignore repeating items. A user with a visual impairment cannot do this and they have to tab through each link every time. To assist these users, the first link on the top text navigation bar should offer a jump to bypass the repeating elements. This link should be an internal link to the beginning of the document text itself.

6.6.1.2 Example

This example illustrates how each of the earlier points is implemented.

- A CSS attribute `class="topnav"` formats the text for display within the web browser.
- The hypertext link tag includes the `accesskey` attribute, allocating a letter for each link.
- The first link in the top navigational bar allows a user to bypass repeating elements and go straight to the document.

```
<p class="topnav">
<a accesskey="S" href="#skip">Skip Navigation bar</a> |
<a accesskey="1" href="index.htm">Home</a> |
<a accesskey="2" href="whatsnew.htm">What's New</a> |
<a accesskey="3" href="sitemap.htm">Sitemap</a> |
<a accesskey="C" href="contact.htm">Contact</a> |
<a accesskey="4" href="search.htm">Search</a> |
<a accesskey="6" href="help.htm">Help</a>
</p>

<a name="skip"><h1>Document Title</h1></a>
```

The resulting web page would be displayed as follows:

Home | What's New | Sitemap | Contact | Search Facility | Help

When inserting a hyperlink it is sometimes advisable to enter some information for users that is not included within the link text or graphic using the 'title' attribute. This is illustrated by the following example:

```
<p>This page is also available in the following formats <a
href="html-doc.htm" title="56kB">[html]</a> <a
href="pdf_doc.pdf" title="120kB">[pdf]</a> <a href="rtf-
doc.rtf" title="61kB">[rtf]</a></p>
```

In this example, the 'title' information is the size of the file to load (HTML file is 56kB, PDF file is 120kB). This information will display in a visual browser when the pointer hovers over the link, while a speech browser will automatically read it.

IMPORTANT

The 'title' attribute can be an excellent tool to help the user but it is important not to make the caption too long-winded. Too long a message, however helpful, will only cause irritation to a visually impaired viewer who will have to listen to it whether they want to or not!

See **section 2.4.4** UK Government accesskeys standard

6.6.2 Graphic navigation	*Core guidance* *If used in website*
Checklist	❑ Graphic buttons must reflect the textual navigation that appears at the top of each page ❑ An 'alt' attribute and value reflecting its contents must be added to each button ❑ The value of the 'alt' attribute should be no more than 100 characters ❑ The text within the graphic button must be clearly legible against its background colour ❑ Each graphic button must use the same 'accesskey' values as those assigned within the top navigation area
Summary	Navigation to pages can be achieved by using pictorial buttons saved in either GIF or JPEG format. It should be remembered that PNG format is not yet widely supported by web browsers. The effect of graphic buttons can be appealing when designing a web page but can be an annoying hindrance to users if implemented inappropriately.

6.6.2.1 Implementation

Any page on a website can benefit from appropriately used graphics. They can be used to illustrate a point, label a document as a department's property or give a more visually rich navigation environment.

When navigation of the website uses graphical buttons the site must always be as easy to use when these graphics cannot be viewed. There must always be a descriptive value to the `alt` attribute given to every navigationally important graphic.

See **section 2.4.5.6** accessible images

IMPORTANT

Turn off the automatic graphics download in your browser to give an indication of what your page is like when you cannot see the graphic buttons.

Is it still easily usable?

When graphic buttons are used, specific values to both the `width` and `height` attributes within the image tag must be set. This helps the browser to render the page on screen with the minimum number of screen redraws.

It is important that graphic navigation buttons are not too large, so that the largest area possible is given over to displaying the document whilst also ensuring that the graphic file sizes are as small as possible.

When graphic buttons are relatively small on screen and a small text font is used, it is important that this text is large enough to be legible for everyone and not anti-aliased (see **section 2.8.10**).

6.6.2.2 Example

An example of the correct implementation of a group of graphic buttons is shown below:

```
<a accesskey="1" href="index.htm"><img
src="images/button1.gif" width="80" height="20" border="0"
alt="Return to Homepage"></a><br>
<a accesskey="2" href="whatsnew.htm"><img
src="images/button2.gif" width="80" height="20" border="0"
alt="What's New"></a><br>
<a accesskey="3" href="sitemap.htm"><img
src="images/button3.gif" width="80" height="20" border="0"
alt="Sitemap"></a><br>
<a accesskey="C" href="contact.htm"><img
src="images/button4.gif" width="80" height="20" border="0"
alt="Contact Details"></a><br>
<a accesskey="4" href="search.htm"><img
src="images/button5.gif" width="80" height="20" border="0"
alt="Search"></a><br>
```

```
<a accesskey="6" href="help.htm"><img src="images/button6.gif"
width="80" height="20" border="0" alt="Help"></a><br>
```

Each of the buttons is 80 pixels wide and 20 pixels in height. The `<br>` tag is there to ensure that each button starts on a new line and is directly below the previous button.

Note that each of the graphic buttons uses the same `accesskey` letter identifiers as the earlier top text navigation bar. This is essential to avoid confusion within the browser itself and to allow users to acclimatise to a standard set of navigational aids within the website.

See **section 2.4.4** UK Government accesskeys standard

6.6.3 Imagemaps	*Core guidance* *If used in website*
Checklist	❑ Always use a client-side map ❑ The `usemap` attribute must be added to your imagemap graphic ❑ An `alt` attribute and value reflecting its contents must be added to each button ❑ The text alternative to the imagemap should be visible beside or underneath the imagemap graphic ❑ Any text within the imagemap graphic must be clearly legible against its background colour
Summary	Navigation to pages can be achieved by using one large graphic. Areas within this graphic can then be designated as live by using the `map` tag and x and y co-ordinates. These imagemaps can be appealing on a web page but are next to useless if the user is visually impaired. This does not mean they shouldn't be used, it just means alternatives should be offered.

6.6.3.1 Implementation

However visually appealing this method of navigation may look; it should only be used sparingly in the website.

There are basically two forms of imagemap, both of which have names that describe how they work, server-side and client-side. The client-side imagemap is the more flexible and therefore the version that must be used.

Server-side imagemaps

Server-side imagemaps are the older variety that will only work if the browser is connected to the Internet at the time the hot spot is selected. Each click on the image will result in a transaction between the user's browser and the content provider's website. This is relatively inflexible and has been overtaken by client-side imagemaps.

Client-side imagemapes

These were developed by Netscape in 1996 and do not require any interaction between the page and the originator's website once the page has been loaded to the user's browser. They can be used offline because all of the co-ordinates are contained within the HTML page.

HTML authors should be aware that some early browsers do not support client-side imagemaps and may wish to include server-side imagemaps as well to cater for them. Browsers that can use client-side imagemaps will use them in preference to server-side ones if both are provided.

When an imagemap is used, a text alternative should be supplied alongside the graphic in question. This text must be formatted using Cascading Style Sheets and must be clearly legible against the page's background colour.

It is essential that each designated area within the client-side imagemap be given an 'alt' attribute with a value that describes the link. This is useful to all users. There is an accessibility requirement to provide a text alternative.

6.6.3.2 Example

An example of a correct implementation of a client-side imagemap is as follows:

```
<img src="images/landsend.jpg" width="301" height="260"
border="0" alt="Lands End Signpost" usemap="#route_map">
<br>
<span class="imagenav">
<a href="landsend.htm">Landsend |</a>
<a href="newyork.htm">New York |</a>
<a href="johnogroats.htm">John 'O' Groats |</a>
<a href="scillyisles.htm">Scilly Isles |</a>
</span>

<map name="route_map">
<area shape="rect" coords="39,73,138,93" href="newyork.htm"
alt="New York">
<area shape="rect" coords="171,72,283,96"
href="johnogroats.htm" alt="John O Groats">
<area shape="circle" coords="149,39,38" href="landsend.htm"
alt="Lands End">
<area shape="poly"
coords="141,116,9,105,14,128,141,139,141,116"
href="scillyisles.htm" alt="Scilly Isles">
</map>
```

In this example there is the image object, called `landsend.jpg`, followed by the text alternative version which is formatted using the `class="imagenav"'` from the Cascading Style Sheet.

The client-side `map` that follows contains the co-ordinates, link attributes and values that makes the imagemap work.

6.6.4 Alphabars	Core guidance If used in website
Checklist	☐ Use Cascading Style Sheets to formats the text links ☐ Give the links as big a foot print as possible ☐ Clearly separate the individual links with spaces or, for example, the vertical bar (|) character
Summary	This method of navigation is designed to allow the efficient location of a part of a very complex or large document or list.

6.6.4.1 Implementation

If an organisation's website is to contain a lengthy list of links or other information, it makes no sense to try and fit it all in to one document and let the user try find the information they want by scrolling up and down an enormous page. This process would be very annoying for many users and almost impossible for people without the use of a pointing device.

The best way of navigating around this sort of information is to offer the user a quick navigational jumping point to the letter or section of interest.

An example of an alphabar for an online Glossary document is shown below.

Glossary

Letter   A B C D E F G H I J K L M N O P R S T U V W X Y-Z

This example uses capital letters. Although these are generally seen as being more difficult to read, they do offer a larger footprint on the page than lowercase letters. The larger the footprint, the easier it is for the user to locate the hypertext link with their pointing device.

The letter or number codes used in the list may be internal links within the document; alternatively they could link to internal reference points within other documents.

It is always advisable to have a link back to the top of the document at the end of each section to avoid having the user scroll back to the top to use the alphabar again.

6.6.4.2 Example

Illustrated below is an example of a correct implementation of an alphabar, it has been slightly truncated for display purposes.

```
<table border="0" cellpadding="2" cellspacing="2">
<tr class="id">
<td class="whitetext" width="60">Letter</td>
<td><a href="#a">A</a></td>
<td><a href="#b">B</a></td>
<td><a href="#c">C</a></td>
<td><a href="#d">D</a></td>
<td><a href="#e">E</a></td>
<td><a href="#f">F</a></td>
<td><a href="#g">G</a></td>
<td><a href="#h">H</a></td>
<td><a href="#i"> I</a></td>
<td><a href="#j">J</a></td>
</tr>
</table>
```

Each of the letters is an internal hyperlink to a section within the document.

The one line that has been highlighted in bold shows how the letter I, which would normally have a very small footprint on the page, has been enlarged by the use of the HTML mark up for a non-breaking space ( ).

See **section 2.4** Building in universal accessibility

7 Annexes

Contents

Annex A. Web browser applications

The following is a short list of the most commonly used web browsers. This list cannot be exhaustive and they are listed by their generic names. To ensure continued relevance, no version numbers are shown.

The majority of these web browsers are free and available for download. The last is available for 30-day free trial but then require a licence payment.

This list does not, in any way, constitute any form of endorsement by Office of the e-Envoy

	Support CSS	Support HTML4	Support Java and JavaScript	Size of Download File	Free / Purchase
Amaya W3C http://www.w3.org/Amaya	◆	◆		4.9 Mb	FREE
Internet Explorer Microsoft http://www.microsoft.com/ie	◆	◆	◆	18.6 Mb	FREE*
Lynx Lynx http://lynx.isc.org/release/				0.7 Mb	FREE
Mozilla Mozilla http://www.mozilla.org	◆	◆	◆	8 Mb	FREE*
Netscape Navigator Netscape http://www.netscape.com	◆	◆	◆	8 Mb	FREE*
Opera Opera http://www.opera.com	◆	◆	◆	1.8 Mb	30 day** free trial available

* Commonly available on CD-ROM

**A free version of Opera is available with identical functionality to the priced edition but is supported by online advertising.

Website specialising in free downloads of old browser applications
http://www.oldbrowsers.com
http://browsers.evolt.org

Freeware and shareware applications can be obtained from the following sites
http://www.tucows.com
http://alcom.tucows.com

Annex B. Disability specific web browsers

The following list should not be considered to be exhaustive. Most of the following browsers are free; some carry a nominal charge. Each can be used in conjunction with a variety of access technologies and they can all be used for testing an organisations website but this is not essential.

They are neither quality tested or rated in any way.

This list does not, in any way, constitute any form of endorsement by Office of the e-Envoy

AVANTI http://www.avanti-acts.org/html/detail/userint.htm	Developed by the AVANTI Project, this browser provides for some of the diverse needs of elderly and disabled people and covers a range of disability-specific requirements.
HomePage Reader http://www.ibm.com/able/hpr.html	This browser from IBM uses their ViaVoice text-to-speech synthesiser and supports JavaScript.
MultiWeb http://mis.deakin.edu.au/multiWeb/MWIntro.htm	Disability-specific browser developed at Deakin University.
PwWebSpeak http://www.prodworks.com/productsindex.htm#pwWebspeak	The first and longest established low-vision browser from the Productivity Works. Only limited support is now available

Screen Readers

A screen-reader is used to allow navigation of the screen presented by the operating system, using speech and/or Braille output, and should therefore enable use of any mainstream application. In the context of browsing this usually means that they are used in conjunction with Netscape, Microsoft Internet Explorer, or, less often, with one of the other non-disability-specific browsers such as LYNX and Opera.

ASAW http://www.microtalk.com	Produced by Microtalk Speech specialist application DOS, Windows 95/98
HAL (and **SuperNova**) http://www.dolphinuk.co.uk	Produced by Dolphin Speech, magnification and Braille specialist application DOS, Windows 95/98 and NT
JAWS for Windows http://www.freedomscientific.com	Produced by Henter-Joyce (a division of Freedom Scientific) Commercial screen reader software for Win95/98 and WinNT systems; also outputs to refreshable Braille displays.
OutSpoken http://www.alva-bv.nl/screenaccess/product.asp	Produced by Alva Speech and Braille specialist application Windows 95/98, Macintosh

Window-Eyes http://www.gwmicro.com/	Produced by GWMicro Speech specialist application DOS, Windows 3.x and 95/98

Adaptive technology browsers

These browsers are all designed for general use, but are of interest because they may give enhanced accessibility in combination with particular adaptive systems, and some have enhanced screen magnification or navigation options.

Amaya http://www.w3.org/amaya	This is W3C's test-bed browser, implementing emerging web technologies. Versions for Windows 95/98, Windows NT and UNIX.
Lynx http://lynx.browser.org/	This is a popular text-based browser for allowing flexible and powerful text-based access from older platforms. Versions for UNIX, Windows 95/NT and MS-DOS.

Voice browsers

These are systems that allow voice-driven navigation, some with both voice-in and voice-out, and some allowing telephone-based web access.

ConversaWeb http://www.speechtechnology.com/otherspeech/conversaWeb_n.html	Voice-activated browser allowing spoken selection of links using 'saycons'.
TelWeb http://www.edson.net/telWeb	Experimental telephone-based browsers allowing access to any site using voice and dialled commands.

W3C WAI Alternative web browsing **This is a collection of pointers to information, and where possible, to demonstration versions of alternative browsing methods** ***http://www.w3.org/WAI/References/Browsing***

Annex C. HTML editor applications

The following is a short list of commonly used HTML editors. This list cannot be exhaustive and they are listed by their generic names. To ensure continued relevance, no version numbers are shown.

This list does not, in any way, constitute any form of endorsement by Office of the e-Envoy

	HTML tag view	WYSIWYG view	JavaScript Library	Website Mgmt Tool	Size of Download File	Free / Purchase
Dreamweaver Macromedia http://www.macromedia.com/software/dreamweaver	◆	◆	◆	◆	11 Mb	30 day free trial available
First page 2000 Evrsoft http://www.evrsoft.com	◆	◆	◆	◆	5.2 Mb	FREE*
FrontPage Microsoft http://www.microsoft.com/frontpage	◆	◆	◆	◆		45 day free trial CD
GoLive Adobe http://www.adobe.co.uk	◆	◆	◆	◆		60 day free trial CD
Hotdog Sausage Software http://www.sausagetools.com/ hotdog/	◆	◆	◆	◆	10 Mb	30 day free trial available
HomeSite http://www.macromedia.com/software/homesite/	◆	◆	◆	◆	14.5 Mb	30 day free trial available
Hotmetal Pro SoftQuad http://www.hotmetalpro.com/products/ eval	◆	◆	◆	◆	12 Mb	30 day free trial available

NetObjects Fusion NetObjects http://ww3w.netobjects.com	◆	◆	◆	◆	27 Mb	30 day free trial available

* Commonly available on CD-ROM

Macromedia product updates support accessibility, eg a free Check for Accessibility extension for Dreamweaver: *http://www.macromedia.com/macromedia/accessibility/features/contents.html*

Free downloadable Accessibility Suites for Macromedia Dreamweaver and Microsoft FrontPage *http://www.usablenet.com/frontend/508as_entry.jsp*

Annex D. Graphic applications

The following is a short list of commonly used graphic manipulation applications. This list cannot be exhaustive and they are listed by their generic names. To ensure continued relevance, no version numbers are shown.

This list does not, in any way, constitute any form of endorsement by Office of the e-Envoy

	Common formats GIF, JPEG, BMP, TIFF	PNG support	Animation	Size of Download File	Free / Purchase
CorelDraw Coral http://www3.corel.com	◆	◆	◆		No free download
Fireworks* Macromedia http://www.macromedia.com/software/ fireworks	◆	◆	◆	18 Mb	30 day free trial of Firework 3
Paint Shop Pro* JASC Software http://www.jasc.com	◆	◆	◆	33 Mb	30 day free trial available
PhotoShop* Adobe http://www.adobe.co.uk	◆	◆	◆		60 day free trial available

*Vischeck Colorblind simulator plug-in available for PhotoShop is also compatible with versions of Paint Shop Pro *http://vischeck.com/index*

Annex E. Plug-ins

The following is a short list of commonly used applications for creating plug-in files. This list cannot be exhaustive and they are listed by their generic names. To ensure continued relevance, no version numbers are shown.

This list does not, in any way, constitute any form of endorsement by Office of the e-Envoy

	Create File format	Windows	Macintosh	Free / Purchase
Adobe Acrobat* Adobe http://www.adobe.co.uk/	◆	◆	◆	No free Download except for the **Reader**.
Flash** Macromedia http://www.macromedia.com/software/flash	◆	◆	◆	30 day free trial available
QuickTime Apple http://www.apple.com/quicktime/products/	◆	◆	◆	30 day free trial available

*the latest version of Adobe Acrobat supports Scalable Vector Graphics (SVG). When downloading the reader be aware that only the full version has accessibility support.

Annex F. General applications

The following is a short list of commonly used applications. This list cannot be exhaustive and they are listed by their generic names. To ensure continued relevance, no version numbers are shown.

They are neither quality tested or rated in any way.

This list does not, in any way, constitute any form of endorsement by Office of the e-Envoy

File Transfer Protocol (FTP) applications	Windows	Macintosh	Other platforms
Bulletproof FTP http://www.bpftp.com	◆		
CoffeeCup Direct FTP http://www.coffeecup.com	◆		
CuteFTP http://www.cuteftp.com	◆		
Winsock FTP Daemon http://www.wftpd.com	◆		
WS_FTP Pro http://www.ipswitch.com	◆		

Fetch http://fetchworks.com		♦	
Vicomsoft FTP http://.www.vicomsoft.com.com		♦	

Readers	Windows	Macintosh	Other platforms
Adobe Arcrobat http://www.adobe.co.uk	♦	♦	UNIX
Microsoft Word http://www.microsoft.com/Office/000/viewers.htm	♦		

Compression packages	Windows	Macintosh	Other platforms
WinZip http://www.winzip.com	♦		
PKZip http://www.pkware.com	♦		
Stuffit http://www.stuffit.com	♦	♦	UNIX
MacZipit http://www.mackzipit.com		♦	

Audio recording/editing/mixing tools	Windows	Macintosh	Other platforms
Cooledit http://www.syntrillim.com	♦		
SoundEdit http://www.macromedia.com	♦	♦	

Web server statistical packages	Windows	Macintosh	Other platforms
Analog http://www.analog.cx	♦	♦	UNIX
WebTrends http://www.webtrendslive.com	♦		

Link checker	Windows	Macintosh	Other platforms
Xenu's Link Sleuth http://home.snafu.de/tilman/xenulink.html	♦		

Route tracing package	Windows	Macintosh	Other platforms
Neotrace http://www.neotrace.com	♦		

Annex G. Changing browser fonts and colours

Although there are many web browsers on the market, the most commonly used applications are Microsoft Internet Explorer and Netscape Navigator. The following information is based on these two browsers. Most others allow the user to configure their browser window and these changes are completed in similar ways.

Any browser will always have a help facility that will explain how these operations are carried out.

All pull-down and selectable menu options within each of the applications have a single underlined letter. This shows how to access the option if a pointing device is not available. This may mean that the 'alt' or 'ctrl' or 'shift' key is held down at the same time as the designated letter is pressed, depending on how a user's computer is configured.

G.1 Microsoft Internet Explorer (MSIE)

MSIE version 4

- Select 'View' from the top pull down menu options
- Select 'Internet Options'
- From this menu screen, illustrated on the right, the user may select the 'Colours' options by clicking on the buttons at the bottom of the screen.
- The user can now change the default colour for the background and font.
- Use windows colours can be deselected by clicking on the box.
- Once this has been done, the Text and Background selections can be changed by clicking on the boxes themselves.
- Selecting the 'Fonts' button will give the user the ability to change the style of font used by the browser
- Once selected any international character set can be selected and any font resident on the computer can be used.

- The Accessibility button allows the user to accept or decline styling put in place by an organisation's Cascading Style Sheet.
- The three options available are to ignore colour, font type and font size declarations.
- The user also has the ability to construct their own standard CSS; this will effect any page accessed and will ensure that the font sizes and colours used are always legible and useful for the user.

As stated, different versions of MSIE work in slightly different ways. In MSIE5.5 this same selection process can be accessed by selecting 'Tools' from the top pull down menu options and then selecting 'Internet Options'

G.2 Netscape Navigator

Netscape Navigator approaches things in a slightly different manner but essentially works in the same way as Microsoft Internet Explorer.

- Select 'Edit' from the top pull down menu options
- Select 'Preferences'
- From this menu screen, illustrated on the right, the user may select the Colours option by clicking on the word.
- The user can now change the default colour for the background and font.
- Use windows colours can be deselected by clicking on the box.
- Once this has been done, the Text and Background selections can be changed by clicking on the boxes themselves.
- Selecting the Fonts option will give the user the ability to change the style of font used by the browser
- Once selected any international character set can be selected and any font resident on the computer can be used.

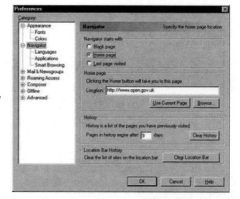

Annex H. Access standards and common file extensions

Delivering online services requires standards and the information standards and specifications for information access browsers and viewers are detailed below. Refer to the latest version of the e-Government Interoperability Framework at www.govtalk.gov.uk.

H.1 Text files

Service	Standard	File extension
Hypertext Markup Language (HTML)	Those parts of HTML4 commonly rendered by web browsers such as MS Internet Explorer (v4/v5), Netscape Navigator (v4/v5/v6) and their associated extensions and plug-ins.	.htm
Portable Document Format	Adobe Acrobat, a postscript, print ready file with free reader software to view. The minimum Viewer is version 3.	.pdf
Rich Text Format	Common format for allowing file produced in one word processor application to be viewed by any other.	.rtf
ASCII	Plain/formatted text file format that is the simplest way of storing text. Similar to HTML with the file formatting.	.txt

H.2 Image files

Service	Standard	File extension
Graphics Interchange Format	Most images on the web are saved in this format it allows the production of static and animated graphics. Benefits from a small file size.	.gif
Joint Photographic Engineering Group	This image format is usually reserved for photographic images. It permits the compression of a great deal of colour information into a small file.	.jpg
Portable Network Graphic	This is an open standard graphics format that is expected to be the long-term replacement for GIF images. A file size will generally be smaller than a corresponding GIF file.	.png
Tag Image File Format	This is a common form for saving and transferring Raster graphics.	.tif

H.3 Spreadsheet formats

Service	Standard	File extension
Microsoft Excel	Proprietary product	.xls
Lotus 123	Proprietary product	.wk1
Delimited (comma separated) file	This flat file format is a common standard within computers and should be understood by all	.csv

H.4 Multimedia

Service	Standard	File extension
Audio/visual streaming formats	Real Audio and Real Video are continuous or streaming sound/multimedia formats that have to be delivered by a Real server.	.rm/.ram
Shockwave	A visual (animation) system from Macromedia.	.swf
Quicktime	A visual playback system developed by Apple.	.mov
Waveform Audio File Format	A sound format from Microsoft that has now become the standard PC-based audio format.	.wav
Audio Interchange File Format	Most commonly used in the Macintosh operating system, it can be outputted via PCs.	.aif
Windows Media Format	A multimedia format from Microsoft.	.wmf
Moving Picture Experts Group	MPEG-1 audio Layer 3 is a standard compression file format for audio. This format is downloaded rather than streamed. MPEG is also the format used for video presentations, eg, on CD-ROMs.	.mp3 .mpg
Webcasting	File format used in webcasting that permits, eg, a logo to be placed within the webcast image	.smil

H.5   General purpose

Service	Standard	File extension
Microsoft Access	Proprietary product that is downloadable rather than streamed	.mdb
Lotus Notes/Domino	Proprietary product.	.nsf
Microsoft Word	Proprietary word processing product.	.doc
	File compression (downloadable only)	.zip
Active Server Pages	A Microsoft format, which is an HTML file with, added scripting. This is processed by a Microsoft web server before being sent to the client	.asp
Microsoft PowerPoint	Proprietary product	.ppt

Annex I. Common HTTP server status codes

The Hypertext Transfer Protocol (HTTP) is relative to the TCP/IP set of protocols, which sets the rules for exchanging data on the World Wide Web. Its name implies that files can contain links to other files via additional transfer requests.

A web server contains a program called an HTTP daemon that handles HTTP requests from web clients (browsers) which are either directly entered URLs or links from existing pages. The server processes this request from the browser and the appropriate file is returned.

The following is a selection of the common HTTP server status codes. Most of these will never be seen be an average web user. They are usually only noticeable when looking through server logs on a web server.

The numerical codes are standard; the reasons text attached to each can be manipulated by the Web manager.

They are broken into five categories, each designated by the first numerical value of the status code:

1xx – Informational
2xx – Success
3xx – Redirection
4xx – Client Error
5xx – Server Error

Each status code shows a transaction between the client web browser and the HTTP server and can be found listed against each individual GET request, the 200 status code is most common as it illustrates a successful request for a file.

200	OK A file has been successfully requested from the server
202	**Request accepted for processing**
301	**Moved** May be followed by a redirection URL
304	**Not Modified** A file that has not been modified has been requested. This message shows the request to the server but the user will have accessed the information from a cache store, either from own PC or local caching service. Covers all file types
400	**Bad Request** Request was impossible or a syntax error occurred
401	**Unauthorised** Request should be re-attempted with a proper authorisation header
403	**Forbidden** A user has attempted to access a password-protected area of the service.
404	**Not Found** This code means that the requested URL does not reside on the server. In modern browsers this may result in a specialised page being displayed directly by the web browser itself. Correctly administered systems should never server a 404-error page; instead, a general search page for the server should be served.
408	**Request Timeout** This either means that the file could not be accessed correctly on the server or that the users connection has failed.
500	**Internal Server Error** This is an exception error that could have resulted from HTTP server overload or a failed server script or program.

Annex J. Error 404 page

When a user enters an incorrect URL a web server will return an Error 404 page.

Everyone will come across this message at some point so it is the department's responsibility to ensure that this page is as helpful to the user as possible.

This annex only applies to departments who manage their own web server(s).

If a department's web presence is hosted by a service provider there will undoubtedly be a shared resource for all clients. In this case, every effort should be made to ensure that this general message is helpful.

Included within the 'Start-up kits' (available from the online version of these guidelines at *http://www.e-envoy.gov.uk/webguidelines.htm* is a template error 404 page.

The text is as follows:

file not found

error 404

The page you have requested on this web server no longer exists, or has been moved to a new location. This error message may have occurred for a number of reasons

- The file may have been moved to a new location
- The file may have been deleted because it is out of date
- The link contained within an external website may be incorrect or out of date
- You may have entered an incorrect URL into your browser
- Our website may be experiencing problems

If you believe that we have caused the error please let us know by contacting us at the following email address *testemail@test.gov.uk*, or alternatively use our feedback form.

Please provide full details on the problems you have experienced and the URL that are trying to access.

You may be able to locate the information you require by entering a query into the search facility provided on this page.

Annex K. Redirect page

When a page is removed from its web location and is not replaced with an alternative at the same URL a web server will return an Error 404 to the user.

This is particularly unhelpful to the user so it is the web manager's responsibility to ensure that a replacement page is provided at the same URL.

When you are redesigning your website or if for operational reasons you are planning to:

    a. close down (delete) an active web page that is considered out of date and it has been decided not to archive it, or

    b. change the location (URL) of a current page;

then you should carefully consider the consequences to:

- search engines and directories that may have listed the page;
- users who may have personal bookmarks of your page, and
- websites that refer to your page and may have established a direct link to it.

You should review the traffic to the page and then consult your server administrator to establish a server-side redirect facility on your original URL. The level of traffic should give some indication has to how long you need to support a redirect page.

When you are removing pages permanently from your website – it is important to check how this conforms to your Department's Electronic Records Management policy.

See **section 2.1.4** Do not change names when moving files
See **section 4.2.5** Uses for metatags

Examples of redirect pages

Draft text

File not found

Redirect

The page you have requested on this web server no longer exists. Please refer to [substitute URL] for information/guidance/search facility [select which is appropriate for your site].

This page will automatically redirect you within 5 seconds. If it fails to do so please use the above hyperlink.

File not found

Redirect

The page you have requested on this web server has moved to a new location at [add new URL]. Please consider updating your bookmark.

This page will automatically redirect you within 5 seconds. If it fails to do so please use the above hyperlink.

Annex L. Archiving websites

The purpose of this annex is to provide government website managers with a framework towards developing within their website management policy suitable procedures and systems to assist in the management, appraisal and preservation of electronic records.

L.1 Introduction

It is necessary for web managers, working with their content providers and those responsible for the management of electronic records, to set in place procedures that will identify material with records potential and ensure that full and accurate copies of web-based services and content are created for preservation. Websites come in many different forms. These range from a collection of static pages that displays the same information to all users, through to pages which are created and displayed dynamically in response to specific queries from users. In addition many websites now do something:

- they enable audio-visual material to be played,
- they enable user details to be captured,
- on-line orders to be taken, and
- personalised information to be displayed based on user profiles.

In the world of managing government websites the identification and preservation of records is generally known as *archiving* and it has three broad aspects:

- working within your department's Electronic Records Management policy to meet legal obligations, eg, Public Records Acts, Health and Safety at Work Act, Freedom of Information Act, specific provisions in primary and secondary legislation relating to a department's core business functions;
- working within your department's Electronic Records Management policy and procedures to meet the needs of the organisation for reliable, authentic records of business activity and to preserve its accountability to the public, Parliament and the courts; and
- meeting your business obligations to retain accessible on-line information to the wider public, ie, your archiving strategy.

L.2 Public Records Acts

L.2.1 Background

The Public Record Office (PRO) has statutory responsibility for guiding, supervising and co-ordinating the selection, safekeeping and transfer of public records created by government departments and agencies. Electronic records are formal records and public records and to assist in this area of the PRO has developed a Website/intranets toolkit.

Managing web resources: managing electronic records on websites and intranets: an ERM toolkit
http://www.pro.gov.uk/recordsmanagement/standards/default.htm

---

This covers a range of issues, for example:

- how websites differ from other electronic sources,
- management control mechanisms,
- model action plan for bringing existing website records under corporate control,
- sustaining web resources over time,
- checklist for the implementation of model action plan, and
- sample entry on a departmental Retention Schedule expressing the disposal arrangements for website content.

L.3 Retention management

It is a core discipline of records management that information is retained for periods appropriate to its business use. The indefinite retention on a website of out of date or inactive material is probably unsustainable. So 'business use' in this context includes openness and public accountability but does not extend to maintaining ephemeral content indefinitely *just in case* someone in the future wishes to access it.

In practice this means developing *class rules* for the retention of information, in all formats, for finite periods until disposal to the Public Record Office or destruction after an appropriate period of time.

These are usually expressed on retention schedules. Implementing them consistently is important to avoid a chaotic built-up of outdated and ephemeral content.

Annex 2 of the PRO's *Managing web resources* is a sample retention schedule illustrating two events – the removal of content from a website and its final disposal at a later date.

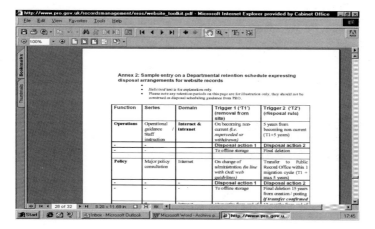

L.3.1 Interactive content

There are many reasons why material published on government websites may be considered as 'out-of-date' or inactive, for example:

- out-of-date because it has been superseded by newer material;
- out-of-date because it has time-expired, eg, the period for responding to a consultation paper has expired,
- the publicity campaign that the website was supporting has ended;
- last weeks press notices, and
- inactive because the material was published under a previous administration.

Under a department's Electronic Records Management system arrangements should be in place to identify and preserve copies of your web-based material in order to meet the requirements of the Public Records Act. However, the Web is a vast online resource and it is part of your corporate memory. Its great business and operational value is in providing 7x24 public access to current and old content. The users of government information, and in particular the media, libraries and similar information services, benefit from the availability of content for a range of reasons, for example:

- provision of accurate background information, eg, consultation papers, statistics, research reports and press notices;
- despite being inactive, it may be the only source of this information, particularly important as increasingly we only publish online;
- it is important for libraries and information services that frequently make long-term references to official material;
- the information can have historical interest;
- the user can experience renewed interest due to later events, and
- 7x24 accessibility can reduce the administration resources required to support home and overseas enquiries/customer relations management/press enquiries, eg, under the requirements of open government and Freedom of Information.

Do we need to avoid a situation of being able to find a run of a research report from 1960 to 1999 which is in a print collection but not the 2000 and 2001 editions because they were only published on the Internet and were removed when the 2002 edition was posted or when that website was reorganised?

Legal Deposit copies in the British Library and the Copyright libraries are aimed at ensuring that publications are preserved for the benefit of future generations, and become part of the national heritage. Materials that departments now publish only electronically, eg, on their websites, deserve no lesser treatment if we are to ensure that information is preserved for future use.

Appendix A lists categories of material that the major libraries, such as Parliamentary Libraries and University Libraries, use for reference on our current work. It is important that many of the documents, which are now being published *only* on departmental websites, are also retained for their on-going reference and use.

L.3.2 Maintenance and cost of out-of-date/inactive content

Short-term
The cost of hard disk space is negligible and the cost of maintaining archive files can be very low. From the point-of-view of good public perception of your website the short-term cost of keeping old content is small and a degree of web management effort is required:

- Old content can be misleading. To avoid this the user should be immediately aware that they are accessing an 'out-of-date' file. So some prominent indication or disclaimer should be provided.

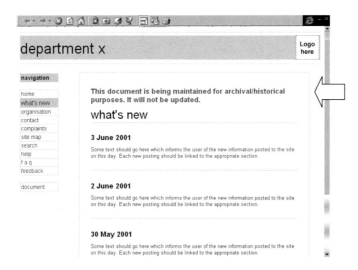

- The date created and date modified should be maintained to reflect the preserved edition that users are accessing.

- The URL of the preserved copy should be the same as when the material was 'originally' published. See paragraph **L.3.3**.
- Indicate in the metadata that the document is 'archived' and consider adding 'Archive copy' to the page title.
- Hyperlinks or pointers should be added to take the user to appropriate newer pages.
- The existence of hyperlinks within old files requires them either to be maintained or to be deleted.
- When reviewing a document consider obsolete or misleading information, eg, email address, telephone numbers, postal addresses provided originally to facilitate response to a consultation; may need to be edited out of the online version but retained in the metadata or an the Electronic Records Management preservation system?

Long-term
The cost of maintaining electronic archive files for long periods – in terms of platform migration and media refreshment – is potentially high. This can involve a high level of web management effort. These issues are discussed in the Public Record Office's Managing web resources: managing electronic records on websites and intranets. Refer to ***http://www.pro.gov.uk/recordsmanagement/standards/default.htm***

L.3.3 The need for stable URLs

There are a number of reasons why URLs on your website should be stable and stay active:

- other sites may have linked to your page(s) – so removal will cause an Error 404 *(known as linkrot)* the consequences of which are poor user opinion and lost business opportunities as you turn away new users;
- users may have bookmarked pages because they want to go directly to a relevant part of your site instead of starting with the homepage every time;
- search engines that have referred to your page(s) are slow in updating their databases, so they will lead users astray if you remove a page, and
- libraries and information services, eg, British Library, the Parliamentary libraries, refer to your web-based documents by URL – so it is important to maintain access directly to these materials.

L.4 Current references

Managing web resources: managing electronic records on websites and intranets
http://www.pro.gov.uk/recordsmanagement/standards/default.htm

Management, appraisal and preservation of electronic records
Volume 1: Principles and Volume 2: Procedure
http://www.pro.gov.uk/recordsmanament/default.htm

Appendix A:

This annex summarises those categories of information, that may be published on websites and that have been identified as being of particular interest to the Parliamentary libraries, university libraries, and the major public reference libraries that maintain collections of official material:

- Departmental annual reports
- Regulatory impact assessments (eg, produced as part of the legislative process)
- Papers laid before Parliament and Papers placed in the libraries of either House by Ministers
- Press notices (eg, announcing major programmes, changes in public policy, delivery performance, etc)
- Departmental circulars (eg, on major programmes, changes in public policy etc)
- Ministerial speeches (eg, on major programmes, changes in public policy etc)
- Consultation papers and possibly responses and analysis to them
- Statistics (eg, gathered for the formulation of public policy)
- Research reports
- Public information leaflets (eg, providing advice on services, programmes, policies)

Checklist: Closing down a website or permanent removal of pages

A decision to close down a website or to remove substantial material from a website should only be taken after very careful consideration:

Project planning – Closing down a website or removal of a document		
Done	Description	
	What is the category of your website/document (in accordance with Annex 1 of the PRO's ERM toolkit) • What is the category of the information being considered for removal (in accordance with the ERM toolkit)	
	What are the reasons? Record them, eg: • Campaign website and use of campaign message/supporting material has ended • Organisation ceases to exist in current form and its role is being merged with an new or existing body • Organisation will cease to exist and its role terminated • The information is out-of-date or misleading • Information is available elsewhere, eg, British Library	
	What will be the Internet consequences of this closure? • Other websites (government/commercial) may link to us, so removing will cause Error 404 • Users may have bookmarked our pages – causing Error 404	

• Search engines have us in their directories – causing Error 404	
Should you maintain the entire website/document as an on-line archive? • What immediate resources would be required to achieve this? • What long-terms resources would be required to maintain this?	
Should you maintain the URL with a redirect page or a page of appropriate follow-up information to users? • Advantage would be to avoid Error 404 pages that provide a poor image of a public sector website • What resources would be required to achieve and maintain this?	
Have you identified what should be preserved as an official record and are your retention and disposal proposals complying with your department's Electronic Records Management policy?	

Annex M. Managing use of email

With the growth of the e-economy organisations have increasingly adopted the use of email marketing as a direct marketing tool. Direct marketing being a term used to cover all those publicity techniques that either involve a direct approach to an individual or seek a response directly from an individual. Like all government publicity, online services should observe the guidance given in the Government Information and Communications Service (GICS) Handbook – Government use of direct marketing.

M.1 Direct marketing

The following paragraphs have been extracted from Annex C of official guidance available online at *www.cabinet-office.gov.uk/central/1999/workgis/annex_c.htm*

7. Direct marketing techniques are a valuable part of a range of publicity media available to government, often offering cost-effective and measurable solutions to many publicity problems.

8. However, some of the techniques are seen as intrusive and some commercial users have sent out material to inappropriate recipients. This has led to unsolicited material being branded as 'junk mail' and has built up resistance amongst some recipients.

9. Against this background, Departments must take care if they are to obtain the benefits while avoiding criticism.

10. As a publicity medium, direct marketing is, of course, covered by the general guidance on government publicity. As that guidance make clear, it is unlikely that unsolicited distribution of material about policies that require, but have not obtained, parliamentary approval will be considered proper.

11. In other cases, direct marketing may be appropriate, but before embarking on it Departments must satisfy themselves that its use can be justified according to the following tests:

- Is direct marketing appropriate for the campaign and is its use in accordance with general guidance on propriety and value for money?
- Will the direct distribution of material be considered over-intrusive by recipients?
- As suitable address lists available and if so are they reliable and accurate and is their proposed use within the guidelines set by the Data Protection Registrar *[now the Information Commissioner]*?
- Are other Departments planning to approach the same audience over the period of the campaign?

M.2 Emails and unsolicited messages

M.2.1 What is Spam?

Email spamming refers to the sending of unsolicited bulk email to users. More often, it occurs through the deliberate or accidental misuse of bulk emailing facilities. This can actually be made worse if recipients reply to the email. It may occur inadvertently, as a result of sending a message to a discussion group or mail list and not realising that the list expands to hundreds or thousands of users. It may also result from an 'out-of-office' responder message that is set up incorrectly.

Unsolicited bulk email (UBE) – also known as unsolicited commercial email, junk mail and junk advertising – targets large number of users with direct mail messages. It is a leading cause of complaints made by Internet users.

Email spamming is almost impossible to prevent because any user with a valid email address can spam any valid email address, newsgroup or discussion forum. When large amounts of email are directed to or through a single site, that site may suffer a denial of service through loss of connectivity, system crash or failure of a service because of, for example, overloading. It costs the recipient time and money to receive and process the email, which is often unwelcome if it occurs without the recipient's prior consent.

M.2.2 Data Protection issues

Currently, using a person's email address to send email for marketing purposes may constitute the processing of personal data for the purpose of direct marketing. Therefore, there is a right to require that the person sending such emails desists by sending them a notice under Section 11 of the Data Protection Act 1998. The sender, if under UK jurisdiction, has no choice but to comply with this notice, and they are allowed a 'reasonable' time in which to do so. An individual recipient has a right of access to the information that the *data controller* holds concerning them. It is therefore incumbent on the email sender to maintain records of an individual's subscription to a mailing list.

The Data Protect Act also restricts the repurposing of mailing lists, that is, re-using for a new purpose a contact list acquired for a different purpose and transferring personal data to third parties.

Email addresses must be obtained legitimately as *harvesting* them without consent or using lists harvested by third parties may violate requirements of the Data Protection Act.

M.2.3 The European Union's position

EU e-Communications Directive (Directive 2002/58/EC) is due to be implemented in Member States by 31 October 2003. This Directive regulates the sending of unsolicited commercial communications by electronic means. It therefore covers a range of communication channels, for example, email, fax, text messages or using the telephone (both mobile and fixed). The default position regarding unsolicited commercial communications sent by electronic methods is that they are prohibited unless the prior consent of the user to receive such messages has been obtained. Consent, has the same meaning as in the Data Protection Directive 95/46/EC – that is it must be freely given, specific and informed. Consent may be given by the recipient ticking a box on a website or submitting a request by email. The new Directive also requires Member States to prohibit the practice of sending direct marketing emails that disguises or conceals the sender's identity. The DTI is due to publish draft Regulations and begin consultation.

M.3 Requested emails

It is recommended that the same guidelines should be followed for emails requested by users as part of a *'subscription to a newsletter'* or *'update request'*. Although these do not count as unsolicited mail or initially as *'spam'*, they can easily fall into this category if mismanaged. For requested emails you should always ensure that:

- distribution lists are not shown in the address field - recipients should not have sight of other recipient contact details;
- requested emails display clearly the sender's address;
- requested emails include a working hyperlink to the sender's privacy policy;
- potential recipients are invited to *opt-in to the mailing list* (rather than opt-out), and an email requesting their confirmation should be sent from the listed address;

- emails should always contain a working online method for the recipient to unsubscribe (opt out) of the mailing or to register changes in email address - these should be implemented within a specified timeframe;
- the content of email should be directly related to the notification that was provided when the individual subscribed to the list; and
- records of 'subscriptions' should be retained.

M.4 Acceptable use

The use of email imposes certain responsibilities and obligations upon users. An acceptable use policy should require that your management of emails will, for example:

- conform to the same rules as issued for conventional departmental or agency external correspondence and for corporate publicity – GICS Direct Marketing – paragraph **M.1** above;
- conform to the requirements of the Data Protection Act 1998;
- not send emails to a recipient who has indicated that they do not wish to receive them;
- controversial statements/opinions should not generally be made and certainly not ones that cannot be supported by the individual making them;
- not contain offensive material;
- not contain messages that are excessive or 'unsolicited bulk email' that could reasonably be expected to provoke complaints;
- avoid emailing children without the prior verifiable and explicit consent of the parent/teacher;
- avoid the mass emailing members of email lists/discussion forums and similar groups;
- not knowingly transmit a virus or other malicious software;
- not be sent in a way that may be illegal, for instance, with forged headers or routed through a non-consenting third party's mail system;
- not violate the terms and conditions under which the sender's email access is provided by their Internet Service Provider; and
- when available, conform to regulations made under the EC Directive (EC2002/58/EC) – see paragraph **M.2.3** above.

M.5 Managing your contractors

When using direct marketing contractors care should be taken to ensure that the guidance recorded in this Annex is followed. A contracting organisation may be liable for errors and abuses made by its contractors. The following additional points should be considered:

- you should be assured that the mailing list to be used has been obtained and maintained legitimately and in accordance with the requirements of the Data Protection Act;
- if you have generated the mailing list and are considering passing it on to your contractor for use, then attention must be drawn to the Data Protection Act's rules on the transfer of personal data between different parties;
- if the mailing list has been created by the contractor or obtained from a third party, a statement of origin should be available that:
  - explains from where the email addresses were obtained;
  - contains a working hyperlink to the website of the list provider; and
  - contains a working hyperlink to the list provider's unsubscribe facility.

M.6 Current references

GICS Handbook – Annex C
http://www.cabinet-office.gov.uk/central/1999/workgis/annex_c.htm

Guidelines for UK government websites – Illustrated Handbook
Section 1.10.2 Data Protection Act
http://www.e-envoy.gov.uk/oee/oee.nsf/sections/webguidelines-handbook-management/$file/102.htm

Office of the Information Commissioner
http://www.dataprotection.gov.uk

See following **Checklist – managing the use of email**

Checklist – managing the use of email

This checklist appended to **Annex M** is intended to assist web managers and publicity managers when planning the use of email lists as a direct marketing tool.

Project planning and management	
Description	Done
Direct marketing email has been considered appropriate for this campaign	
The risk of this being considered over-intrusive has been assessed	
Suitable email address lists have been identified and are available with any third-party origins of the lists being known to us	
Address lists are reliable and conform to the requirements of the Data Protection Act	
The proposed use of the lists is in accordance with the guidelines set by the Information Commissioner	
Checked if other departments/agencies are planning to approach your audience over the period of your campaign	
The email distribution list will **not be shown** in the address field	
Potential recipients are invited to **opt-in** to the mailing list rather than opt-out	
An email requesting a recipient's confirmation to opting-in is to be sent	
The email contains a working online method for a recipient to unsubscribe off the list and/or to register changes in address	

Acceptable use	
Description	Done
We dot not email a recipient who has indicated that they do not wish to receive emails	
We will be emailing children	
Children – we have obtained all prior verifiable and explicit consent of parents/teachers and these records have been retained by us	
The email clearly identifies the department/agency by name and has a working hyperlink to our published privacy policy	

Managing your contractor(s)	
Description	Done
Mailing list(s) being used have been obtained and maintained legitimately and in accordance with the Data Protection Act?	
We are passing our mailing list(s) to a third-party and have checked that the DPA rules on the transfer of personal data permit us to do so	

Checklist – specifying your website

This checklist can be used by web managers to assist in planning a website and to ensure that the HTML presented on the site is as accessible as possible to the largest possible audience. Use this checklist in conjunction with the 1.12 procurement choosing an ISP/hosting checklist, 1.4 Evaluation checklist and 2.4 Universal usability checklist.

Project Planning

Done	Description	
	What does the website need to do?	
	What is the timescale of the development process?	
	Will the website development be stepped in order to evaluate progress and make alterations?	
	If so, what change control processes will be used?	
	Who will be in control of this change control procedure?	
	How will the communication channels be controlled?	
	Plan and register URL and any supporting URL(s)	
	If private sector developers are employed what guarantees will be put in place to ensure that the price quoted will be the final price?	
	Arrange where your website will sit within your Department's electronic records management policy/system	
	Are all parties clear as to the requirements and expectations of the project?	

Audience Targeting

Done	Description	
	What is the target audience of the website?	
	How will this target audience access the website?	
	Do certain sections of the target audience have special requirements (ie blind, deaf, motor disability)?	
	How will these special requirements be best met?	
	If planning a Content Management System – are you undertaking internal user testing?	
	Will the completed website be tested on as many browser applications (including disability browsers) and as many operating systems as is reasonably practical, throughout the entire design and population of the website?	

Standards

Done	Description	
	How will you ensure that the website conforms to the requirements of the Guidelines for UK Government Websites? Specifically, will your website achieve at least the minimum	

level of accessibility specified in the W3C's Web Accessibility Initiative?	
Will you provide an ALT attribute for each individual image?	
Will all the HTML files contained within the organisation's website conform and validate to the open standards of HTML and CSS?	
Will all the pages incorporate the appropriate DTD?	
Will all new documents include metadata?	
Which standard file extension will be used throughout your website, either htm or html?	

Design Standards

Done	Description	
	Does your organisation already have a corporate design style?	
	If so, how will this translate on to your website?	
	If this is to be ignored, why?	
	What are the websafe colours for use on the website?	
	What are the Red, Green, Blue, Pantone and hexadecimal values for these colours?	
	If your colours are not websafe how do you propose to make them so?	
	What typeface is required?	
	If the organisation's typeface is not a standard web font, what is the closest available?	
	Will your website's font and colour styles be formatted using an external Cascading Stylesheet file?	
	Are frames to be used in any part of the website?	
	If so, what will be put in place for users who cannot utilise frames?	
	Will your website avoid the use proprietary formatting techniques (ie browser specific)?	
	Will your organisation's website be organised through a set of templates?	

Images

Done	Description	
	What images are to be used throughout the site?	
	Who will write and supply the 'ALT' attributes for every image?	
	Are you going to supply these images?	
	If so, does the organisation have copyright ownership of these images?	
	If not, how are they going to be found by the web design company, and how much will copyright free images cost?	

Content

Done	Description	
	What are the basic content elements required within the website?	

	Has a navigational model been constructed?	
	How flexible is this navigational model?	
	Is this navigational model expandable and future proof?	
	Does the organisation have the appropriate Crown Copyright cover for all of the intended content for the website?	
	Who will populate with website with the organisation's information?	
	If this is to be completed by the design agency, what control mechanisms will be in place to ensure the information is correct and typos etc are removed?	
	Who will edit the content for grammar, style and consistency of message and style?	

Documentation

Done   Description

	Will the website design be fully documented?	
	Will the website construction be fully documented?	
	Once delivered, can your web manager alter, delete and add new information to the website simple and easily?	
	Will training be required for your organisation's staff to allow editing and maintaining of the website?	
	If so, will this requirement be met by the design agency?	
	Is the intellectual property of the site assigned to the Crown?	
	If the Crown does not have ownership of the source code, do you have a full licence to use this code and what is the duration of the license and its geographical scope?	
	Do your homepage, content and cross-government requirements comply with the Guidelines for UK Government Websites?	
	Will you register with ICRA and insert a PICS label and display the ICRA logo?	
	Can you display the W3C WAI logo?	
	Who will register the domain name(s)?	
	Who will be responsible for the renewal of the domain name(s)?	

Scripting techniques

Done   Description

	Will any scripts be used on any of the pages of the website?	
	If so what is the essential reason for this technology being used?	
	Are these scripts essential to the running of the website or are they just being used for presentational reasons?	
	If they are to be used, will they work on all browser applications?	
	If they fail to work on specific browser applications, can the pages still be used without loss of content, functionality or usability?	

Specific references	
Done	Description
	Will your website use cookies? Have you a planned cookie regime?	
	Is there a requirement for discussion groups?	
	Discussion groups -- how will these be moderated?	
	What content of the website will be presented in such a way that a plug-in will be required? (ie flash, audio streaming, video streaming, video players etc)	
	If a plug-in is required will the same information be presented in standard HTML format?	
	Will all or part of the website be delivered through a dynamic application?	
	If so, will the complete pages be accessible to all browser applications and available URLs?	
	Is there a requirement for a mailing list server?	
	Advertising – are any commercial credits being used, including within the markup?	
	If you need to use a text only/EasyAccess version on your site, document why?	

Glossary

This glossary explains the most often used acronyms and keywords associated with using and publishing on the World Wide Web.

It is by no means exhaustive, but will certainly help in understanding much of the shorthand used within these guidelines.

absolute URL

The URL/URI that includes the full path to a file, for example
http://www.e-envoy.gov.uk/webguidelines/index.htm;
these are required for links to information that is located on a different server than your own website. Also specified as fully qualified URLs. See **relative URLs**.

Adobe Acrobat

Software from Adobe for saving, reading and manipulating files saved in a proprietary PostScript format, known as PDF files. PDF files can be read with the free Adobe Acrobat reader available from *http://www.adobe.co.uk*.

acceptable use policy

Published policy statement regarding the terms and conditions attached to the use of a service or facility such as an Internet connection or a website.

access control list (ACL)

The set of rules used by a computer operating system or system component (such as web server software) that specifies which usernames are to be allowed access to specific resources and the level of access that they are to be granted. For example, a file named index.htm may have an ACL that specifies it to be readable by anonymous (ie not logged in) users accessing it via web server software running on the computer, but only to be modifiable by a user who is logged in with the username 'webmaster'.

access log

A web server access log is a list of all the requests for individual files that people have requested from a website. These files will include the HTML files and their embedded graphic images and any other associated files that are transmitted. In general, an access log can be analysed to tell you:

- The number of visitors to each page on the site
- How many requests for each page at the site, which can be presented with the pages with most requests listed first
- Usage patterns in terms of time of day, day of week, and seasonally

ADSL (Asymmetric Digital Subscriber Line)

A digital line that brings 'always-on' high-speed, (for example 256 kbps) Internet connections to the business and home market using existing telephone cabling.

airgap
A security term used to describe the absence of any connection between a free-standing workstation that has a direct or dial-up connection to the Internet and any other network, such as the organisation's local area network infrastructure.

animated GIF
A GIF image file that creates an illusion of motion through the use of multiple images displayed sequentially.

anonymous FTP
Refer to **FTP**.

API (application programming interface)
The set of rules governing the communication between application software components and the operating system on which they run. For example, an operating system's API defines how it communicates the occurrence and location of a mouse click within a window to the application that owns the window.

applet
Term used to describe the small applications written in Java that can run inside a web page.

ASCII (American Standard Code for information Interchange)
This is the common denominator of Latin script character sets comprising encodings for upper- and lower-case letters, numerals and a few punctuation and special characters.

attack
Describes an intentional attempt, by a person or system, to obtain unauthorised access into a computer system and the data held on that system.

ASP (Active Server Pages)
Active Server Pages is the name for the server-side scripting technology that is a part of Microsoft's Internet Information Server (IIS). ASP applications are able to build HTML pages for delivery over the World Wide Web and are able to interact with other Microsoft applications such as SQL Server and Access databases.

ASP applications are written in either JScript (Microsoft's proprietary implementation of JavaScript), VBScript or a mixture of both scripting languages.

ASP pages usually have the .asp filename suffix.

assistive access technology
Assistive technology is a user agent component that augments one or more other user agents to help people with disabilities interact with a computer. For example, screen reader software is an assistive technology because it relies on browsers or other application software to enable web access, notably for people with visual and learning disabilities.

auditing

The monitoring of a system to detect security breaches and to ensure that only authorised users have access to the site or network. It can also apply to other aspects of computer system operation, for example, website traffic auditing, accessibility auditing.

authenticated FTP

Refer to **FTP**.

authentication

Refers to identifying and verifying legitimate users of computer resources such as applications software and attached devices.

backward compatible

A term used to describe an information system component that is able to interwork with older components. For example a web page that is updated to work with Internet Explorer version 5.5 and continues to work with earlier versions of that browser would be described as 'backward compatible'.

bandwidth

The amount of data that is, or can be, sent through a given communications circuit in a fixed amount of time. Usually cited as a measure of the capacity of a data link or network.

binary

The term *binary* refers to a numbering scheme in which there are only two possible values for each digit or logical state: 0 and 1. The semiconductor electronics at the heart of today's electronic computers use binary logic and arithmetic.

In binary counting and arithmetic, the digits' weight increases by powers of 2, this means that in a digital numeral, the digit furthest to the right is the "ones" digit; the next digit to the left is the "twos" digit; next comes the "fours" digit, then the "eights" digit, then the "16s" digit, and so on. The decimal equivalent of a binary number can be found by summing all the digits. For example, the binary 10101 is equivalent to the decimal $1 + 4 + 16 = 21$.

bookmark

A record kept by web browsers of World Wide Web addresses (URLs) selected by the user, any of which can be readily returned to by the user by accessing their bookmark file. Referred to as 'favorites' in Microsofot Internet Explorer.

bounce

If you send an email and it fails to be delivered to the addressee, the message is returned to you with a messaged indicating that it has been undelivered. This is known as a bounce.

browser

A browser is an application or program (software) that is used to view or interact with various kinds of Internet resources. The browser interprets the HTML markup, used to format web documents, to recreate the page on your screen. There are numerous browsers available: most are graphic based but some have been specially developed for the disabled. The two most common browsers are Microsoft's Internet Explorer and Netscape's Navigator.

cache

A cache (pronounced *cash*) is a place to store something more or less temporarily. Web pages you visit are stored in your computer's memory and in your browser's cache directory on your hard disk. When you return to a page you've recently looked at, the browser can get it from the cache rather than the origin server, saving you time and saving the network the burden of additional traffic. You can usually vary the size of the cache, depending on your particular browser.

There are two different types of caches:
- Intermediate caches such as content providers' reverse-proxy caches, ISPs' perimeter caches, and organisations' proxy caches. These capture a copy of web content on its way from origin servers to users' browsers. They are designed to re-serve captured content to other users, thereby conserving upstream bandwidth.
- Your web browser's cache, which contains the most recent web files that you have downloaded and which is physically located on your hard disk.

case-sensitive

This is a condition in which usage and interpretation of a resource (such as a filename) is affected by the use of UPPERCASE and lowercase characters. The incorrect specification of case in the web URLs of resources hosted on computers with case-sensitive filesystems is a common cause of broken hypertext links.

CFML (Cold Fusion Markup Language)

Proprietary language used in the Macromedia Cold Fusion system to generate dynamic HTML pages using templates.

CGI

CGI (common gateway interface) is an API for writing software components that handle communication between web server software and other programs running on the server.

challenge-and-response system

A system that validates authentication by means of specific user names and their associated passwords.

chat

A shortform used for Internet Relay Chat and other similar text-based real-time communications systems. See **Internet Relay Chat**

client, client program

The component of a client/server architecture implementation that makes requests for service from the server component. For example, a Web browser is a client that issues requests for the delivery of web pages to a web server system

client-side
Functionality that exists on the user's computer (your PC) rather than being provided by the server. For example, with a client-side image map you have the necessary code for your PC to the take the action selected.

client-side imagemap
An image in an HTML page that most often functions as a navigational aid. Various parts of the image (hot spots) are 'mapped' as hyperlinks to other areas of the site or CD-ROM, or to other web sites.

ColdFusion
A cross platform web application server – see **CFML**.

comments
Notes included in HTML page mark-up which are ignored by browsers, but which can be seen by viewing the source code.

compressed file
A file that has been squeezed down to a smaller size by the application of compression techniques during the saving of a file. See **Zip files**.

connectivity
The physical connections of network hardware, such as cables, telephone lines and other connection systems. A principal connectivity issue is bandwidth – the maximum amount of data that a connection can carry per unit of time.

content developer
A term used for one who authors web pages and/or designs web sites.

cookies
A cookie is a token which may be sent to your browser when you fetch content from a website and which the browser stores in a file on your hard disk. This token is usually sent back to the sever when you reconnect to the website that issued it. Refer to **section 4.7**.

cyberspace
A loose generic word for the world of computers and the society that gathers around them, as referred to by William Gibson in his fantasy novel *Neuromancer*.

cybersquatting
A term referring to the practice of buying up domain name reflecting the names of existing organisations with the intention of selling the names to the organisations for profit. It has also come to refer to the acquisition of such domain names for vexatious and other 'bad faith' purposes, such as, passing off. The 1999 Federal Domain name Piracy Prevention Act aims to provide remedies in the US.

data corruption
Term used to describe the unexpected and/or unauthorised alteration or destruction of data.

dedicated connection
A communications link reserved exclusively for one type of use. Often used to refer to a leased circuit or private circuit.

dial-up connection
Internet access provided through a modem or ISDN connection.

denial of service attack
On the Internet, a denial of service (DoS) attack is an incident in which a user or organisation is deprived of the services of a resource they would normally expect to have. Typically, the loss of service is the inability of a particular network service, such as email, to be available or the temporary loss of all network connectivity and services. In the worst cases, for example, a website accessed by millions of people can occasionally be forced to temporarily cease operation. A denial of service attack can also destroy programming and files in a computer system.

digital signature
A digital code that can be attached to an electronically transmitted message that unambiguously identifies its sender.

DOM (Document Object Model)
The W3C defines DOM as follows:
The Document Object Model is a platform- and language-neutral interface that will allow programs and scripts to dynamically access and update the content, structure and style of documents. The document can be further processed and the results of that processing can be incorporated back into the presented page.

domain, domain name
A name that represents one or more IP numbers.

Domain names are hierarchically organised with the highest-level component of the name at the right-hand end. Examples of global top level and high-level domains are:

- com – global top level domain, used to be seen as a commercial company domain name registered in the USA
- .net – global top level domain, which historically used to indicate that the owner was in some way connected with the operation or management of the Internet, for example, an ISP. Today the .net top level domain is used in the same way as .com..ac.uk – UK academic institutions
- .gov.uk – UK Government organisations
- .co.uk – a company registered in the UK

Domain names have to be registered with the appropriate naming authority to be valid and usable on the Internet. It can take at least three days before a new domain name becomes active. All Internet providers must update their DNS tables to record a new site's location. See **propagation.**

DNS (Domain Name Service)
This is an Internet infrastructure service that translates fully qualified domain names

into the corresponding IP number, and vice versa.

For example, the DNS name www.uk online.gov.uk might translate into 123.123.12.12.
See **section 2.1**.

DNS poisoning

See **spoofing**.

download

To retrieve a copy of a file from a website and save it onto a users computer. It may, for example, be a PDF document that is to be read at a later date or an application program which is to be installed on the user's computer.

Dynamic HTML (Dynamic Hypertext Mark up Language)

There is no formal open standard that defines DHTML. It is a term applied to a mixture of standards including HTML, CSS and client-side scripting. Both Microsoft and Netscape claim to implement something called DHTML despite the fact they are quite different arising largely from differences in their Document Object Models (DOMs) and also from the differences in their JavaScript implementations.

electronic journal

A periodical that is published online. Sometimes these have paper equivalents and simply provide archives of back issues or supporting online services. See **e-zine**.

email (electronic mail)

A system with which computer users can exchange messages with each other over a network. Email is probably the most widely used communications tool on the Internet. One of advantages of email is its ability to be forwarded and replied to easily.

email alias

This is just another term for an email address. For example, John Doe's email alias may be 'john.doe@cabinet-office.x.gsi.gov.uk'.

email forwarding

Email forwarding automatically redirects email destined to one email address to another. For example all email messages to the advertised generic email address webguidelines@cabinet-office.x.gsi.gov.uk might have a forwarding rule to have the mail system deliver it to john.doe@cabinet-office.x.gsi.gov.uk.

encryption

The conversion or transformation of readable data into an unreadable steam of data using a reversible encoding process.

error codes

A code (typically numeric) issued by a software component to indicate that an operation did not complete successfully. Refer to **Annex J** for a list of HTTP server status error codes.

event handler

A software component that responds to certain events. For example, on web pages, events are usually user actions such as clicking the mouse, typing, etc. An event handler controls the response to such action.

extranet

An extranet is a private network that uses the Internet protocol and the public telecommunication system to securely share part of a business's information or operations with suppliers, vendors, partners, customers, or other businesses. An extranet can be viewed as part of a company's intranet that is extended to users outside the company.

An extranet requires security and privacy. These require firewall server management, the issuing and use of digital certificates or similar means of user authentication, encryption of messages, and the use of virtual private networks (VPN) that tunnel through the public network.

eye-candy

This term is used to describe graphics that are used in a purely ornamental context. See **screen furniture**.

e-zine

Terms used for small or self-published electronic journals.

file formats

Files are stored and accessed across the Internet in many different formats. The most popular is HTML but other common formats include plain text, GIF, JPEG, PDF and MPEG. For further information of these and others refer to **section 4**.

firewall

This term conveys the idea of a barrier between a computer or network of computers and the rest of the Internet. A firewall allows control over the network traffic that passes through it. There are two categories of firewall:
Network-based (generally packet-level and port filters mostly built into routers on a network or at an ISP's site. They look at the information's IP packet header and/or port number requested in order to determine whether a packet can pass through).
And
Application-based (generally the host on the Internet side of the firewall runs proxies for each Internet service that is permitted, for example HTTP, FTP, DNS, SMTP. When a message goes through, a proxy interprets/filters it and relays the data, if allowed by the firewall's rule base).

FAQ (frequently asked questions)

FAQs are widely published on the Internet and usually take the form of instructional text files in question-and-answer format. They are written on a wide variety of topics, and are often the most up-to-date source for specialised information.

frames

Frames is the use of multiple, independently controllable sections in web pages. This effect is achieved by building each section as a separate HTML file and having one 'master' HTML file that identifies all of the sections and the location on-screen at which they render.

When a user requests a web page that uses frames, the address requested is actually that of the "master" file that defines the frames. This file contains instructions to the browser to fetch the other files that contain the substantive data. The ultimate result of the request is that multiple HTML files are served, one for each visual section. For comprehensive detail refer to **section 6.4**.

freeware
Software that is made available for use at no charge by its publisher. However, the publisher almost always retains copyright over it. The Internet is often used as the distribution mechanism for freeware.

FTP (File Transfer Protocol)
A widely used way of downloading and uploading (getting and putting) files across the Internet. File Transfer Protocol is a standardised way for Internet hosts to communicate so that files can be transferred back and forth between them. There is a set of commands in FTP for making and changing directories, transferring, copying, moving and deleting files. Originally, FTP connections were text based, but graphical applications are now available that make FTP commands as easy as dragging and dropping. Numerous FTP clients exist for a number of platforms. **Anonymous FTP** allows anyone who has access to the Internet to access the files on a server; user identification is not necessary. **Authenticated FTP** is a site that requires user identification and a password before allowing access by a user.

gateway
A generic term for a 'go-between' system that connects one network with another, for example when the two networks use different addressing schemes or communication protocols.

GeT (Greenwich Electronic Time)
GeT provides a global time standard and infrastructure. Its global network of atomic time servers and freely available tools facilitate accurate time in the networked economy by enabling synchronisation, measurement, management and co-ordination of time across the Internet. See **NTP**. Refer to ***http://www.get-time.org***

GIF (graphic interchange format)
One of the many file formats used for storing computerised images. Generally, this format is used for line-art images (such as icons and other non-photographic images) on web pages.

gopher
An application that presents, in menu form, information found all over the internet. Gopher programs will also permit searches on the internet for hosts, directories and files, based on keywords supplied by the user. Now largely obsolete having been superseded by the World Wide Web.

GUI (graphical user interface)
The interface provided by the computer's operating system between the user and software applications running on the computer. The GUI has often been likened to

the conductor of an orchestra, while the software applications are the musicians. A graphical interface such as those in Windows 95 and the Macintosh Operating System can be learned rapidly and used intuitively.

hacker

Common term for a person (or system) that intentionally seeks to obtain unauthorised access into computer programs or data.

helper applications

Term used to describe software to which a web browser 'hands-off' the processing of downloaded files that are in formats it cannot itself work with.

hexadecimal number

This is a compact way of representing binary numbers. It is also the encoding used for expressing colour values in web pages. For example, the 'hex' code for the colour white is "#ffffff" and for red is "#ff0000". Sometimes referred to as RGB numbers.

host name

Name assigned to a computer. In an Internet environment it is often machine's DNS name.

hit

A hit is a request for a single file from a web server. A request for an HTML page with three graphic images will result in four hits in the log: one for the HTML file and one for each of the graphic image files. While a hit is a meaningful measure of how much traffic a server handles, it can be a misleading indicator of how many pages are being looked at. A better way of understanding accesses to an organisation's website is to count page impressions.

homepage

There are three distinct meanings of homepage. (1) **Server homepage** – the page that a server returned when it is addressed with a URL that contains only a DNS name. In the case of a server that is configured with multiple virtual servers, there will usually be a homepage for each virtual server.

(2) **'Department' or 'publication' homepage** – which may, or may not, correspond with a server or virtual server homepage. (3) **Browser homepage** – a preference setting in browsers that selects the URL to navigate to when the browser is launched. Individual users can change this setting.

host

A computer connected to the Internet. See **node**.

hub

A hardware device that has ports or outlets that interconnect the cables in a computer network thereby enabling the distribution of information amongst the devices connected to it.

HTTP (Hypertext Transfer Protocol)

The communications protocol that makes the World Wide Web work over the Internet. For example, it specifies the rules by which browsers request resources from servers and how the servers respond to those requests. HTTP actually sends more than just a file to the client, it also sends information about the file, for example title of the file, when it was last updated, its size, and the file's MIME type. The browser uses this additional information for administrative purposes, for example displaying status information at the bottom of your screen. Refer to **http://www.ietf.org/rfc/rfc2068.txt**.

HTML (hypertext markup language)

This is the mark-up language used to indicate to web browsers how to render, ie layout and display, documents. HTML consists of elements that are delimited with 'tags'. Each tag begins and ends with an opening and closing angle bracket -- < >. Refer to **http://www.w3.org/MarkUp/**.

icon

Term used to describe a small picture intended to represent something (a file, directory, or action such as navigating to the target of a hyperlink) in a graphical user interface. When an icon is clicked on, some action is performed, such as opening a directory, aborting a file transfer or navigating.

impersonation

Refer to **spoofing**.

information architecture

Term increasingly used to define the aspects that have to be built into a website – functionality, navigation (buttons, search engine, top-of-page, etc), interface, interaction and visual design.

Internet

Internet refers to the global information system that:

- is logically linked together by a globally unique address space based on the Internet Protocol (IP) or its subsequent extensions/follow-ons;
- is able to support communications using the Transmission Control Protocol/Internet Protocol (TCP/IP) suite or its subsequent extensions/follow-ons, and/or other IP-compatible protocols; and provides, uses or makes accessible, either publicly or privately, high-level services layered on the communications and related infrastructure described herein.

Internet backbone

The very high bandwidth interconnections with fast, high capacity routers, which interconnect major parts of the Internet – the motorway network of the Internet.

Internet datacentre

A terms used for (commercial) facilities whose operators rent out rack-space and/or caged off areas within which their customers can install their own web servers together with other associated servers and networking plant. Also known as 'collocation facilities' and sometimes as 'Internet hotels'. A defining feature of Internet hosting datacentres is their very high-speed, resilient Internet connections that would be inordinately expensive for their individual customers to provision at their own location. Internet datacentres typically also feature multiple redundant mains electricity feeds with battery and diesel powered uninterruptible power supplies.

In view of the very high value of the equipment aggregated within, Internet datacentres are typically also hardened against physical penetration.

Internet hosting centre

See **Internet datacentre**

IP number (address) (Internet Protocol number (address))

The 32-bit address defined by the Internet Protocol. Every device interface connected to the Internet or an Internet-compatible network has a unique IP number. IP numbers are usually represented in dotted decimal notation. IP addresses are the closest thing the Internet has to telephone numbers. When you 'call' that number (using any number of connection methods such as FTP, HTTP or Gopher) you are connected to the computer that 'owns' that IP address. The following is an example of an IP address or number 212.58.224.35. For an Internet host, each of the four component elements comprising its IP number will be in the range 1 to 254.

ISP (internet service provider)

An ISP (Internet service provider) is a company that provides individuals, companies and other organisations access to the Internet and usually other related services such as website building and virtual hosting. Refer to **chapters 1** and **2**.

IRC (internet relay chat)

A text-based conferencing system that allows users to communicate synchronously. Users log into a 'channel' on which other users are 'chatting' and their communications takes place in real-time on the screen.

Intranet

A computer network that is internal to an organisation. Increasingly, the term is understood to mean that the organisation's internal network includes a web server for publishing information within the organisation Intranets provide access to information held and managed locally.

ISDN (integrated services digital network)

With ISDN data is sent as a digital sequence as opposed to an analogue waveform over conventional telephone circuits. ISDN come in various configurations, for example, a 2 x 64 channel basic rate interface (BRI) referred to as ISDN-2 allows a user to send digital information at 128 kbps. To send voice (analogue data) over an ISDN circuit involves digitising it at one end and reconstructing the analogue waveform at the other end. Many ISDN terminal adapters contain a digitiser and digital to analogue converter (DAC) and have a socket into which an analogue telephone handset can be plugged.

Java

Java is a programming language and a run-time environment (the latter also known as Java Virtual Machine). It was designed to have the "look and feel" of the C++ language, but to be simpler to use. Java can be used to create complete applications that may run on a single computer or be distributed among servers and clients in a network. It can also be used to build a small application module or 'applet' for use as part of a web page. Applets make it possible for a web page user to interact with the page. Java can also run server-side in the form of 'servlets'.

Java was introduced by Sun Microsystems in. Both of the major web browsers (Microsoft Internet Explorer and Netscape) include a Java virtual machine.

JavaScript

JavaScript is a script language from Netscape. It is somewhat similar in capability to Microsoft's Visual Basic Scripting. In general, scripting is easier and faster to code in than the more structured languages such as C++.

JavaScript is used in website development to do such things as:
- Automatically change a formatted date on a web page
- Cause a linked-to page to appear in a popup window
- Cause text or a graphic image to change during a mouse rollover

JavaScript code can be embedded in HTML pages and interpreted by the web browser. JavaScript can also be run at the server as in Microsoft's Active Server Pages before the page is sent to the requestor. Both Microsoft and Netscape browsers support JavaScript, but in slightly different ways.
Visual Basic Scripting should not be used client-side, as it will only work in Internet Explorer.

JPEG (Joint Photographic Experts Group)

A compressed file format for images commonly used for including images included in websites. Especially suitable for photographs.

kB (and MB)

Kilobytes and megabytes. A kilobyte is actually 1024 bytes and a megabyte is 1024kB.

kbps (and Mbps)

Kilobits per second and megabits per second – the measures of communications links speed.

LAN (local area network)

A system for networking a group of computers at a single physical location. 'Ethernet' is probably the most commonly used LAN technology.

library

A term used to describe (1) a collection of precompiled routines that programs can use, and (2) a collection of files.

life episodes

A term used to describe a concept whereby events are linked together over time so as to be felt or understood as *this* or *that* episode in someone's life. For example, moving home takes time and involves a series of events, such as choosing an area to live, getting a mortgage, packing and so one. But is recalled as a single life episode – 'moving home'.

(mail) list server

Programs that act as message switches for email on specific subjects. When you subscribe to a list server, you receive all messages that are sent to that list. If you reply to messages all other subscribers will see your response.

log files

Computer server software typically stores a record of its activity in disk files. For example, web server log files contain information about the resources accessed by users of the site.

mailing list

Also called list servers, list processors, distribution lists, etc. These are discussion groups formed around a specific area of interest, which correspond via email. Interested users simply subscribe to a given list by sending a single line email message to a central server. All emails to the lists are distributed by email to all subscribers, sometimes via a moderator (moderated lists) or automatically (unmoderated list). Facilities to unsubscribe are usually also available.

MathML

A mark-up language designed to represent mathematical equations. These can be displayed on a screen and read by a screen reader.

metadata

An electronic document's metadata is information about that document. Metadata in web pages is used by many Internet search engines to catalogue the content of websites. This information is contained in the head element of web documents and is not seen by users unless they choose to look at the HTML code underlying the document. Metadata may also be found in native format documents, such as Microsoft Word, where it is searchable by using MS Index Server. Document metadata can also be stored separately (for example in a database) and linked to the documents to which it applies.

meta-language

A language for describing or specifying other languages. An example of a meta-language is XML.

MIME (multipurpose internet mail extensions)

An encoding scheme originally designed to enable the inclusion of media types other than plain text, such as formatted and styled text, images, audio and video in Internet email messages. The MIME encoding scheme is also used by HTTP and enables web servers to tell browsers about the content of the files they are sending.

MPEG (Motion Picture Experts Group)

A set of audio and video file encoding and compression schemes. To hear or see MPEG audio or video you will need to install a helper application or a web browser plug-in. MPEG-1 Layer 3 (known as MP3) is the popular high quality standard for audio compression.

mobile users

Users who access the Internet (or other network) from a number of different physical locations, usually via a dial-up or cellular telephone modem.

moderator
Content manager for a discussion group who maintains the day-to-day messages ensuring that content is both relevant and complies with the owning organisation's Acceptable Use Policy.

modem
An electronic device for connecting a computer to the Internet over ordinary 'dial-up' telephone lines. The name stands for MODulator-DEModulator because it converts digital signals into sounds for transmission over phone lines by modulating a carrier wave and extracts (demodulates) the digital signal from the audio signal at the far end.

mouse
Refers to the most popular pointing device used by computers.

navigation mechanisms
The mechanisms by which a visitor can navigate a web page or website. Typically these include: *Navigation bars* – a collection of links to the most important parts of a document or site.
Alpha bars – an alphabetic list (A to Z) that links into a document that is structured alphabetically, for example an index. *Site maps* – provide a global view of the organisation of a web page or site.
Table of contents – generally list and links to the most important sections of a document or site.

netiquette
Internet etiquette – term to describe proper and friendly behaviour by users of an internet system towards other users.

network
A network is two or more computers that are connected. The common types of network are, for example, (1) LAN, local area network – computers are in close proximity to one another, typically within the same building, and (2) WAN, wide area network – the computers are in different geographic locations connected by long-haul digital data circuits ('leased circuits').

Network address translation (NAT)
NAT is the technique of translating one IP number or network's set of IP numbers to another at the point of attachment of the two networks. NAT is typically implemented in devices, such as routers and firewalls. It enables the use of a private IP numbering space on organisations' and domestic networks. The use of NAT is one solution to the world-wide shortage of IP numbers. Refer to Internet RFC 1918 'Address Allocation for Private Internets' *http://www.ietf.org/rfc/rfc1918.txt* and RFA 2663 'IP Network Address Translator (NAT) Terminology and Considerations *http://www.ietf.org/rfc/rfc2663.txt* .

newsgroups
A global discussion group system that uses the Usenet NetNews and related software. These groups have formed around common interests, some of which cover

controversial issues. Each group's users exchange comments on topics of interest. As a user raises a topic, it becomes a 'thread' that other users can respond to, expand upon, and/or answer.

node

Another name for 'host'. Any device that is attached to the network, including workstations, servers, shared printers, etc.

NTP (Network Time Protocol)

NTP provides a mechanism to synchronise time on computers across the Internet. The current protocol is version 4. XNTP is a public domain software package that uses NTP for synchronising computer clocks. See **UTC**. Refer to *http://www.eecis.udel.edu/~ntp/*

offline

Used to describe a computer or other resource that is not attached to or not accessible from the Internet or other network.

Open source

Software whose source code is in the public domain and that can therefore be modified or further developed by anyone. The term Open Source is also a certification mark owned by the Open Source Initiative (OSI) which adds some further requirements to the way open source software is distributed and licensed for further development.

open standard

Standards whose specifications are in the public domain and are widely accepted and adopted by national and international organisations and companies.

operating system (OS)

The operating system (sometimes abbreviated as "OS") is a set of programs that are loaded into a computer when it is first switched on. A computer's operating system controls the computer's hardware resources and manages the applications programs that perform useful work for the computer's users.

Application programs make use of services provided by the operating system by making requests for them through a defined set of rules referred to as an application program interface (API).

Microsoft's Windows 98, Compaq's Open/VMS, IBM's OS/2, AIX, and OS/390 are all examples of operating systems. UNIX is the name of a family of related operating systems that are based on a set of Open standards.

packet

The term for a unit of data sent across a network. When you send or request data over a network, it is broken up into packets for transmission and routing and is reassembled at their destination.

Port address translation (PAT)

Also referred to as 'Network Address Port Translation' (NAPT) and terms, such as

'NAT overflow', 'NAT overloading' and 'port-level multiplexed NAT'. This is a variation of NAT (see **Network address translation**) that allows a larger number of IP number on a private network to access the public Internet using a smaller number (or even just one) external IP number. Refer to RFC 2663 'IP Network Address Translation (NAT) Terminology and Considerations *http://www.ietf.org/rfc/rfc2663.txt* .

penetration test (pen test)
Penetration testing is a series of controlled attacks on a server (such as a web server) attached to the Internet, carried out by an authorised body. These attacks are designed to discover any weaknesses in the server's security.

permissions
Security measures, imposed on a system by the system administrator, that limit access to system resources to authorised users or groups of users See **access control list**.

PHP (PHP Hypertext Pre-processor)
A server-side scripting system that is popular and freely available. There are implementations available for a wide range of popular web server software on UNIX and MS-Windows platforms. PHP applications are able to build HTML pages for delivery over the World Wide Web and are able to interact with other applications such as MySQL databases.

ping
A simple way to test or time the response of an Internet connection. A Ping program sends an Internet Control Message Protocol (ICMP) request to an Internet host and waits for a reply. The program will report whether or not the reply was received and, if it was, the round-trip time. Pinging a host will indicate whether a distant host is alive and give an idea of the quality of the end-to-end connection to it. A Ping will also reveal the IP number of the server.

pipe size
Slang term for **bandwidth**.

pixel
Pixel is a contraction of 'picture element' and is sometimes expressed as PEL. These are the tiny squares of colour that are arranged in a raster (rows and columns, like a chessboard), and which together produce an image on your computer screen. A VGA screen is 640 pixels wide by 480 pixels deep. An SVGA screen is 800 x 600 and an XGA screen is 1024 x 768.

platform
A term that generally refers to a computer, its operating system and perhaps other software that it runs.   For example a web server platform might comprise Microsoft Windows 2000 Server and Internet Information Server version 5 running on a Compaq DL360 machine.

plug-in
Additional software, which works in conjunction with web browsers to enhance their capabilities, such as in playing audio or video (for example RealPlayer) or complex graphic effects (for example, Shockwave or Flash). Many plug-ins are available free

for downloading over the Internet.

PoP (point of presence)

A term used to describe a physical location at which an ISP has connection equipment located. Historically, ISPs used to have to locate connection equipment around the country in order to provide local call charge rate dial-up access. Nowadays, PoPs are generally 'virtual' in that carrier networks (such as BTs) are used to route dialled calls to central locations where the ISPs equipment is consolidated.

POP3

POP3 (Post Office Protocol version 3) is used to collect and read email from a server. Typically, when email is sent to you it is stored on a POP3 server until you access it. Once you are logged-in, POP3 is used to collect the stored mail from the server to the local mailbox on your PC. See **SMTP**.

portal

The term 'portal' is often used to refer to websites that organise and categorise collections of links to other online information resources and services. The large Internet directory services are portals by this definition but the term is often used to refer to websites that aggregate links to other sites dealing with specific subject areas. Portal sites typically also include their own original information such as reviews or other guidance as to the usefulness of the sites to which they link. www.ukonline.gov.uk is the authoritative portal to government information and services on the Internet.

posting

An Internet term for publishing or uploading content or messages.

PPP (point to point protocol)

A widely used communication protocol for accessing the Internet over ordinary analogue telephone lines. It is a more modern and flexible protocol than its predecessor SLIP.

propagation

Generally this is used to describe the period of time after a domain name is registered or transferred until it has become visible to all the Internet Domain Name Servers around the globe. This period can last anything from three to seven days and may result in users not being able to find your domain name until the period is over.

The term is also sometimes used, (for example in the Microsoft-using world) to mean staging content up from development web servers to live servers.

protocol

Simply, the 'language' spoken between computers to help them exchange information. More technically, it is a formal description of message formats and the rules for the exchange of messages that two computers must follow in order to communicate.

prototyping

The process of using building and developing a website or online service for the purpose of demonstrating functionality, and to proof the information to be published.

proxy server

Server acting as an intermediary between a client's computer and the computer they wish to access. If a client makes a request of a web server, the request may be directed to a proxy that then makes the request of the server on behalf of the server and forwards to the result to the client. Proxying is frequently used as a part of a firewall scheme.

publishing

The copying of files from a development machine to the web server so that your web resource becomes available to the public.

pull technology

The means by which users request and download information from the Internet.

push technology

The means when a service automatically sends requested information downloads and updates to users (subscribers) whenever the information becomes available. A simple example is an email alert system.

re-engineering

A term increasingly used to describe the rebuilding and restructuring of a website, particularly when this leads to files being renamed and URLs changing.

relative URL

A relative URL is an address expressed relative to the originating document on the same server. A relative URL makes it easy to move a set of pages or other resources, but only if the positions of the pages relative to each other remain constant. Best used when files are 'related' to one another and kept in proximity to one another. See also **absolute URL**.

remote access

The ability to access a computer from outside the building in which it is housed, this requires communications hardware, software and physical links for example telephone lines.

RGB number (red, green, blue number)

A number representing a colour that tells a browser (or other computer software) how much red, green and blue to put into the colour. See **hexadecimal number**.

rollover

A function on a web page whereby an action or event is triggered when the cursor passes over a specific icon or label.

router

A device that forwards traffic between networks with the forwarding decision being made based on network layer information and routing tables, for example IP addresses in the case of Internet routers.

scalability

The proportion in which the resources required to host and manage a website (or other network component or service) scale with the size of it and/or the amount of use that is made of it by users.

screen furniture

This term is used to describe those elements visible on-screen that are used to effect the page design, for example logos, banners, dividers, etc that contribute towards the informability and usability objectives of the website. See **eye-candy**.

screen magnifier

A computer program that magnifies a portion of the screen, so that it can be more easily viewed. Computer users who have impaired vision often use screen magnifiers.

screen reader

A computer program that reads the contents of the screen aloud to a user. Primarily users with visual impairment employ screen readers.

search engine

Search engines are network services that maintain searchable databases of websites and use 'robot' or 'crawler' programs to collect the information, for example, AltaVista. Similar services called 'directories' maintain catalogues of websites that users can search, for example Yahoo.

search tools

Search tools are mechanisms for finding information on the Web. Search tools allow users to search in any or all of the following ways – by subject (for example, Yahoo), by keyword (for example InfoSeek, WebCrawler) and by surfing (for example, the 'what's new' listings that are a part of many web sites).

server

A computer configured to store and retrieve information and service requests for that information from other computers. On the Web this usually means a server using the client/server model and the World Wide Web's Hypertext Transfer Protocol to serve the files that form web pages to web users.

server-side

Functionality that is provided by the server rather than on your PC. For example, with a server-side imagemap, mouse co-ordinates are sent to the server, which then decides the appropriate action to take.

shareware

Software that is freely available, if you like the product and decide to continue using it, you are generally required to make a registration and pay a fee requested by the publisher.

SHTTP (secure HTTP)

A protocol that provides server authentication, digital signatures and encrypted sessions for web traffic.

site map

A web page that uses a graphical outline or other structure to illustrate the relationship among all the major parts of a website

Simple Object Access Protocol (SOAP)

SOAP is a W3C initiative. It specifies a way of 'wrapping up' XML data structures so that they can be used to exchange information between computer systems. SOAP is a communications protocol that allows messages to be transmitted as XML documents. SOAP is one of a category of developments known as 'Web services' that allow the technologies underlying the WWW to be used for computer-to-computer communication as well as for communications between computers and humans. Refer to *http://www.w3.org/2002/ws/* .

SLIP (Serial Line Internet Protocol)

A communication protocol for accessing the Internet over an ordinary telephone line. It is an older and less flexible protocol than PPP that has largely superseded it.

SMIL (Synchronised Multimedia Integration Language)

A mark-up language designed to present multimedia files together. For example, instead of running a video with an integrated sound track, a separate video and audio file can be used and synchronised via SMIL. The would permit users to choose different combinations, for example, the sound track in a different language or to present the sound track as a text transcript.

SMTP (Simple Mail Transport Protocol)

On the Internet this is the protocol that used to relay email messages from server to server.   It is also typically used to send email messages from Internet connected PCs. However, it is not usually used to retrieve email to mailboxes on PCs: see **POP3**.

spider

A spider (or web spider, web crawler or robot) is a computer program that automatically searches the Web for information. The retrieved information can then be used to construct catalogue indexes of websites that will form the raw material used by a search engine.

spoofing

Computers and individuals can be impersonated and their identities forged. Computers can be configured with false IP addresses that could subsequently allow access to specific networks, resources and information. Email messages can be sent purporting to have been sent by someone other than the read sender.

The technique known as 'DNS cache poisoning' involves exploiting weaknesses in some DNS server software in order to have a DNS name translate to a different IP number from the one intended.

SQL (Structured Query Language)

SQL is a standard interactive and programming language for getting information from and updating relational databases. SQL is an ISO standard.

SSI (server side includes)

Important web server technology that instructs a server what content to include in a document to be served to a client. For example, when a static web page needs customisation but a full dynamic page generation application is not warranted, SSIs may be employed. These are mark-up instructions that the web server processes before delivering the page to the client. They can be used for tasks such as putting today's date at the top of a page, incorporating a file containing a standard navigation bar (that would consequently only need to be built once) or including the size of a downloadable file against the hyperlinks to it.

SSL (Secure Sockets Layer)

A technology originally developed by Netscape for encrypting data sent between client and server. Refer to *http://home.netscape.com/security/techbriefs/ssl.html*

SGML (Standard Generalised Mark up Language)

SGML stands for Standard Generalised Mark up Language (ISO 8879), the international standard for defining descriptions of the structure and content of different types of electronic document. It is this language that was considerably downsized and simplified to construct XML.

streaming

Streaming on the Internet refers to audio, video and text files that are sent are in compressed form and displayed by a viewer as they are in the process of loading to your machine from a website. A browser plug-in is usually required in order to receive streamed content.

These files are more user friendly than standard file formats which require an entire file to download before a user can access the information.

style sheet

Term used to describe the default template(s) for one or more web pages. Style sheets generally include information on the 'shape and feel' (appearance, layout) of a web pages and is applied to attain consistency and accessibility compliance.

splash screen

The name given to the welcome screen increasingly found at the 'front door' of websites. Functioning like a book cover, the splash screen is intended to entice the visitor into the body of the site.

subdomain

The name of the components in a DNS name that are to the left of the domain name, for example the component 'shipping' in *www.shipping.detr.gov.uk*

system administrator

A technician responsible for the maintenance, security and other system-related functions on a computer or network of computers.

system intrusion

The hacking of a computer system and the ability of the hacker to 'wander' around a networked system with the ability to tamper with program and data files. These activities often involve establishing a 'backdoor' through which future undetected access can be gained. An Intrusion Detection System (IDS) is a computer running special purpose software designed to detect intrusion attempts on a network.

tags

Term used to describe the syntactic components of the HTML mark up language.

telnet

An Internet protocol to make command-line connections to remote hosts. Telnet clients are available for most platforms. When you Telnet to a UNIX computer, for example, you can issue commands at the command-line prompt as if the machine was local.

thumbnails

Small versions of larger graphics, which are used in web pages to link to the full-size graphic images.

TCP/IP (Transmission Control Protocol/Internet Protocol)

TCP/IP is the standard communications protocol required for Internet computers. Almost all server and personal computer operating systems available today include TCP/IP.

Unicode

Officially called the Unicode Worldwide Character Standard, it is a system for "the interchange, processing, and display of the written texts of the diverse languages of the modern world." It also supports many classical and historical texts in a number of languages.

Currently, the Unicode standard contains 34,168 distinct coded characters derived from 24 supported language scripts. These characters cover the principal written languages of the world. Refer to *http://www.unicode.org/*

Universal Description Discovery and Integration (UDDI)

UDDI is a sweeping industry initiative designed to create a platform-independent, open framework for describing services, discovering businesses, and integrating business services using the Internet. The UDDI project aims to achieve this by exploiting technologies, such as SOAP, XML and HTTP. Refer to *http://www.uddi.org* .

URI (Universal Resource Identifier)

Most people may be familiar with the term "URL" and not the term "URI". URLs form a subset of the more general URI naming scheme. Globally, this covers for example, email addresses, FTP addresses and web addresses.

URL (Uniform Resource Locator)

A URL (Uniform Resource Locator) is the address of a file (resource) accessible on the Internet. The type of resource depends on the Internet application protocol. On the world wide web, the resource can be an HTML page, an image file, a Java applet, or any other supported file type. The URL contains the name of the protocol required to access the resource, a domain name that identifies a specific computer on the Internet, and a hierarchical description of a file location (path) on the computer.

upload

To transfer a file to a server from a client's personal computer. Used to describe the process of installing new content on a web server (which may involve the use of FTP).

usage statistics

Statistics that show how a website is being used. These often indicate which times of the day the site is busy and what type of operations it is being asked to perform. Such statistics often include traffic peaks and troughs, performance statistics and average daily user loads.

Usenet

Usenet groups are more commonly known as 'newsgroups'. There are tens of thousands of groups hosted on thousands of servers around the world, dealing with various topics. Newsreader software is required to properly download and view 'articles' in the groups, but you can usually 'post' an article to a group by emailing it.

UTC (Universal Time Co-ordinated)

UTC evolved from Greenwich Mean Time (GMT) and is official standard for the current time. See **GeT**.

version control

A system of managing what edition (or version) of a web page is being published and of indicating to the user the edition that is being delivered to them.

virtual domain

A domain that does not have a unique IP address but shares an IP address with another domain name.

virtual hosting

Virtual hosting allows a server to respond to requests from several different domains.

Virtual Private Network (VPN)

The term Virtual Private Network refers to the technique of carrying or extending private networks over (also known as 'tunnelling through') a second public network, such as, the Internet. The network or its extensions are 'virtual' in the sense that they do not employ any physical resources of their own, but instead use the circuits and other equipment belonging to the underlying public network. Privacy is typically achieved by having the systems at each end of a VPN connection authenticate each other and by encrypting the private network data before placing it onto the public network. Typical applications of VPN include extending an organisation's network out to its business partners and to its own staff working at home or on the road.

virtual server

When one rents web server space from an ISP you are generally provided with space space on a machine that is shared with other users – a 'virtual server' as opposed to an 'actual server'. However, you can usually have a unique IP address and your own domain name.

virus

A program that replicates itself through its incorporation into other programs. Generally has malicious intent.

WAI (Web Accessibility Initiative)

These are the guidelines established in 1998 to highlight and improve the difficulties experienced by many web users on a day-to-day basis. Many of the initiatives are simple to implement and can make all the difference to many users. Refer to *http://www.w3.org/WAI/*

webcast

This term is used to describe the delivery of live or delayed `sound/video broadcasts using Internet/Web technologies. Conventional television cameras and sound systems capture the AV feed. It is then digitised and streamed live or from an archive on an appropriately configured web server.

web page

A resource (document or file containing HTML mark-up) and stored on a web server.

web resources

A general term for the web pages, HTML files, graphic files, sound files, and so on, stored on a web server for delivery on request.

webmaster

A generic term used to cover the administrator and/or creator and/or maintainer of a website.

web server

The hardware, operating system and HTTP server software that together are used for storing and serving web pages web resources and other services.

web server software

Software that receives, processes and responds to client requests for web resources, for example, Apache, IIS, Zeus.

website

A collection of interconnected web pages and resources stored on a web server under a common domain name.

whois

A search tool used, for example, to find out who is responsible for a specific domain name on the Internet.

WWW (World Wide Web)

The 'Web' is a collection of online documents housed on Internet servers around the world. Web documents are written or 'marked-up' in HTML. To access these documents, you have to use a web browser, such as Netscape Navigator or Internet Explorer.

W3C (World Wide Web Consortium)

The W3C is the international organisation chaired by Time Berners-Lee. Their aim is convince the Web community of the need for universality and standardisation. Refer to *http://www.w3.org/*

worm

A program that replicates itself. Worms, as opposed to viruses, are meant to replicate in network environments. Generally has malicious intent.

XML (eXtensible Mark up Language)

XML, short for eXtensible Mark up Language, is an emerging universal format for structured documents and data. Developed originally with web documents in mind, XML enables web publishers to create their own customised tags to provide functionality not available with HTML.

XSL Extensible Stylesheet Language

XSL is a language for expressing stylesheets used in conjunction with XML.

Zip files

Files that have been squeezed (compressed) down to a smaller file size by the application of a Zip compression algorithm and have a .zip extension. A Zip file can contain a number files and their directory structure. On the Internet programs and large graphics are compressed into Zip files and then made available for download. After you download a Zip file, you need to use a decompression program to 'unzip' the file.

Index

The notation *n* against a section number indicates a boxed note.
The notation *ck* against a section number indicates that a checklist is also provided.

Section

G

Games consoles	5.3.4
Generic email addresses	2.2.4, Annex M
Ghost copies	1.2.5
GICS	1.3.2, 1.3.3
GIFs (file format)	2.8.14.1, Annex H
— animated	2.8.14.1
— transparent	2.8.14.1
Government Interoperability Framework	1.12, 4.3.7, 5.4.2, Annex H
Government Metadata Framework	1.7
Government publicity, Conventions on	1.2.3
Government website (definition of)	Introduction 1.1
Government's Information Asset Register (IAR)	2.3.5
Graphic formats	2.8.14
Graphics	2.8, 4.2.3.5, 6.6.2
— Applications	Annex D
— navigation	2.8.9, 6.6.2
— text alternatives	2.4.6.2, 2.8.4
Green papers	see Consultation papers

H

Headings	4.2.4.1
Help facilities	2.4.4, 4.1.3.4
Hexadecimal values	2.8.3,
HMSO	1.10.3.9
Homepage	2.1.1, 2.2.3, 2.4.4
Hosting	1.12.2, 1.12.4
— offshore	1.12.4
Hspace	2.4.5.6, 2.4.6.2, 2.8.7
HTML	4.2, 6.1
— editors	6.3.2, Annex C
— forms	6.5
— frames	6.4
— markup standards	4.1
— tables	6.3
HTTP	2.1.2, Annex I
Human Rights Act	1.10.7, 1.11
Hyper Text Markup Language (HTML)	2.1.2, 2.4.3.1, 2.4.6, 4.2 , 6.1, Annex H
Hyper Text Transfer Protocol	see HTTP
Hyperlinks	1.2.8, 1.10.3.7, 1.10.8.3, 1.10.8.7, 2.4.3.1, 2.4.5.11, 4.2.4
Hyphen	3.1.3.3

I

ICRA labelling	1.8
Imagemaps	2.4.3.1, 2.4.5.5, 2.8.8, 6.6.3
Images	2.4.3.1, 2.4.5.5, 2.4.6.2, 2.8, 4.2.3.5, 6.6.2
Index page	2.1.1, 2.2.3, 2.4.4
Info4local	2.3.6
InfoRoute	2.3.5,
Interactive Digital Television	See Digital Television
Internet Content Rating Association	1.8.3

Web metrics	1.4
Web page navigation	6.6
Web safe colours	2.8.3
Web TV	5.2.13
Webcasting	Annex H
Website(s)	
— structure	2.1.3, 2.6, 3.2
— contents	1.2.2.3, 2.2, 2.6.2
— management	1, 1.2, 2.6.6.2, Annex L
— types of	1.1.1
Welsh Language Act	1.10.6, 2.7
What's New	2.2.3, 2.4.4, 2.6.6, 4.2.3.4
White Papers	2.2.2, 2.3.3
Windows Server	3.1.3.1
Winzip	4.3.6
Wireless Application Protocol (WAP)	5.3.3.2
Wireless Markup Language (WML)	5.3.3.2
Word (Microsoft)	4.3.4
World Wide Web Consortium	see W3C

X

XIS format	4.3.5, Annex H
XHTML	6.1.7
XML	5.4
XML, accessibility	5.4.3
XSL	5.4

Z

Zip format	4.3.6